Civic Revolutionaries

Douglas Henton
John Melville
Kim Walesh

Foreword by
Becky Morgan

Civic Revolutionaries

Igniting the Passion
for Change
in America's Communities

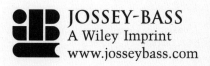

JOSSEY-BASS
A Wiley Imprint
www.josseybass.com

Published by Jossey-Bass
A Wiley Imprint
989 Market Street, San Francisco, CA 94103-1741   www.josseybass.com

Jossey-Bass books and products are available through most bookstores. To contact Jossey-Bass directly call our Customer Care Department within the U.S. at 800-956-7739, outside the U.S. at 317-572-3986 or fax 317-572-4002.

Jossey-Bass also publishes its books in a variety of electronic formats. Some content that appears in print may not be available in electronic books.

Credits are on page 266.

Library of Congress Cataloging-in-Publication Data
Henton, Douglas C.
   Civic Revolutionaries: igniting the passsion for change in America's communities/ Douglas Henton, John Melville, Kim Walesh; foreword by Becky Morgan.—1st ed.
      p. cm.
Includes bibliographical references and index.
   ISBN 0-7879-6393-3 (alk. paper)
1. Social action—United States. 2. Community organization—United States.
3. Community development—United States. 4. Civic leaders—United States. I. Melville, John, date. II. Walesh, Kim. III. Title.
   HN65.H46 2003
   361.2'0973—dc22   20033017299

Printed in the United States of America
FIRST EDITION
HB Printing   10 9 8 7 6 5 4 3 2 1

Contents

Dedication

We dedicate this book to JOHN W. GARDNER, who inspired us and countless Americans to answer his call to civic responsibility. He set the standard for thoughtful and courageous action in tackling seemingly insolvable problems in our society. As secretary of Health, Education and Welfare, father of public television, creator of the White House Fellows program, founder of Common Cause and the Independent Sector, chair of the National Civic League, and mentor to many, John W. Gardner was an uncommon American who practiced the principles he taught.

Gardner believed that civic responsibility is everyone's business. He believed citizens who have the ability to influence others should not evade their responsibility to their community. To be a civic revolutionary in the spirit of John Gardner is to act boldly on the fundamental values that have made America the land of great promise—values that include justice, liberty, and equality of opportunity. Every generation has the responsibility to search for better ways to fulfill this promise—to act as stewards of the American Experiment. In the last year of his life, Gardner (2002) predicted that today's Americans would indeed rise to the challenge: "I see the rebirth of this nation rising out of the nation's communities. Periodically, throughout our history, 'the folks out there,' out and around America, far from power but close to the good American earth, have shown not only their creativity but their capacity to move the nation. This is such a time. The next America will be forged in America's communities. That's where the fabric of our society is being rewoven" (p. 21).

Gardner's last book, *Living, Leading, and the American Dream* (2003), reflects his deep belief in every American's ability to play a role in realizing our nation's promise.

In Gardner's final years, his search for a better way to fulfill America's promise led him to the concepts and practices of regional stewardship. He felt that America needed to tackle problems across jurisdictional and organizational boundaries by tapping a reservoir of civic talent that was only beginning to emerge. He was encouraging of a new generation of regional stewards, who "have first of all a deep sense of responsibility about their region. They want it to thrive economically, to be sustainable environmentally and to have a web of mutual obligations, caring and trust and shared values that make possible the accomplishment of group purpose" (Alliance for Regional Stewardship, 2000, p. 2). It is in the spirit of John Gardner that we offer this book as a resource to today's civic revolutionaries as they assume responsibility to advance the ongoing American Experiment.

August 2003

Douglas Henton
Mountain View, California

John Melville
Mountain View, California

Kim Walesh
San Jose, California

Foreword

At this time of both great challenge and opportunity for America, citizens across this country are increasingly answering the call to stewardship because it is a more effective way to deal with our complex problems. Beginning as a grassroots movement in regions of our nation, this powerful idea will create what has been called a *tipping point*, where little things make a big difference. This book tells the story of civic revolutionaries, acting as regional stewards, who are following in the great tradition of our nation's Founders.

The definition of *stewardship* that I prefer is "the careful and responsible management of that to which one is entrusted." Because I grew up on a farm in Vermont, stewardship came naturally to me. If the animals and the land were not well cared for, the family livelihood would suffer. As a local and state elected official in California, I undertook to be a vote for and a leader for the careful and responsible management of the people's resources. In recent years, working with business, government, and nonprofit leaders at the regional level, through Joint Venture: Silicon Valley Network, I saw the benefits to communities when stewards addressed the economic, environmental, and educational issues in a collaborative, caring manner. Real solutions were possible when people joined together across sectors—what we called the "bottom-up" approach to responsible stewardship.

The late John W. Gardner—distinguished citizen, teacher, and mentor—has inspired us with his vision of stewardship. The authors of this book, working in many regions of the United States and the world, have helped craft blueprints for improving the collaboration between businesses, the public sector, and nonprofits that have led to regional progress. They and hundreds of others in diverse regions formed the Alliance for Regional Stewardship to promote a renewed commitment by all citizens to improving their communities.

In one of his last speeches, Gardner said, "I keep running into highly capable, potential leaders all over this country who literally never gave a thought to the well-being of their community. And I keep wondering who gave them permission to stand aside!" I wonder this, too. How dare people with skills and economic and intellectual capacity withdraw from giving back, from being responsible stewards within their regions. Gardner also said, "I am asking you to issue a wake-up call to those people."

This book is the wake-up call. It tells the story of how citizens across the nation are becoming civic revolutionaries, answering the call to stewardship as a way to resolve tensions and create solutions in our regions and communities. By returning to the roots of the nation's Founders, the authors examine the core principles that have guided the nation and reexamine them in light of current realities. Applying lessons learned from promising experiments by regional stewards, the book draws critical insights and points toward core principles that can help resolve fundamental tensions. In short, this book is for both emerging and existing regional stewards who want to connect deep values and core principles with day-to-day practices in a way that will help stimulate civic action. Never before have Americans needed one another more, neighbor to neighbor, than we do today. It is in our own local regions that we can take responsibility for the well-being of that to which we have been entrusted. We cannot wait for state and federal action. I urge you to become a civic revolutionary, so that we may, collectively, enhance the security of our country and the well-being of all our people.

August 2003   Becky Morgan
                        Founding Chair, Alliance for
                            Regional Stewardship
                    President, Morgan Family Foundation

Acknowledgments

In writing this book, we have described a journey of discovery. Since we met in the 1980s, the three of us have had the privilege to work with and learn from civic revolutionaries from all walks of life and every region of this country. The most recent leg of our journey began soon after the publication of our first book, *Grassroots Leaders for a New Economy,* in 1997. In the six years since, we have heard more stories of civic success and struggle, found new leaders answering the call to action, helped launch new experiments in civic problem solving, and learned a lot more about the promise and resiliency of our communities and regions. We often felt on the cusp of something new and important for our nation.

The emergence in the 1990s of more than twenty collaborative regional initiatives, led by civic revolutionaries in California, our home state, convinced us that we were witnessing the beginning of a broader movement. Becky Morgan was an early inspiration to us and many others as she broke down old barriers and forged new alliances to tackle pressing issues such as education, regulatory reform, and economic development in Silicon Valley. Nick Bollman, previously at The James Irvine Foundation and now president of the California Center for Regional Leadership, was our sponsor and partner in building a statewide network of regional initiatives and continues to be an inspiration for new regional thinking in California and nationwide. With Becky's and Nick's encouragement, we hosted a national gathering of regional leaders in 1999 and found that the California experience was not unique.

From that initial national gathering, the Alliance for Regional Stewardship, a national peer-to-peer network, was born. Since then, the alliance has grown to more than six hundred leaders from more than thirty regions, who regularly share best practices and work together on common regional issues. We appreciate the support given to the alliance by the Irvine, Morgan Family, Hewlett-Packard, Bank of America, MacArthur, and Ford Foundations as well as the Heinz Endowments, which has helped this group of remarkable people come together and learn from one another (www.regionalstewardship.org). We also appreciate the support and partnership of John Parr, the CEO of the alliance and former president of the National Civic League. This book is part of the intellectual foundation for the alliance's John W. Gardner Academy for Regional Stewardship, an intensive mentor-based experience that will help develop more regional stewards.

We owe a debt of gratitude to the mentors and professional colleagues who have shaped our thinking about the American Experiment. All three of us have been profoundly influenced by the life and writings of John W. Gardner, to whom we dedicate this book. We also recognize the intellectual contributions of academic mentors and thought leaders, including William Miller, Manuel Pastor, Robert Reich, AnnaLee Saxenian, and Aaron Wildavsky.

We thank the many gifted practitioners who have inspired us with their passion for community and for this emerging field, including Carl Anthony, Frank Beal, Christine Chadwick, Jim Gibson, David Harris, Richard Hollingsworth, Sheila Hurst, Brian Kelley, Keith Kennedy, Neil Kocurek, Sunne McPeak, Deborah Nankivell, John Neece, Pike Powers, George Ranney, Ethan Seltzer, David Soule, Ashley Swearingen, Glen Toney, George Vradenberg, Mary Walshok, Dan Whitehurst, Carol Whiteside, Julie Meier Wright, and Bob Yaro.

And for their friendship and contribution to our shared journey, we acknowledge our colleagues Diane Bone, Jay Harris, Karen

Keane, Trish Kelly, Jim King, Dara Menashi, Neal Peirce, Curtis Johnson, Ed Kawahara, Stephen Levy, and Mary Jo Waits. We thank everyone who reviewed and helped improve drafts of the book.

We want to recognize the central role of our families—not only for their support in our journey of discovery and the writing of this book but as the inspiration for our work. They remind us every day why we choose to work with people who are trying to make their community a better place. John is grateful to Sue for her generosity of spirit and Sam for his wisdom, to Millie for her fearlessness and Jan for her persistence, and to John Stanley Melville for his boundless faith in people. Kim thanks Steve, her parents, and her extended family for their steadfast support of her work and life. Doug recognizes his wife, Carol, and his daughter, Liz. Building community of all kinds—regional, church, school—remains his family's number one priority.

This book would not be possible without the outstanding contributions of the entire Collaborative Economics family—in particular, the project management of Chi Nguyen and the research assistance of Liz Brown. This dynamic young duo has taught us new ways of working and seeing the world. We also appreciate the first-rate administrative support of Hope Ebangi and Antoinette Buggle.

We thank our friends at Jossey-Bass, especially our editors, Ocean Howell and Johanna Vondeling, for their encouragement and thoughtful suggestions throughout the writing process. Of course, all errors and omissions are our responsibility alone.

Most of all, we honor the countless civic revolutionaries across the country who are tinkering away, experimenting with new approaches to complex problems, often with little fanfare or recognition. It is time that the stories of these American heroes be told and celebrated. May they inspire others to become stewards of their communities and regions.

The Authors

Like the civic revolutionaries that we write about in this book, despite having very different beginnings, we found one another traveling a similar path. After growing up on a farm in Kentucky, DOUGLAS HENTON attended Yale and the University of California–Berkeley, where he had the privilege to study political science, economics, and public policy with some of the leaders in their fields, including Robert Dahl, Charles Lindblom, and Aaron Wildavsky, as well as distinguished members of the President's Council of Economic Advisers, including Nobel Prize winner James Tobin, William Nordhaus, and William Niskanen. Their intellectual contributions along with that of Yale historian John Morton Blum are deeply reflected in this book. In 2000, Henton returned briefly to academe and participated in a strategic leadership program at Oxford to develop ideas for this book.

JOHN MELVILLE grew up in suburban California. His academic preparation at Stanford fueled his deep interest in political science and history, especially in the founding of our nation and the endless struggle to fulfill the promise of America.

After growing up in Wisconsin, KIM WALESH worked for the governor of Indiana, in corporate America, and in India. These experiences led her to economics and public policy, the Kennedy School at Harvard, and a passion for helping leaders improve their communities.

We first worked together at Stanford Research Institute (SRI International) in the 1980s, leaving to form our own company, Collaborative Economics (www.coecon.com), in 1993. In the decade since founding Collaborative Economics, we have worked as strategic advisers to civic leaders in dozens of regions across the country, helping to form the Alliance for Regional Stewardship, a nationwide network of practitioners. In 1997, we authored a book on civic entrepreneurship entitled *Grassroots Leaders for a New Economy*, published by Jossey-Bass. We have also authored numerous reports and articles and have contributed to the work of many others in the field.

Civic Revolutionaries

Introduction

The Creative Tensions of the Continuing American Experiment

The American Experiment is still in the laboratory.
And there could be no nobler task for our generation
than to move that great effort along.

John W. Gardner

Individuals who accept the call to stewardship are following a long and noble American tradition.

The Continuing American Experiment

Our country's founding generation grappled with a fundamental question: how to balance and reconcile competing values in the birth of the first modern democracy. Individual and community, freedom and responsibility—the Founders worked through these and other tensions of their time and laid down the nation's guiding philosophy in the Declaration of Independence and the Constitution. The task of every succeeding generation has been to revisit these values under changing conditions, within the framework of the nation's guiding philosophy, and to try to reconcile them so that America can move forward. This is the continuing American Experiment.

The American Experiment is our most important tradition and the key to our enduring success as a nation. No single achievement

1

is as enduring as our freedom to keep trying to get it right. No single misdeed is as significant as the process by which we learn to correct our mistakes over time. The idea that we are engaged in a timeless experiment to "form a more perfect Union" makes anything possible, despite our failings at any given moment. This process is what the first generation of revolutionary leaders expected to take place—and believed would be the only way the new republic would endure. Every generation would have to produce its own leaders to continue the American Experiment.

The American Experiment has endured precisely because succeeding generations have stepped forward and made their contribution. In those generations, individuals provided the catalyst for experimentation and progress. Sometimes these people have been well-known—like Abraham Lincoln, Theodore Roosevelt, Martin Luther King, Rachel Carson, or Cesar Chavez—but often they have done their work in small community settings with little fanfare. They have made their neighborhoods, cities, regions, and states, in the words of Supreme Court Justice Louis Brandeis, "laboratories of democracy." As in the case of the abolitionists, the suffragists, and the leaders of the Civil Rights, environmental, and farmworker movements, among others, the work of these individuals ultimately had national impact.

John W. Gardner called us to our responsibility to participate fully in the continuing American Experiment, reminding us that the work is never done, that the "experiment" is still very much in the "laboratory" (O'Connell, 1999, p. xiii). The growing complexity of public issues, the diversity of American society, and the imperfections of representative democracy will always keep us there. We can never rest, because the world keeps changing. But it is in our power to see that the American Experiment progresses rather than regresses on our watch. It is our responsibility to be *stewards* of the American Experiment. As was true for generations before us, our duty is to answer the call to stewardship in our time.

Stewards of the American Experiment

Today *civic revolutionaries* across the nation are answering the call to stewardship, igniting the passion for change in America's communities. They are revolutionaries in the sense that they are willing to experiment with new approaches to complex community problems. Although their methods differ and the pace of change varies from place to place, the essential motivation of civic revolutionaries is the same: a long-term commitment to fundamental change that improves the well-being of people and their communities.

Following in the footsteps of generations before, people of great ability and imagination are today stepping forward as leaders in a grassroots movement to transform how our nation solves its most pressing problems. In communities across America, leaders from business, government, education, and community are struggling to move forward on critical economic and social issues—how to succeed in a volatile economy, how to prepare people for a new world of work, how to safeguard environmental assets, how to create a sense of community in a pluralistic society.

Although important work is taking place on critical issues nationally, we believe that the most interesting and powerful civic innovation is happening from the bottom up—in communities and regions across America. Although most of these civic revolutionaries are not household names and probably never will be, their determination to change their communities makes them part of a great American tradition of experimentation and fundamental optimism about the future.

Grappling with Tensions Between Competing Values

Like the founding generation, today's civic revolutionaries are grappling with an enduring challenge—how to reconcile competing American values. Although American life clearly includes many tensions over competing values, we believe that a few of them have proved to be fundamental to the American experience over time, and are therefore the focus of this book. These are not meant to be an inclusive list of competing values. Undoubtedly, a case could be made for other sets of competing values—and should be made if those values need to be reconciled in order for a community to move forward. The competing values that serve as the core of this book are the following:

- *Individual and Community*—the tension between the values of individual freedom and liberty and community duty and responsibility

- *Trust and Accountability*—the tension between the values of implicit trust and explicit forms of accountability in civic life

- *Economy and Society*—the tension between the values of economic prosperity and societal stability and progress

- *People and Place*—the tension between the advancement of people and the vitality of places

- *Change and Continuity*—the tension between the potential benefits of change and the comfort of continuity

- *Idealism and Pragmatism*—the tension between the inspiration of idealism and the action of pragmatism

Each of these tensions is a healthy competition between two "goods," not a clear choice between right and wrong, good and bad, democracy and totalitarianism. This fact makes the task of reconciling these values more difficult. Neither side can claim the moral high ground. Reasonable, ethical people can disagree. For example, even though virtually everyone values individual liberty or community responsibility—and most believe that some of both are required for a successful society—the devil is in the details. Where exactly does individual liberty end and community responsibility begin? Or better yet, how can both be served and actually reinforce each other?

In fact, each tension requires a balancing act, an understanding of the positive attributes of each good and an ability to define a relationship between the two goods that preserves and strengthens their positive attributes as much as possible. Neither too much nor too little of each value will work. Instead the central and enduring task of civic revolutionaries is to create a workable reconciliation of competing values, an explicit or implicit, widely accepted "bargain" or social contract, or as Gardner put it simply, "Freedom and responsibility, liberty and duty, that's the deal" (O'Connell, 1999, p. 126).

The bigger opportunity is not only to find a workable balance but to create a dynamic combination that produces a whole greater than the sum of the parts. The interaction between the two goods can produce a positive-sum, rather than a zero-sum, result. Individual freedom and community responsibility can reconcile in ways that not only protect their best attributes but also produce larger societal benefits. For example, the combination of freedom and responsibility embodied in the GI Bill, which provided educational and other benefits for veterans returning from World War II, not only expanded educational freedom for individuals in return for their community duty but also produced enormous societal benefits by creating a better-educated population.

Each of these tensions is dynamic, changing with the ebb and flow of events and generations, defying any ultimate solution. The American Experiment never ends but is rather an ongoing process of trial and error, finding what works and changing course when necessary. It is a series of creative tensions between competing values, practical challenges to community, and ultimately national progress.

This book suggests that Americans can find ample common ground in the process of reconciling positive American values—values that otherwise compete with each other and can clash in a struggle for supremacy, with negative consequences for people and communities. By focusing on how to reconcile and maximize the positive impacts of these American values, civic revolutionaries can ignite the passion for community change.

Meeting the Crises of Today

Today we face both a crisis of confidence and a crisis of capacity in how we deal with economic and social problems in America, while we are also addressing international challenges that include war and terrorism. A crisis of confidence is growing, fueled by reports of scandal and ethical lapses in major institutions in our society—government, business, and civic. At the same time, we are experiencing a crisis of institutional capacity because of the increasing complexity of the problems that we face. Difficult economic, social, and environmental challenges are increasingly interdependent and beyond the scope of local jurisdictions. They also defy easy solution with national or state-level programs or policies.

To meet the complex challenges of the twenty-first century, we will have to revisit the fundamental questions that frame the American Experiment, remembering the founding philosophy of our republic and reconciling competing values given the new realities of our time. In fact, the ongoing process of renewal is at the core of our nation's public philosophy, which enables us to reinvent how we govern ourselves and how we approach both new and enduring issues in our communities. It is ultimately how we must recover confidence in our institutions and rebuild our capacity to solve problems in our society.

The first generation of American civic revolutionaries was deeply inspired by the core ideas of freedom and liberty, as well as by the broader public or community interest. These individuals introduced a framework of public ethics for America and translated it into a workable set of operating principles for governing the nation. They set an example for how subsequent generations could grapple with their unique challenges within a basic framework of public ethics.

Now is not the first time that the American people have felt restless and uneasy about losing touch with the fundamental principles of our republic. At the end of the nineteenth century, as we moved from an agricultural to an industrial era, dislocations caused by the rapid growth of cities and the economic decline of farms gave rise to populist and later progressive movements that influenced political thinking well into the middle of the twentieth century. In response, Theodore Roosevelt reinvented the national government and brought renewed leadership to the public sector to deal with abuses and ethical misconduct. Roosevelt saw himself as a steward of the people. He not only believed in cleaning up corruption and reforming government institutions to deal with abuses of corporate power. He also believed that Americans should practice new moral and civic virtues.

Are we entering a similar period, in which political and economic crises could rekindle a civic spark and restore public commitment to virtue? Communities across America are being disrupted by fundamental changes in their economies and societies. Some would say that we have entered a "perfect storm" of foreign and domestic challenges. Our communities are struggling, with no road map for how to navigate through these challenges. New realities require rethinking how we will govern ourselves in the future based on a combination of a strong sense of public ethics, hard-nosed realism, and tough-minded optimism, especially in light of our recent business and political scandals, economic challenges, and the harsh new world of global terrorism—as well as the sheer complexity of the problems that we now face.

This book is a call to action for civic revolutionaries, to guide our communities and our nation back to a strong commitment to public ethics and effective problem solving. As Randy Cohen (2002), the "ethicist" for the *New York Times Magazine*, has observed, "Just as individual ethics can only be understood in relation to the society within which it is practiced, it is also true that individual ethical behavior is far likelier to flourish within a just society. Indeed it might be argued that to lead an ethical life one must work to build a just society" (p. 9). In recent years, often with little national fanfare, in communities across the country, civic revolutionaries have begun to rise to the challenge.

The fundamental questions that face communities have not changed very much through the years. Knowing how the Founders addressed such questions is still useful in helping us frame our challenges and search for reconciliation of competing values in our time. Many leaders in America are tackling these difficult challenges today. Michael Walzer of the Institute for Advanced Studies at Princeton University observes that "civil society is a project of projects; it requires many organizing strategies and new forms of state action. It requires a new sensitivity for what is local, specific and contingent— and above all a new recognition that the good life is in the details" (Dionne, 1998, p. 143). *Civic Revolutionaries* is about those projects, the people who undertake them to improve their regional communities, and the simple rules and ethical principles that guide a new public philosophy for regional governance in the twenty-first century.

We face difficult challenges, but strong civic leadership is the response to those challenges. Although this book does not attempt to provide all the answers to these critical questions, it does try to help civic revolutionaries who want to relate their day-to-day practices to core values in a more fundamental way. In the process, the book will help leaders design more effective ways to address their critical problems.

At a critical moment in our nation's recent history, during the 1960s when every institution in society seemed to be under attack, Gardner wrote *The Recovery of Confidence* (1970). He said the following words that are still relevant today:

> Why are we having such difficulty in getting at our problems? One might blame our apathy, or our unwillingness to spend or failure to understand the problem, or resistance to change. But something else is wrong, something central, and something crucial. As we examine the

intensive and multitudinous efforts to cope with the problems we are driven to the significant conclusion: there are some things that are gravely wrong with our society as a problem solving mechanism. . . . The crucial task is to design a society (and institutions) capable of continuous change, continuous renewal and continuous responsiveness [p. 7].

This book is about identifying and applying those underlying principles and practical insights from the field that will help today's civic revolutionaries create the type of self-renewing institutions that Gardner told us were so important.

Finding Regional Collaboration to Be Critical

Typically, we see the tensions of competing American values under discussion at the national level, when we reflect on what defines us as a country or what fundamental rights may be at stake. The flurry of dialogue about individual rights and community interests sparked by the federal government's security response to the September 11, 2001, tragedy is a case in point. Our experience suggests, however, that there is an equally important but largely untold story of how these competing values are playing out in communities and regions today. In fact, groups of connected communities are feeling these tensions acutely, and their leaders are struggling to address them as stewards not just of a single community but of an interdependent region.

We believe that a grassroots civic movement is currently under way in this country at the regional level—one that is making a distinctive contribution to the continuing American Experiment. Civic revolutionaries, acting as *regional stewards*, are experimenting with new ways of addressing critical, complex issues that cut across multiple political jurisdictions and constituencies—transportation, housing, economic competitiveness, social equity, disaster preparedness. This is a pragmatic approach to problem solving born of necessity from multiple forces, including devolution of federal and state programs, global competition, decentralization from central cities, fiscal limitations, increased diversity and demands for participation.

Over the last decade, a growing number of researchers and practitioners have called attention to this emerging regional movement. Neal Peirce, Curtis Johnson, and John Hall have made a strong case for the growing importance of regions in the global economy. In *Citistates: How Urban America Can Prosper in a Competitive World* (1994), they point out that regional *citistates* must be a central focus for leadership and policy because metropolitan areas are the real labor markets, the functioning economic communities, the commute sheds, and the environmental basins.

In *Regions That Work*, Manuel Pastor of the University of California-Santa Cruz observes that "regions, then, may offer the minimum size at which markets and business networks achieve the low-cost economies of scale necessary to compete in international markets," while "at the same time, they may offer the maximum size at which working relationships can be crafted and sustained" (Dreier, Grigsby, Lopez-Garza, and Pastor, 2000, p. 5). Metropolitan regions—rather than individual communities—are the places where assets important to economic prosperity are aggregated and where economic, environmental, and equity issues necessarily come together in our modern society.

This new reality poses difficult challenges for civic leadership, and for the institutions of government and processes of governance. The need for regional approaches and cohesiveness stands in sharp contrast to governmental fragmentation and parochial governance. But as Allan Wallis (1996) of the University of Colorado at Denver explains, "Expanding the power of the metropolitan region runs counter to the cultural preference for keeping government as small as possible with power exercised close to the people affected. The inherent conflict between ends and means has made achieving effective regional government or governance extremely difficult" (p. 15).

The result is the emergence of networks of regional stewards who influence regional direction through ad hoc approaches, rather than new, formal government structures. These leaders work pragmatically across traditional boundaries of geography and sector to deliver results. Kathryn Foster (2001) of the Lincoln Land Institute describes this emergence of a *new regionalism* or a civic-based "we are all in this together" approach to problem solving:

> From these trends emerge new forms of regional leadership driven more by the need to inspire, motivate and empower action in a networked power sharing world than by traditional paths of command and control in a hierarchical, someone-in-charge world. One practice-based model to emerge from these realities is that of 'regional stewardship' which emphasizes commitment to place rather than an issue, an integrated approach to issues and solutions, and the development of broad coalitions sharing a regional vision [p. 26].

The work of civic revolutionaries acting as regional stewards has only just begun. We are in a transitional phase, working to develop new patterns of collaboration and partnership, experimenting with new ways of doing business.

We see this experimentation that is taking place at the regional level as a catalyst for national innovation. In fact, a strong tradition embodied in the American Experiment is the role of grassroots innovation in national transformation. Before coming together to produce the national constitution, the Founders had gained experience in framing constitutions for their individual colonies, testing the practical impacts of their ideas. Each one was a steward of sorts in his community before moving to the national stage.

The opening words of *The Federalist Papers* noted that the nation was about to decide "whether societies of men are really capable or not of establishing good government from reflection and choice." The American Experiment is about the continuous process of reflection and choice—of working through trial and error to reconcile competing values for our time. Regions composed of interdependent groups of communities are now laboratories where experiments to reconcile these values are under way, producing new forms of regional stewardship and governance that are more suited to the global economy and the more decentralized and diverse society of the twenty-first century.

The Need for Guiding Principles and Practical Insights

After more than a decade of vigorous experimentation, the movement toward regional collaboration to address complex problems is a growing field of thought and practice but remains just below the national radar screen. A new generation of civic revolutionaries has stepped forward in many regions, but the current perspective and preparation of business, government, and community leaders remain insufficient to meet today's complex challenges. These challenges require a broader outlook and a heightened ability to work across political, sectoral, and organizational boundaries to resolve conflict and take advantage of opportunity.

We wrote this book because we believe that this emerging movement—led by civic revolutionaries—is producing new guiding principles and powerful practical insights. We have been fortunate to work with many civic revolutionaries, who, as community and regional stewards across the nation, are by necessity and through the real-life experience of working on complex problems showing how we can reconcile important American values for our time. Inspired by the life and writings of Gardner and other stewards of the American Experiment, we offer this book as a practical tool to move this great effort along.

The central question of this book is how today's civic revolutionaries can reconcile enduring American values for success in our time. To answer this question, the book defines each set of competing values and explores the nature of the tension between them, from its historical revolutionary roots to its contemporary effects. In each case, the chapters describe promising experiments from around the country, showing how the current generation is grappling with the timeless tensions of the American Experiment. These experiments have experienced some success and offer insights for civic revolutionaries who are grappling with similar challenges.

Each chapter also identifies specific insights from the field of experimentation, strategies and techniques that might be useful to civic revolutionaries in regions across the country. We base these observations on two decades of experience advising civic leaders in more than forty regions across the country, including interactions with innovative practitioners who are members of the Alliance for Regional Stewardship, a national peer-to-peer network, which we helped launch and continue to support. We also consulted with leading researchers and foundation executives who have helped support this field of experimentation.

Anyone who wants to be a more effective civic revolutionary should read this book—especially people who are dissatisfied with the status quo and are tired of gridlock or halfhearted solutions. Such people include the following:

- Business executives

- Civic leaders

- Elected officials and public managers

- Community organization and nonprofit leaders

- Economic and community development practitioners

- Leaders in philanthropy

- Faith leaders

- University and educational leaders

- Community residents

We hope that our book will help civic revolutionaries, acting as regional stewards, to have more productive discussions in their communities and make better-informed, more confident choices. The book provides many practical insights into how civic revolutionaries in other regions are addressing competing values. But perhaps most important, we hope that this book helps leaders ask the right questions. They will be able to frame alternative approaches in ways that reflect timeless values.

We also hope that this perspective on regional innovation will help leaders connect to one another across regions for learning, communication, and support. We hope to give leaders a common language for talking about their experience and reflecting on what they have learned. And we hope that seeing themselves as part of an important, ongoing American experiment will provide some inspiration for continuing their difficult work of building better communities.

Igniting the Passion for Change

Based on the experiences of the leaders and communities discussed in this book and rooted in the experience of the Founders, we believe that there are three major roles that civic revolutionaries play to ignite the passion for change and navigate the process of experimentation in their communities. Civic revolutionaries *discover*, then they *decide*, and then they *drive* change. (See Figure I.1.)

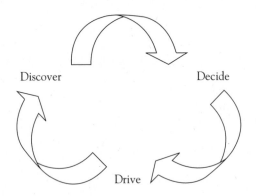

Figure I.1. Civic Revolutionary Cycle.

Discover: Building a Compelling Case for Change

Civic revolutionaries build a convincing case for change in their communities—accumulating information, ideas, and allies in the process. They diagnose the challenges facing their communities, the tensions between competing values that must be addressed in new ways. They creatively describe, reframe, measure, and connect issues and root causes. They try to understand what is working, what is not working, and what might work. They seek out the experiences of other communities, to expand the view of what's possible and to find other civic revolutionaries who might be able to help them frame problems or develop solutions. At the same time, they seek out and discover allies in their communities, individuals that can help make the case and become part of the coalition for change. All of this preparation helps them discover or rediscover problems, possibilities, and people and in the process builds the case for experimentation.

The Founders themselves went through a period of discovery by being active at the local and state level before moving onto the national stage, finding allies in other parts of the country, connecting with one another in *committees of correspondence*, and drawing liberally from the literature and experience of other countries when they seemed to fit the aspirations and needs of the fledgling republic. Through these efforts, they built the case for change. They went through a particularly intensive search as they recognized the limits of the Articles of Confederation and created the Constitution during what the historian Samuel Eliot Morrison calls the "creative period," between 1785 and 1788. The Articles created a national government that had neither the resources nor the authority to govern the new nation of three million people spread along the eastern seaboard, and an alternative had to be found.

Like the Founders, today's civic revolutionaries broaden their horizons through the discovery process, but they also stay focused on the applications of what they have learned with the allies that they have found. Making the case is not an academic exercise, but one that marshals information, resources, and people to take action.

Decide: Making Critical Choices in Experimentation

Civic revolutionaries use what they learn from the discovery process to make decisions. They make choices from among the many actions they could take to tackle their challenges. Though they may consult with those in other communities and tap into national sources of research and ideas to consider options for action, they sort through different ideas and decide on how best to apply what they have learned. They decide about focus, scope, and priority in designing experiments in community change—immediate actions connected to an overall vision (or story) of change that will provide opportunities for continuous feedback and adaptation.

The Founders themselves engaged in focused decision-making sessions to agree to the Declaration of Independence and the Constitution. In the case of the Constitution, after much experience with experimentation at the state level and the Articles of Confederation, individual Founders came together to sort through specific ideas and create an overall framework for action, essentially agreeing on a set of operating principles for governing the republic. As Morrison observed, "The Federal constitution was the capital achievement of the creative period. This reconciling of unity with diversity, the practical application of the federal principle, is undoubtedly the most original contribution of the United States to history and the technique of human liberty" (Harris, 2002). Just as important, they introduced a system of renewal that would allow future generations to make adaptations.

Like the Founders, today's civic revolutionaries do not find answers to all the problems but set out a new approach based on guiding principles that can be put into practice immediately, with tangible and visible results. Above all, they do not shrink from the responsibility and risk of making decisions and moving forward with much-needed experimentation.

Drive: Mobilizing Allies for Change

Civic revolutionaries are relentless in their drive for change. Although they are thoughtful and reflective in preparation and in decision making about what to do, they neither succumb to "paralysis by analysis" nor engage in an endless search for the perfect solution. They embody the spirit of experimentation—they reflect, decide, act, then reflect on initial results, make more decisions, pursue new actions, and start the process again. They drive a realistic, opportunistic, and adaptable experimentation process.

Even with their preparation and decisiveness, the Founders were ultimately drivers of change. After agreeing to the Constitution, they engaged in a campaign to put it into practice, working to ensure that each state would vote to ratify the document. Although we recognize and celebrate their contribution in our time, the Founders faced an uphill battle in their time. Supporters of the Constitution would not have won a Gallup poll.

Key to the effort to drive adoption of the Constitution was a series of essays (essentially op-ed pieces) in a New York newspaper, the *Independent Journal*. We now know these essays collectively as *The Federalist Papers*. They made the case to a wary American people that a new structure of governance was necessary and that the Articles of Confederation were inadequate to the demands of the day. They articulated how the new Constitution addressed the problems that the country faced and how it addressed the major concerns of opponents and the numerous competing interest groups in our already diverse nation. The essays were reprinted in other newspapers and circulated as pamphlets and were arguably one of the key drivers for adoption of the Constitution by the states. Only with these efforts did the Constitution transform from a thoughtful synthesis of governing principles into the blueprint for action to launch a new nation.

Once the ratification process was completed, the Founders participated in the implementation of the new governing model. They quickly added the first ten amendments, collectively known as the Bill of Rights, and over the next few years through experimentation fine-tuned the content and application of the document through legislative changes and judicial review. The Constitution was never about getting it perfect the first time around. Even in their time, the Founders tinkered with their creation to make it a practical, workable blueprint for action.

A Cycle of Continuous Change

The three practical roles for civic revolutionaries mirror the experience and beliefs of Gardner. For him, life was a continuous cycle of reflection, decision, and action. He made important contributions playing each role and demonstrated how to move back and forth among the three roles to drive positive change in America. With the inspiration of the Founders and subsequent civic revolutionaries like Gardner, as well as the contemporary experiences of practitioners across the country, we offer the following chapters as explorations of enduring tensions between competing values in American life and suggest practical roles for civic revolutionaries who seek to reconcile them—a continuous cycle to discovery, decision, and action to drive change.

How to Navigate the Book

This Introduction frames the overarching themes and purpose of this book as a principled, practical guide for civic revolutionaries. It focuses on the challenge of the American Experiment, providing perspective on the competing values and the creative tensions that have existed since the founding of the nation—and that each succeeding generation must revisit and resolve for its time. It suggests the emergence of a grassroots movement for change at the regional level and describes practical roles for civic revolutionaries who want to ignite the passion for change in their communities.

Each of the following six chapters is organized around a specific creative tension of the American Experiment, a set of competing values that every generation of Americans has had to reconcile— Chapter One: Individual and Community, Chapter Two: Trust and Accountability, Chapter Three: Economy and Society, Chapter Four: People and Place, Chapter Five: Change and Continuity, and Chapter Six: Idealism and Pragmatism.

As most effective leaders seek to do, this book operates at two levels: the conceptual and the pragmatic. The first section of Chapters One through Six is The American Experience, providing historical perspectives on the tension between competing values. The second section of each of these chapters is The Tension Today, offering perspectives on the situation facing today's civic revolutionaries. The third section focuses on Promising Experiments, exploring examples of innovative approaches to reconciling competing values in communities today. The final section of each chapter focuses on the lessons learned from civic revolutionaries in action, Insights from the Field, offering practical guidance to readers.

The concluding Chapter Seven describes how a new generation of civic revolutionaries acting as regional stewards can advance the American Experiment in our time. This chapter summarizes and connects a set of guiding principles and practical roles for civic revolutionaries, based on the key insights and lessons from the preceding chapters. It concludes with a prediction that the grassroots process of reconciling competing values, driven by civic revolutionaries, will renew the *social compact* between Americans and their communities, regions, and nation.

We hope you enjoy this book and its new perspective on the civic innovation taking place in regions today. May you find some inspiration and practical insights that will help you transform your place and encourage you to share your experience with many others. As modern-day civic revolutionaries, we can all answer the call to stewardship and make our contribution to the continuing American Experiment.

1

Individual and Community

Creating Common Purpose

Individual residents naturally want personal freedom, and local governments want control over what happens in their jurisdiction. But regional trends such as economic change, traffic congestion, and land use patterns are constraining individual freedom and undermining local control. An adversarial environment among jurisdictions and special interests has created gridlock on important issues. Most people agree that the value of freedom for individual residents and jurisdictions is important, but so is the value of working together to take responsibility as a community for solving regional problems that affect everyone. The practical question is how to reconcile the competing values of individual and community to meet the challenges of today.

At the core of the American Experiment is the balancing act between two powerful concepts: the individual and the community. The Founders believed that both are critical ingredients to a successful society. Individual freedom and liberty are the wellsprings of creativity and initiative. Community duty and responsibility are the glue that allows individuals to live together peacefully and productively. Or as Gardner (1995) put it simply, "Humans are social beings, and to discuss individuality without talking about the social system that makes it possible is to talk nonsense" (p. 86).

The American Experience: Resolving the Tension Between the Individual and the Community

Our nation's founders sought to create a framework that would prevent the individual and the community from overwhelming each other—resulting in neither freedom without responsibility nor duty without liberty. The resulting framework addressed two fundamental questions:

- How to balance competing interests (or factions) in a diverse society

- How to manage the growing complexity of interests of a geographically dispersed and economically diverse nation

They succeeded well enough to ensure the survival of the new nation and set the standard for subsequent generations. Every generation since has inherited this balancing act—some in times of war, depression, civic unrest, and social upheaval that have severely tested their ability to preserve both individual freedom and community responsibility.

Where individual freedom is guaranteed and flourishes, differences of opinion and clashes of freedoms are inevitable. The Founders understood and appreciated the realities of human nature and knew that any enduring American system had to find a way simultaneously to encourage the diversity of ideas while tempering the conflict among interests. They sought to preserve the benefits of pluralism while guarding against the danger of factions.

James Madison in *The Federalist Papers* offered perhaps the best articulation of the Founders' concern about the practical challenge in balancing "the multiplicity of interests" in a diverse society. In *Federalist* No. 10, Madison introduced the challenge of *faction*, defining it as "a number of citizens, whether amounting to a majority or minority of the whole, who are united and actuated by some common impulse of passion, or of interest, adverse to the rights of other citizens, or to the permanent and aggregate interests of the community" (Quinn, 1993, p. 71). He identified two distinct dangers: the threat that some individual interests would overwhelm the rights of some citizens and the threat that factions could undermine the broader community interest.

At the same time, Madison recognized the reality that "the latent causes of faction are thus sown in the nature of man" and "have, in turn, divided mankind into parties, inflamed them with mutual animosity, and rendered them much more disposed to vex and oppress each other than to co-operate for their common good." In fact, "liberty is to faction what air is to fire." However, this reality did not lead Madison to argue for removing the causes of faction: "It could not be a less folly to abolish liberty, which is essential to political life, because it nourishes faction than it would be to wish the annihilation of air, which is essential to animal life, because it imparts to fire its destructive agency" (Quinn, 1993, pp. 70–73).

The challenge then, as Madison defined it, is that "the *causes* of faction cannot be removed and that relief is only to be sought as a means for controlling its *effects*." What effects? In *Federalist* No. 62, he observed that "liberty may be endangered by the abuses of liberty as well as by the abuses of power." Alexander Hamilton described another effect in *Federalist* No. 6 when he noted the tendency for neighboring states to be natural enemies unless bound together voluntarily in the common cause of a republic, "extinguishing that secret jealousy which disposes all states to aggrandize themselves at the expense of their neighbors" (Quinn, 1993, pp. 55, 73, 137).

The Founders answered the *challenge of competing interests* by creating a constitutional framework that preserved liberty generally but also constrained liberty in specific instances in which the liberties of some would overwhelm those of others, or when the effects of factions would compromise the broader community interest. Defining exactly where those lines are drawn is a continuous process of refinement.

Just as the competition of interests in a pluralistic society is inevitable, so is the complexity of a problem-solving environment in a dynamic world. However, an important distinction exists between the competition of interests and the complexity of the problem-solving environment. The former deals with individual differences and often conflicts, and it requires a better understanding of underlying values among participants in order to develop creative solutions or even compromises that allow for some degree of progress.

With the latter, the challenge is less about resolving major differences and conflict and more about finding new ways to mobilize a multitude of sometimes similar, often complementary interests into solving a shared, but complex, problem. It is about transforming a multitude of independent agents into a whole that is greater than the sum of its parts.

For the Founders, meeting the *practical challenge of complexity* meant creating a nation out of thirteen independent states. The first attempt, in the Articles of Confederation, failed to reconcile competing interests but—just as important—collapsed under its inability to manage the growing complexity of a geographically dispersed and economically diverse nation.

This growing complexity of interests was magnified by the growing complexity of state lawmaking. State constitutions varied greatly and were regularly altered, creating a sense of confusion and chaos within and between states. As one observer from Vermont wrote in 1786, laws were "altered—realtered—made better—made worse; and kept in such a fluctuating position, that persons in civil commission scarcely know what the law is" (Wood, 2002, p. 142). Altogether, the complexity of the problem-solving environment exposed the inherent weakness of the Articles of Confederation and drove the Founders to develop a national constitution that would be able to manage complexity.

In *Federalist* No. 37, Madison recognized the complexity of the problem-solving environment when he grappled with how to partition powers between national and state governments. He identified three specific challenges: "indistinctness of the object, imperfection of the organ of conception, and inadequateness of the vehicle of ideas." In other words, he described a problem-solving environment in which the problem will be hard to define, the problem solvers will be imperfect in their abilities to solve the problem, and "vehicles" to describe and advance solutions will be inadequate. Despite theses obstacles, Madison argued for moving ahead, to manage complexity as well as possible, acknowledging the obstacles, but "with a deep conviction of the necessity of sacrificing private opinions and partial interests to the public good" (Quinn, 1993, p. 104).

Thus the Founders created the Constitution not only to manage differences among factions but also to manage complexity in a diverse and dynamic nation. In fact, according to Michael Meyerson, author of *Political Numeracy* (2002), the Constitution is a document that sets up a *complex adaptive system* driven by feedback. Complex adaptive systems are based on simple rules that recognize the need for constant change and improvement and provide a framework for an open society.

For more than two centuries, the Constitution has managed to adapt repeatedly to an extraordinary array of small alterations and grand upheavals, both external and internal, while at the same time maintaining coherence under change. The Constitution in general and the Bill of Rights in particular are relatively short and simple principles or rules. However, their application over time is parallel to the concept of iteration or feedback. As we see with chaotic systems, the smallest changes can lead ultimately to quite significant developments through a process of dynamic adaptation. The Constitution provides simple rules that act as the framework for complex, nonlinear systems. Elections, legislation, and judicial decisions all act as self-correcting mechanisms.

In short, the framers created a chaotic Constitution that is well suited to the changing nature of our complex political and economic environment. As Jay Harris, former publisher of the *San Jose Mercury News* commented, "The genius of the Constitution lay in what the framers did not attempt to do—they had a clear grasp of the general ideas and left the details to later interpretation" (2002). The beauty of the Constitution is its elegant simplicity. It is a simple set of rules for governing complex behavior.

The Founders established the framework for problem solving for future generations but did not solve all the problems in their time. They did not address the issue of slavery, which led to the great division of the Civil War. In his Gettysburg Address, Abraham Lincoln finally connected the promise of equality in the Declaration of Independence (that all men are created equal and have certain unalienable rights) with the idea of the national Union of "We the People" created by the framers of the Constitution. Lincoln makes clear that lives were lost in the Civil War to ensure that everyone had a place in America's future and that the Union "of the people, by the people, for the people, shall not perish from the earth." Out of the Civil War, America redefined its social compact based on core values of freedom, equality, and opportunity for all.

A half century after Lincoln, Herbert Croly in *The Promise of American Life* ([1909] 1989) gave the turn-of-the-century Progressive movement a rationale in his famous formula of seeking Jeffersonian ends (equality and opportunity) through Hamiltonian (centralized) means. This rationale justified the creation of a strong central government to compete with the increasingly centralized economy dominated by the large monopolistic industries of that era, known as "trusts." This general formula has endured for almost a century through wars, depression, the New Deal, and the Great Society. However, the creative tension between the individual and the community resurfaces as times change and new circumstances force us to consider new ways to address this issue.

The Tension Today: Practical Challenges to Address

Among the important challenges that today's civic revolutionaries experience in balancing the values of the individual and the values of the community are the following:

- *The challenge of community building:* from forced compromise to free choice

- *The challenge of competing interests:* from conflict to complementarity

- *The challenge of complex environments:* from chaos to cohesion

Alone, the compromise of federalism (the framework that provided a separation of powers between the national and the state governments) created by the Founders of the Constitution, and subsequent refinements, may not fit our current situation very well. The national government may simply be too far removed from the real problems facing individuals and communities today. In many respects, a government that was designed as a workable model for a nation of a little more than three million people has become more of a distant bureaucracy that is ill equipped to solve the increasingly complex problems of today.

Current circumstances suggest that the Croly formula may no longer be viable. In fact, the reverse may be necessary: Hamiltonian ends (vital economy and community) through Jeffersonian means (decentralization). We may need a more distributed model based on regional networks or compacts forged through cooperation and bargaining among leaders at the neighborhood, city, region, state, and national levels. A distributed model may be the way we need to resolve the tension between individual interests and community responsibilities.

Gardner (1970), who spent much of his life working to resolve the creative tension between individual freedom and liberty and community responsibility and duty, suggests a balance between these values:

> The significant question is not whether the individual should be completely free of his society or completely subjugated. It is a question of what are the ties and what are the freedoms. The ties must be the life-giving ties of shared values, a sense of community, a concern for total enterprise, a sense of identity and belonging, and the opportunity to serve. The freedoms must be the freedom to dissent, to be an individual, to grow and fulfill oneself, to choose in some measure one's own style and manner of serving the community [p. 46].

In his writings, Gardner grappled with how to resolve the tension. Through his actions, he promoted practical efforts that offered individuals creative opportunities to serve the community. To the end of his life, he sought ever better ways to engage people in their community, to define through action the relationship between individual freedom and liberty and community responsibility and duty.

Addressing the creative tension between the individual and the community is not an academic exercise, but rather an exercise that offers specific, practical challenges. For the Founders, these challenges were as real and practical as they are today. The major challenges that the Founders faced—and that leaders continue to face today—are how to make the following shifts:

- *From forced compromise to free choice:* how to create an environment in which people voluntarily choose to exercise their freedom (rather than unwillingly compromise their freedom) to build a community of place, believing that they will gain more in social benefits than they give up in individual liberty

- *From conflict to complementarity:* how to turn competing interests into working relationships based on complementary values and roles

- *From chaos to cohesion:* how to transform complex problems into manageable tasks and channel independent efforts into collaborative action based on simple but elegant guiding principles

The struggle of the Founders over the competition of interests is relevant to us today. Across the country, communities and regions are struggling with factions. Jurisdictions fight over transportation, land use, and other issues whose impacts cross political boundaries. Special interests often dominate political discourse and government decision-making processes. Bureaucracies fight for the preeminence of their narrow agendas. The framing of problems and the range of possible solutions become extreme or fixed as advocacy groups battle to sell their "remedy" to their "grievance."

Gardner (1970) believed that to preserve and advance the broader community interest, factions would have to revolutionize their communication: "The advantages of pluralism are diminished if the various elements of the society are out of touch with one another. . . . Communication in a healthy society must be more than a flow of messages; it must be a means of conflict resolution, a means of cutting through the rigidities that divide and paralyze a community" (pp. 36–37). It is important to note that Gardner distinguished between communication whose purpose is to win and communication that results in problem solving.

Despite the proven effectiveness of the Constitution as a vehicle for managing complexity, each generation must address anew the practical challenge of turning a complex array of individual initiatives into collaborative action. How do decentralized systems that return power to the individual and small communities through devolution work together to create networks of responsibility to address common regional concerns? Can this work be done with the hierarchy of traditional government structures? Or can centrality of purpose really be achieved through decentralization of means?

The answer to the practical challenges of community building, conflict, and complexity is *common purpose*. The objective is to achieve a "productive balance (perhaps *tension* is a better word) between pluralism and a concern for the shared purposes of all segments of society. Pluralism without a concern for common purposes moves toward chaos and the anarchic play of vested interests" (Gardner, 1970, pp. 33–34). In effect, achieving common purpose is a process of working through this tension toward a productive balance.

Complexity of interests, without regard to one another, can lead to a "tragedy of the commons," a classic zero-sum result that can worsen the situation. Elinor Ostrom, in *Governing the Commons* (1991), has suggested that the solution is that the parties need shared information and self-organization. No requirement exists for decisions imposed from the outside (hierarchy) or for private-property rights (markets). Between hierarchies and markets are networks of mutual relationships based on shared responsibility. What is key to making networks function is shared information as well as shared responsibility (both individual responsibility and group responsibility).

Defining a common purpose and creating the appropriate vehicle to advance that public good was the practical challenge that faced the Founders and subsequent generations. What seems to be necessary are new kinds of *networks of responsibility*, like those that helped build this country at its founding. We need to create networks in ways that reengage citizens in their own communities and across communities.

Individuals value freedom, but they also seek community. Matt Ridley (1997), an evolutionary biologist, has observed that most people are happy to accept that selfish behavior is "natural," whereas good deeds require self-sacrifice. But he finds that our cooperative instincts may have also evolved as part of our nature: by exchanging favors, we can benefit others and ourselves. In reaching his conclusion about the importance of cooperation, he provides the following prescriptions:

> The collapse of community spirit in the last few decades and the erosion of civic virtue are caused not by the spread of greed but the dead hand of Leviathan. The bureaucratic state makes no bargain with the citizen to take joint responsibility for civic order, engenders no obligation, duty or pride and imposes obedience instead.
>
> The roots of social order are in our heads, where we possess the instinctive capacity for creating not a perfectly harmonious and virtuous society but a better one than the one that we have at the present. We must build our institutions in such a way that draws out those instincts. Preeminently this means the encouragement of exchange between equals. Just as trade between countries is the best recipe for friendship between them, so exchange between enfranchised and empowered individuals is the best recipe for cooperation. We must encourage social and material exchange between equals for that is the raw material of trust and trust is the foundation of virtue [p. 265].

Gardner (1990) believed that to create common purpose, we must focus on shared values. He suggests a path forward: "Every successful society we know about has created a framework of laws, unwritten customs, norms of conduct and values to channel behavior toward purposes it deems acceptable. Social commentators have an understandable impulse to focus on our disagreements over values. But if we care about the American Experiment, we had better search out and celebrate the values we share" (p. 75). In fact, promising experiments nationwide are trying to create new ways to channel individual initiative into collaborative action based on shared values.

Promising Experiments: Creating Common Purpose

Civic revolutionaries can create common purpose between the individual and the community in the following ways:

- Forging common ground through dialogue that leads to action

- Mobilizing complex interests through new networks

In the face of clashing freedoms and factions, civic revolutionaries are experimenting with new approaches. They are creating common purpose out of competing interests and complex environments. They are searching and finding shared or complementary values among diverse interests, rather than accepting that different interests mean different or conflicting values. They have taken different paths, used different methods, and focused on different issues, but they share the belief that common ground can develop through mutual understanding and collaborative action.

Forging Common Ground Through Dialogue
That Leads to Action

A growing number of communities and regions are employing *dialogue* to find a realistic common ground, fully recognizing choices and consciously making whatever trade-offs are necessary. These places are experimenting with a mode of interaction that differs significantly from the traditional pattern of discourse between competing interests: *debate*. Daniel Yankelovich, one of America's leading social scientists and public opinion experts, explains the difference between debate and dialogue in his book *The Magic of Dialogue: Transforming Conflict into Cooperation* (1999). Whereas the goal of debate is to defend one's position and critique the opposition, the goal of dialogue is to establish mutual understanding through a process that suspends judgment, reveals assumptions on both sides, and includes diverse perspectives through empathetic listening. This process replaces the adversarial dynamic of debate with a collaborative one that builds trust, an essential quality that helps shift people's orientation from an individual to a community point of view.

In most regions today, debate continues to be the primary mode of interaction in public settings, from legislative bodies to city council meetings. For leaders who are baffled at why well-intentioned civic engagement efforts produce more conflict than consensus, they should consider that it might be because the community is using debate—not dialogue—to address the issues. Debate is about winning. It is an approach that is well suited to special interests that have decided on a fixed position and are trying to prevail over other interests, but it can get in the way of finding creative solutions to difficult problems or of finding common values that can serve as the basis for common action. On complex regional issues, Yankelovich suggests that people care as much about values as about facts and want the opportunity to discuss them in a thoughtful way.

The use of dialogue or bargaining is proving to be effective in addressing the tension between individual and community interests. Promising experiments from San Diego, California, and Charlotte, North Carolina, are described here.

San Diego Dialogue

In the late 1980s, San Diego experienced significant economic and social changes. With the downsizing of the defense industry, the region lost thousands of jobs. Residents were disenchanted with the political process, the lack of regional planning, and the deteriorating quality of life. At the same time, waves of immigrants who were crossing the border put pressure on public services and became an increasingly contentious issue. Malin Burnham, chair of the University of California San Diego Foundation and longtime civic leader, recalls the tension: "You could feel the conflict within the region and the frustration caused by inadequate long-range planning. Most organizations were concerned with today's problems and their own survival. We needed an organization to fill this gap."

A group of civic leaders asked the University of California-San Diego (UCSD) to set up an independent organization—San Diego Dialogue—to help put facts on the table and bring the community together around regional challenges. The university was a natural home for neutral convening. "People said the university could serve as the honest broker. When you don't have established companies or large foundations, a university like this can be the vital partner," explains Mary Walshok, associate vice chancellor of UCSD. With the divisions that existed in the community, it was critical for San Diego Dialogue to be independently funded, free of politics, and a source of objective research on regional issues.

San Diego Dialogue began with twenty-five to thirty diverse leaders and eventually increased to a hundred. They came from business, civic, and educational backgrounds and had a common agenda: a commitment to creating a better place. At the first focus group, the Dialogue asked, "Who are we, where are we going?" Participants realized that the San Diego region did not stop at the border—things like crime, pollution, and culture transcended state lines. According to Burnham, "We couldn't be effective and have a long-range view without a regional approach. We quickly came to describe our region as including at least some part of the Tijuana area." Walshok adds, "We started out thinking that the future was north—Orange County and Los Angeles. It was a great surprise when we figured out that we needed to look south. Today 35 percent of the Dialogue is about Mexico. Here's what we do. We poll leaders on issues. We develop a research agenda. We produce in-depth analysis on key topics. We have dialogue sessions on finding new solutions."

How did San Diego use the process of dialogue to address the tension between individual and community? It helped the region build trust and break old habits that discouraged real problem solving. Richard Barrera, executive director of the Consensus Organizing Institute and a leader in the Hispanic community, observed at a May 2002 forum of the Alliance for Regional Stewardship:

At a meeting of business leaders and school principals, the conversation began with us telling them all the things they were doing wrong. The principals then, patiently, said, "Let us describe what's going on." They talked about having 70 percent turnover rates and fifty or so languages spoken by students. People got quiet. What started as a clear agenda shifted. We began talking about the principles of community building very pragmatically. We also talked about leadership and the challenge of a constantly changing community, where you can't talk to one person and trust that they represent everybody else. You have to have lots of conversations and do a lot of listening—not with a set agenda but by allowing an agenda to emerge, taking it slowly.

Through patient listening, dialogue fostered a deeper understanding of issues and created new relationships in the region. Barrera notes that the process of building connections has helped break down borders between groups. Conversations began to focus on community solutions rather than on individual grievances. The power of dialogue in San Diego has led to specific breakthroughs: improving border-crossing infrastructure, university-industry collaboration, education, and land use and transportation, as well as larger issues of regional governance. The economic transformation of San Diego in recent years has been significantly aided by these improvements, including the development of new biotechnology and communications industries.

Recently, the ChoiceWork Dialogue approach developed by Daniel Yankelovich and his company, Viewpoint Learning, was used to help San Diego leaders determine how regional land use, transportation, and housing issues might be addressed more effectively and be better aligned with public priorities. Like many regions, San Diego has been exploring different governance options for more integrated approaches to growth issues, including a directly elected regional model such as Portland Metro, an appointed model such as the Twin Cities, and a more ad hoc model such as Denver. A commission was created by the legislature to study the issue and recommend one plan to consolidate regional organizations and another plan to coordinate their activities. ChoiceWork Dialogue contributed to this process by engaging representative groups of citizens in a structured discussion of the issues and options as well as the trade-offs that each would require. After wrestling with the issue over the course of an eight-hour dialogue, participants broadened their views from a focus on their needs in individual communities to a desire for more regional solutions. Viewpoint Learning is now using its new public-learning model in other communities in California, including Orange County.

ChoiceWork Dialogue is based on an insight about how the public reaches judgment on difficult or emotion-laden issues. The conventional model holds that public opinion is formed through a simple two-stage process: information leads to public judgment. However, when issues involve conflicting values and hard choices, a complex process of "working through" intervenes between information and resolution—and issues can remain stuck at that stage for months, years, or decades. ChoiceWork Dialogues are designed to help participants progress through the four critical steps of the working-through stage: (1) taking in the facts, (2) connecting the dots, (3) facing up to conflicting values, (4) shifting from an individual to a community-based point of view. They help people move beyond their initial impulse to avoid hard choices and disagreeable realities, encouraging them to come to grips with difficult issues in dialogue with one another and to work together to reconcile their views with their deeper values.

For San Diego and elsewhere, Daniel Yankelovich (1999) argues that dialogue is essential for transforming conflict into cooperation. He believes that "increasingly we find ourselves facing problems requiring more shared understanding than in the past. . . . The traditional top-down style of leadership in semi-isolation from others is increasingly out of vogue. It is being replaced by what I have come to think of as 'relational leadership' with others rather than handing down visions, strategies and plans as if they were commandments from mountaintops" (p. 13). Like Gardner, Yankelovich understands the need for a new form of communication to identify common, underlying values that move past traditional, adversarial debate on issues. Even when interests are based on conflicting values, dialogue can be a way of developing better mutual understanding and can set the stage for bargaining without rancor. In this more diverse, less hierarchical world, decision makers need to learn to argue less and dialogue more so they can learn and act more effectively.

Charlotte Voices & Choices

A different example of how dialogue can lead to new forms of regional action is demonstrated in Charlotte, North Carolina. In 1995, four regional organizations—Foundation for the Carolinas, the *Charlotte Observer*, Carolina's Regional Partnership (now Charlotte Regional Partnership), and the Urban Institute of University of North Carolina-Charlotte—cosponsored a Citistates report for the Charlotte region. Written by national journalists Neal Peirce and Curtis Johnson, a Citistates report provides an independent assessment of the region's major problems and opportunities—most notably, the impacts of growth—through a series of in-depth articles published in a major local newspaper. In this case, the sponsor was the *Charlotte Observer*. Peirce and Johnson (1995) suggested that Charlotte needed "multiple forums—regionwide and locally—to put the decisions about your physical growth, your educational future, your parks, towns and neighborhoods, into the hands of thousands of citizens." Their recommendation ultimately led to the creation of a new platform for civic engagement, Voices & Choices.

The Citistates report provoked a spirited civic dialogue on the impacts of growth. Mary Newsom, associate editor of the *Charlotte Observer*, recalls the public's response: "The public reaction was incredible. We got several hundred phone calls, a lot of letters, a lot of just regular folks saying, 'You guys are right on target.' There was a dramatic increase in the talk about trying to manage growth." Newsom also describes how the report challenged individual notions and opened new avenues for discussion: "After the report, one of our most conservative local politicians said, 'Maybe that outer-belt highway is a mistake.' Indeed we had a semipublic debate about that issue. Until recently, even to question the outer belt was the civic equivalent of going to a dinner party and mooning the hostess. The Peirce report made it OK to question those things."

Voices & Choices (originally called Central Carolina Choices) formed to facilitate further regional dialogue and engagement across the region. In 1997, the Mecklenburg County Commission asked Voices & Choices to facilitate an environmental summit that would focus the region's attention on economic and environmental sustainability issues. In preparation for the summit, Voices & Choices developed three different growth scenarios for the region and held numerous town hall meetings to discuss the scenarios with residents. The grassroots effort encompassed the fourteen-county region of Charlotte and engaged more than five hundred diverse residents—community members, business leaders, and environmental activists—over four months. Betty Chafin Rash, founding executive director of Voices & Choices, notes the shared vision that began to emerge: "Through dialogue, we found remarkable consensus on a vision for the future. We may have held different views on how to get there, but we agreed on where we wanted to go." Common ground was being forged one conversation at a time.

The community engagement efforts culminated in a regional environmental summit held in November 1998, where more than 550 people worked together to craft a regional vision and establish priorities. By the end of the summit, participants had affirmed the need for regional cooperation and recognized the connections between environmental health, economic sustainability, and quality of life. Rash describes the event: "The summit was significant in that, for the first time, so many diverse stakeholders came together to focus on the environmental challenges of our region. I saw business leaders, chamber executives, government officials, planners, environmentalists, community activists . . . a true cross section of the region. All fourteen counties were represented. Most people left wanting to stay engaged in some way. The challenge was how to keep them engaged." The success of the environmental summit rested, in large part, on the ongoing efforts of the local media, community groups, and civic leaders to raise awareness and encourage discussion of environmental issues.

Beyond finding common ground through dialogue, Voices & Choices was successful because it effectively transformed dialogue into action. "Concern about regional problems had been building for several years," according to Bill Spencer, former president of the Foundation for the Carolinas. "The dialogue was already there in local communities across the region. Voices & Choices helped move the dialogue from opinion to plans for action." The key is to maintain the momentum with actionable next steps. Following the summit, Voices & Choices formed six action teams in the areas of land use, open space, transportation, air quality, water quality, and resource recovery and recycling. Hundreds of citizens participated on the teams, which deliberated from May to December 1999 and ultimately recommended more than 150 action items. A final report was issued in early 2001, detailing the committees' action items and one principal recommendation: an integrated land use–transportation plan with an open-space commitment under the guidance of a regional body.

Currently, Voices & Choices is working toward implementing the regional plan while continuing to engage citizens. Some early achievements include the passage of a half-cent sales tax increase to finance a comprehensive regional transportation system. The system will cost almost $3 billion, uses regional funds to leverage three times the amount in federal and state funds, and will consist of a mix of rail, bus, and streetcar lines. The system will explicitly include significantly better service to disadvantaged, predominantly African American and Latino neighborhoods, a result that would likely not have happened without Voices & Choices dialogues. Furthermore the Business Committee for Regional Transportation is supporting the creation of a regional planning alliance and the notion of a true regional transportation authority. Most recently, city and county officials are planning to connect their separate greenway projects into a new four-county, 150-mile Catawba Regional Trail.

Voices & Choices is an example of a regional stewardship initiative that has used dialogue to connect leadership with grassroots citizens to address complex regional issues in more effective ways. Although many would agree that more work is necessary in this complex bistate region to promote boundary crossing along racial, income, and political lines, the critical first step has been taken by creating a platform for understanding and reconciling competing interests through dialogue.

Mobilizing Complex Interests Through New Networks

To move from competing interests to complementarity, a growing number of communities and regions are experimenting with new kinds of problem-solving alliances, teams of diverse interests that traditionally have not worked together, to create and implement solutions. In Silicon Valley, for example, an uncommon alliance between environmental groups and developers was formed to address a severe housing shortage while business and education leaders teamed up to wire every school in the region. In other places, leaders are creating cohesive networks—within and across communities—to tackle a complex issue of shared concern. In Detroit, the faith community mobilized its participants to tackle transportation issues. In California, facilitated by the California Center for Regional Leadership, a coalition of regional organizations from throughout the state worked collectively to influence state policy.

The Housing Action Coalition

The Housing Action Coalition (HAC) was formed by the Silicon Valley Manufacturing Group (SVMG) in 1993 to advocate for affordable housing for the Silicon Valley region. The lack of relatively affordable and accessible housing has been a chronic concern to Santa Clara County residents and employers. It threatens not only the area's overall quality of life but its economic vitality as well. The lack of affordable housing contributes to continued urban sprawl and the destruction of natural resources and results in increasing traffic congestion, air pollution, and difficulties in attracting and retaining employees.

The idea for the Housing Action Coalition originated with Don Weden, planning director for Santa Clara County. At the time, housing projects were easily defeated in city council meetings because public input often opposed projects on the basis of increased traffic congestion, neighborhood crowding, or other unwelcome changes. Without a broader, community voice in support of specific housing projects (that is, projects that would benefit the region as a whole), Silicon Valley would continue to neglect its housing needs.

Don Weden approached SVMG and said, "What we need is something like a housing action coalition to advocate for homes people can afford." The idea fit well with SVMG's "smart-growth" agenda, and Carl Guardino, president and CEO of SVMG, helped form the Housing Action Coalition with others from the community, including representatives from the city of San Jose, Hewlett-Packard, the Home Builders Association, and the Greenbelt Alliance. Drawing on builders, environmentalists, labor organizations, apartment interest groups, real estate organizations, major employers, faith groups, the Sierra Club, and the League of Women Voters, Guardino organized a coalition that knit together different interests in a common cause. "The first six months were rocky. It took several months to get people off of their soapboxes and onto common ground."

The coalition developed a set of general goals and specific criteria for housing proposals that it could support and adopted those goals and criteria in 1993. The general goals adhere to smart-growth principles: they discourage urban sprawl; promote the use of public transit; provide for mixed uses within a neighborhood; promote affordability, innovative community design, economic development, and sustainability; and minimize the cost of city services. The specific criteria help HAC members decide which housing proposals to support by detailing the location, density, affordability, design, size, and safety features that must be in place. As an example, housing proposals must have an overall density of at least fourteen units per acre and must be located within an existing urban service area. Once HAC gets behind a project, it mobilizes its membership to attend public hearings, where typically such housing proposals are killed by NIMBY ("not in my backyard") attitudes.

To date, the coalition has successfully advocated for more than thirty-two thousand new homes, many of them transit oriented and about half of them affordable to low- and moderate-income earners. The coalition has successfully advocated for high-quality, higher-density housing that uses land efficiently and keeps costs relatively low. Coalition members speak on behalf of future residents and burst myths about the likely effects of new housing on the quality of existing neighborhoods. The coalition today includes more than 150 individuals from local companies, the Home Builders Association, the Sierra Club, the Association of Realtors, Valley Transportation Authority, the City of San Jose, and the Greenbelt Alliance, among others.

Early on, HAC members decided that the group would only support development projects, not oppose them. According to Guardino, "The decision to be a positive voice in the community for housing builds a system of trust both internally [within HAC of diverse interests working together] and externally [in relation to the Silicon Valley community]. We knew that there was no way we would have the support of the developers or the cities who approached HAC for various projects if we shut them down and didn't support them. It had to be positive."

Looking ahead, the greatest challenge to HAC is keeping the coalition together. People come to the table from very diverse perspectives, some from business and others from a nonprofit perspective. According to Shiloh Ballard, HAC program manager, "Ultimately, this coalition is a place where we all agree, if an issue is too contentious, we will take it off the table. It means that we have a broad membership and that our focus is very narrow." HAC's narrow focus delivers tangible results, which allows HAC to hold the interest of its diverse membership. "It is part of the [Silicon] Valley makeup that we want to solve problems rather than whine about them, and that's one of the chief reasons for the success of the HAC. . . . People stay involved in the HAC because they are making a quantifiable difference."

Silicon Valley's NetDay Initiative

The rapid spread of the Internet in the mid-1990s created a natural interest in wiring schools. The cause became a priority of then President Clinton and then Vice President Gore, and regions across the country took up the charge. Many efforts fizzled out, however, never reaching scale or leaving behind wiring and technology that made little difference in educational performance. This was not so in Silicon Valley, however, where armies of volunteers successfully connected nearly every public school and at least 75 percent of classrooms in each school to the Internet over a period of three years.

The regional effort in Silicon Valley turned out differently for several reasons. Success hinged more on the application of social innovation than on physical technology. The catalyst was Smart Valley, a regional initiative that emerged out of a participatory civic process called Joint Venture: Silicon Valley. Smart Valley mobilized an alliance of technology workers, venture capitalists, community leaders, school administrators, and thousands of volunteers around NetDay, an ambitious three-day event to wire public schools. In addition to creating new collaborative partnerships, Smart Valley used a few simple organizing principles to manage the project's complexity. The key ingredients were the following:

- *Flexible, self-organizing teams.* To manage the volume of volunteers interested in becoming involved, Smart Valley created a flexible network infrastructure. Volunteers registered on a Web site and specified the day and the task that most matched their interests and abilities. They were assigned to a nearby school with the most need and received updates electronically. Anyone with ten or more volunteers was eligible to come to a training session as a team leader and received more direct support. Smart Valley encouraged people to expand the system and modify it for their use. In this way, more than twenty thousand volunteers were mobilized and distributed to schools regionwide—in wealthy and disadvantaged neighborhoods alike.

- *An integrated approach for technology donations, standards, and implementation guidelines.* Smart Valley worked with companies to negotiate donations of compatible equipment and with technical experts to set uniform standards for implementation. Smart Valley then assembled a step-by-step guidebook to ensure effective implementation of wiring and technology.

- *A commitment to capacity development.* Recognizing that donations and willing volunteers would be ineffectual if schools did not have the capacity to make use of them, Smart Valley also tried to build organizational capacity. Every school district was required to name a project manager, create a district technology plan (with assistance from community experts), and plan for what would happen after NetDay. Smart Valley also hosted a series of expert workshops to train project managers and team leaders. "The most valuable thing for most school districts," reports Karen Greenwood, project director of NetDay, "was the assistance they received with planning and training."

The Silicon Valley NetDay Initiative was successful because it created an infrastructure well suited to complexity, meshing together volunteers, donations, and capacity-building assistance in a flexible, yet disciplined, fashion.

To channel individual initiative into collective action, some civic revolutionaries are pursuing their work through voluntary networks for action. In a growing number of communities across the country, new models of community-to-community mobilization have emerged, with the express purpose of participating in regional decision-making processes. These efforts seek to unite dispersed local interests around a shared purpose, linking with regional interests in common cause.

Detroit's MOSES

To win support for a regional transportation equity campaign, an organization called Metropolitan Organizing Strategies Enabling Strength (MOSES), a faith-based network affiliated with the Gamaliel Foundation, mobilized an uncommon coalition of urban and suburban interests to improve public transportation options in the Detroit region. With its strong ties to the city, MOSES had historically taken on urban issues such as drug enforcement and access to public facilities. MOSES decided to take up the issue of regional transportation because "it is a unifying issue that brings both city and suburban congregations together. Better regional public transit benefits people across geographical boundaries. It cuts across age, race, and income by improving access to jobs, health care, and education," according to Vicky Kovari, a member of MOSES.

Detroit is now the only major city in America that does not have a rapid transit system. Part of the problem is structural: the state constitution stipulates that at least 90 percent of state transportation dollars must be spent on roads and bridges (leaving only 10 percent that can be spent on public transportation). In the past few years, however, state spending on public transportation has hovered closer to 8 or 9 percent of the total transportation budget. With three in ten residents too poor to own a car, the lack of public transportation was posed not only as an equity issue but also as one that has negative impacts on suburban retailers, who draw their workforce primarily from the city.

To bridge the deep divisions between Detroit's urban population (which is 85 percent African American) and its suburban population (which is 80 to 90 percent Caucasian), MOSES reached out to congregations outside the city of Detroit. They held thousands of what they call "one-on-ones" and gave group presentations in suburban cities. The goal was to understand the views of their counterparts and to find common, or at least compatible, interests for changes in the prevailing transportation system in metropolitan Detroit. As a result, MOSES was able to create a network of multiple interests, whose membership was one-third suburban. Bill O'Brien, the executive director of MOSES believes that "the secret of success is bringing others in the same room. How big is the room? Larger than we thought because it has the cities, suburbs, and farms in it" (Bonfiglio, 2002).

MOSES created a campaign mechanism that built in roles for the business community, including the Detroit Metro Chamber of Commerce and the Big Three automakers, as well as mayors, labor unions, and legislators. Through a series of public meetings organized by MOSES and other regional actors, momentum has begun to build for a regional transportation agenda. In November 1999, MOSES brought leaders to the first-ever regional meeting on transportation, attended by eight hundred citizens, all three county executives, and other local elected politicians. In 2000, it successfully lobbied to pass an appropriations bill that increased public transit funds by $50 million. Two years later, MOSES rallied five thousand people—a cross section of urban and suburban residents, business leaders, faith leaders, young and old—to meet with gubernatorial and congressional candidates to express their support for a regional transportation plan. This public support was instrumental to the passage of a state bill to create the Detroit Area Regional Transportation Authority (DARTA).

"Our power comes from being able to mobilize hundreds and thousands of people," says Kovari. "No other organization around here can do that. People were amazed that we could get five thousand urban and suburban residents to turn out for our public meeting—especially in a region as segregated as Detroit. We are serious about using power to make our voices heard." MOSES leaders start by building relationships with the community through their one-on-ones. Delegations spend a significant amount of time doing outreach in the community and training every member to become a leader. The result is extensive and inclusive networks that can be mobilized around a common purpose.

The bill to create DARTA was vetoed in December 2002 by John Engler, the outgoing governor of Michigan, but thanks to the persistent efforts of MOSES and other community organizations, a revised bill is being reconsidered in the new legislature. The coalition continues to grow, as the dispersed interests of faith communities, environmentalists, labor, and business unite across urban-suburban lines to work toward an improved regional transportation system.

California Center for Regional Leadership

If solving problems at the regional level presents a complex set of challenges, then imagine the considerable complexity of organizing competing interests in California, the most diverse and populous state in the country. That is exactly what the California Center for Regional Leadership (CCRL) encountered when it began to organize a network of twenty-one collaborative regional initiatives (CRIs) throughout California. CRIs—civic organizations or partnerships led by people from business, government, education, and the community—are at the forefront of a new type of governance that is regional in scope, collaborative in nature, and grounded in the interdependence of economy, environment, and social equity. Initially supported by the Irvine Foundation's Sustainable Communities Program, CRIs are self-organizing systems that have emerged from the bottom up in response to complex regional problems.

CCRL was established to support, facilitate, and promote innovative solutions among the CRIs. In addition to helping each CRI become more effective, CCRL plays an important role in connecting these groups into an effective coalition that influences California state policy. By identifying statewide issues that are important to regions— such as tax reform, infrastructure planning, and economic strategy— CCRL found a common agenda to bring to legislators in Sacramento.

In particular, CCRL was instrumental to the California Assembly Speaker's Commission on Regionalism, initiated by Speaker Robert Hertzberg in 2000. Nick Bollman, president and CEO of CCRL, was appointed chair of the commission, which included thirty-one commissioners from California's many different regions. The need for the Speaker's Commission on Regionalism arose because, according to Hertzberg, "California has had the same fifty-eight counties since 1907 even though the state has transformed itself over and over again. That's why it is no surprise that California's government structure is outdated and poorly equipped to deal with many of the issues of the day. If government is going to provide Californians with the services they deserve, it is going to have to change. If government is going to be effective in this mobile new economy, it is going to have to start to think regionally."

After fourteen months of study, commission outreach meetings in eight regions across the state, a hundred presentations, and fifteen newly commissioned research papers, *The New California Dream: Regional Solutions for Twenty-First Century Challenges* was issued in January 2002, with more than a hundred policy reform recommendations addressing a wide variety of issues: the economy, workforce, social equity, state-local finance reform, growth, schools, the environment, regional collaboration, state government reform, and building a new regional civic culture. Today significant outcomes have been realized as a result of the report. These include

- Reinvigoration of the California Economic Strategy Panel, a public-private entity established to advise and lead state government on policies that will support the competitiveness of California's economic regions

- Consolidation of workforce investment programs into a single state agency, to bring greater coherence to state strategies supportive of improved worker preparation for the dynamic needs of regional economies

- Adoption of new state-planning legislation (AB 857), which requires state agencies to adopt explicit goals and strategies, and in a manner integrated across the spectrum of agencies, to achieve regional planning goals: urban infill; protection of open space, habitats, and working landscapes; and more efficient use of the land wherever development occurs (including new towns and suburbs)

Through the speaker's commission and the network of connected CRIs, CCRL has helped mobilize complex interests into a common, actionable strategy. As Bollman puts it, "The twenty-first century governance model for California requires that the state government become an authentic and reliable partner to California's diverse regions. This requires in turn that regional leaders understand and embrace the long-term needs and interests in their regions and act together to bring the state to the regional table. Though there is much more to do, working together the regions and the state have begun to head in that direction. Stay tuned."

Insights from the Field

Every region and community must find its own way, its own resolution of the creative tension between individual freedom and liberty and community responsibility and duty. At the same time, civic revolutionaries in every region and community can benefit from the experiences of others. With growing experimentation in American regions, some insights from the field are useful to consider, organized in the following sections according to the practical roles for civic revolutionaries—to discover, decide, and drive change.

Discover: Building a Compelling Case for Change

Start by considering both the competition of interests and the complexity of the problem-solving environment. What civic revolutionaries have found is that the tension between individual and community interests is a product of two important but different challenges. Competition of interests requires new forms of communication and commitment to seek out any underlying shared values, which could serve as the basis for agreement. A new kind of communication is responsible for breakthroughs in places such as San Diego, Charlotte, and Silicon Valley, where civic revolutionaries did not assume that different interests meant different values. They may, but if one begins with the assumption of irreconcilable differences, one will end up with a self-fulfilling prophecy.

The complexity of the problem-solving environment requires a new kind of networking of interests—one that breaks down "silos" (barriers separating interests) and leverages the efforts of likeminded leaders. Assume that many people do share values about moving the region forward, and create a civic "space" where they can congregate, as civic revolutionaries in Silicon Valley and Detroit have done. In California, the statewide "network of regional networks" provides a diverse set of examples for how to provide new forums for complex, but often common, interests to congregate and learn about one another, setting the stage for collaborative action.

Diagnose your situation, using a variety of methods to frame challenges and possibilities for change. In many regions, such as Sacramento, Jacksonville, and the Washington, D.C., region, civic revolutionaries have championed indexes of economic, environmental, and social indicators that help put the facts on the table, frame challenges in a more integrated fashion, and stimulate a new kind of conversation about the future. In places such as Indianapolis, they have used comparative analyses of other regions to give people a sense of context about where the community stands and to instill a sense of competition and urgency for change. In regions such as Portland, the Sierra Nevada counties of California, and Pittsburgh, they have done public opinion surveys to quantify data that are otherwise unavailable or to gauge public values and attitudes. In many places, such as Atlanta and Columbus, they have taken intercity visits to learn about the experiences of other places. In regions such as San Diego and Cincinnati, they have also invited practitioners and experts to their community to provide outside perspectives on regional challenges. All of these approaches can help frame current realities and possibilities for change.

Build a database of potential civic revolutionaries and identify the key bridge builders. One of the most important roles for civic revolutionaries is discovering allies. There are many different ways to recruit, and civic revolutionaries in Richmond, Virginia, offer a useful example: begin with your immediate network and identify people who could be potential civic revolutionaries, people who have shown a flair for working through tensions between competing values, are dissatisfied with the status quo, and are open to new ideas from within your region and beyond. Then ask each individual in your immediate network to do the same, further building the database of potential civic revolutionaries. By going to the third level of networks, you are probably going to tap into a pool of people who are not visible, well-known leaders; perhaps they are younger or are leaders of certain communities (for example, racial, neighborhood, issue specific, industry, professional). From this exercise, identify key bridge builders, those who have extensive networks that reach into multiple communities of interest.

Break from traditional patterns of civic engagement to diagnose real needs and discover real allies. What is clear from experimentation across the country is that one cannot expect to get new results from traditional processes. We have more than enough forums for debate that lead to winners and losers in American society and too few arenas for dialogue that lead to a real exchange of views, collaborative action, and positive-sum outcomes. Create a new arena for dialogue as has been done in Charlotte, San Diego, and other places, initially to help diagnose the situation facing the region or interpret the index, survey, or other analytical work that tries to put the facts on the table. Use this initial work to recruit like-minded civic revolutionaries to the core team that is championing change. Such a forum can also provide an open learning environment for considering the experiences of other places and how they might apply in your community or region.

A number of tools and techniques are now available to support new patterns of civic engagement, including visualization tools, simulation, geographic information systems and modeling techniques, and other community process tools. Although many tools and techniques are available, civic revolutionaries need to customize and experiment through trial and error to arrive at the civic process that best fits their region. Beware of letting the tools drive the process. Too often, high-tech tools can complicate or distract from the process of real exchange among participants. A 2000 report for the California Center for Regional Leadership, *Informed Regional Choices*, found that although civic organizations had a need and a desire to use new participation tools, many faced practical barriers to their effective use, including a lack of the following:

- Awareness of and readiness to use new tools both in the organization and among constituents

- Resources to enable use of tools, at a moment in time and sustainable over time

- Feedback systems to improve choices and uses over time, internal learning systems and peer-to-peer systems

- Technical readiness, especially telecommunication infrastructure

- Feedback to suppliers for continuous tools improvement

The most important lesson learned from regional experiments with civic engagement is that tools must be connected to effective community problem-solving *processes* to be effective. Tools should help amplify and extend what is already an effective process design.

Decide: Making Critical Choices in Experimentation

Create a decision-making framework. There is great risk in diagnosing needs, opening up new ideas and possibilities, and exciting new allies without any framework to make decisions about what to do next. It is a formula for frustration or, even worse, cynicism. The design of the decision-making framework should be inclusive, not top down. Civic revolutionaries should build it together and agree to the final formulation. Based on the rich diversity of experience from around the country, such a framework can be based on a few simple guidelines or decision-making criteria or a series of decision-making steps. Important lessons include

- *Clearly defining the scope of decision making.* Reframe and connect issues based on the diagnosis of community challenges, the diversity of regional voices, and the discovery of innovations from other places. You cannot be all things to all people or "solve world hunger" overnight, nor do you want to aim too low, just moving organizational boxes around or endorsing what would likely happen anyway. So the challenge is in defining the scope of decision making to be big enough to make a difference, but bounded enough to get something done.

- *Articulating a few breakthrough choices.* Within the scope of decision making, agree on what the breakthrough choices are, key decisions that represent bold experimentation with new approaches rather than tinkering with the status quo. One way to identify key breakthrough points is to map a *story of change*, linking a chain of actions that could lead to major results.

However, do not try to make thousands of tactical decisions up front, setting out detailed tasks or an elaborate plan. Instead focus on the few fundamental choices that will shape the environment for later decisions that must be made in implementation.

- *Creating a road map for decision making.* Provide a discipline and timetable for coming to decisions, rather than a well-meaning but open-ended process of weighing alternatives that puts off decisions as long as possible. Give people a sense of expectation for forward movement. Instill a sense of urgency by creating a pattern of *task, deadline, event.*

Define simple rules or operating principles that can transform the complexity of interests into the commonality of purpose. Complexity without simple rules quickly devolves into chaos and confusion. However counterintuitive it might seem, the agreement to simple rules or operating principles for collective action can channel complexity into impressive results. Of course, a critical difference exists between arriving at a set of simple rules that have great weight and utility and following a set of simplistic guidelines that are little more than wishful thinking. To agree on a set of simple rules to cope with complexity (like the Constitution) requires time and sometimes difficult interactions to discover underlying values and articulate workable guidelines for joint action.

Remember that common purpose is not the same as consensus. Many regions have engaged in visioning processes or consensus-seeking efforts that produced either vague goals or limited least-common-denominator actions that made little difference. Consensus is important, but gradients of agreement can be defined that offer an acceptable degree of consensus, allow for creative but generally consistent interpretations, and enable a networked effort to move forward. For example, in Sacramento, regional Hewlett-Packard manager Larry Welch introduced such guidelines into efforts to

choose the best mix of economic, social, and environmental measures of regional progress.

Civic revolutionaries in regions such as Chicago, Boston, and
Denver have agreed to operating principles that channel complexity in a common direction. In some places, such as Chicago, these
principles define desired behavior (for example, taking availability
of affordable housing and access to public transit into account in
corporate location decisions). One of the models for these kinds of
approaches is the Sullivan Principles, which emerged as an answer
to opposing apartheid in South Africa specifically and defined a set
of actions for individual companies to adopt in their operations in
countries around the world.

In other regions, such as Boston and Denver, the "terms of
engagement," or guidelines for action, are embedded in a more comprehensive compact for change. In these cases, and similar examples across the country, much effort is focused on creating the most
powerful and useful set of guidelines, rather than on getting the
implementation details just right. Charles Euchner of Harvard's
Rappaport Institute for Greater Boston describes what is emerging
in his region as a system "that would establish a relative handful of
simple but strong rules to guide the innumerable decisions of individual actors—and then back off and let those individuals create
their own order and rich networks rather than trying to impose a
single order. The state would establish clear rules and processes for
highways, transit, housing, open space and economic development.
Those rules and processes would establish the parameters for policy
for local government but would otherwise leave local government
alone" (Euchner, 2002, p. 28). In these regions, it is not about creating regional government, but rather about new forms of regional
collaboration that are both disciplined and open to innovation.

Drive: Mobilizing Allies for Change

Create new networking vehicles to initiate change. New platforms, not
new organizations per se, are indispensable. Channeling individual
initiative into collective action requires new platforms—networks,

campaigns, projects—that can be widely owned and are adaptable in design and implementation. Civic revolutionaries in regions such as Detroit and Silicon Valley developed new kinds of problem-solving "platforms"—structured like campaigns—to network complex interests. New vehicles that are not organizations per se also help limit the natural opposition of existing organizations and their benefactors. They initiate change immediately, and if designed effectively, they offer an alternative to traditional approaches in a relatively short amount of time. They also tend to stimulate a conversation about organizational restructuring as the energy and results generated by the new approach begin to ripple across the region. In contrast, starting with formal organizational restructuring, without an emerging alternative, is unlikely to succeed.

What these new vehicles have in common is that they are network models, operating somewhere between hierarchies and markets. Both researchers (for example, Oliver Williamson, Elinor Ostrom, and others) and practitioners have found a strong rationale for networks in the kind of complex problem-solving environment of our time. Hierarchical, market, and network approaches work best under different conditions:

- *Hierarchies.* In stable environments, hierarchical forms of organization make sense because they can reduce transaction costs through formal vertical integration within the organization.

- *Markets.* In fluid environments, market forms of organization make sense because maximum flexibility and creativity are required to try out many approaches and move quickly from failures to new experiments.

- *Networks.* In complex environments, networks make sense because they can direct the creative power of markets toward common purposes by using simple rules and trust relationships typical of hierarchies.

In today's environment, the network model that channels a complex array of efforts in a common direction works much better than a hierarchical model that attempts to allocate roles and focuses on a single strategy. In fact, we have entered a new era of networked or distributed governance, which requires a combination of dialogue, simple rules for guiding complex action, and new networking platforms to mobilize action.

Mobilize networks of people, not committees of organizational representatives. Focus on budding civic revolutionaries and their interests, aspirations, and expertise, not on their organizational positions. Although organizational roles are important considerations, experience shows that people drive revolutions, often going way beyond their job descriptions to experiment with new approaches. Even if they are not in a formal position of organizational leadership, or one of several board members, they can use their influence with formal organizational leaders.

Civic revolutionaries have networks, and every person in their networks has networks. Understanding and mobilizing these networks is the key to driving change. Civic revolutionaries have to be modern-day community organizers—but often operating at the regional level. As MOSES in Detroit has demonstrated, such a mobilization requires careful preparation and extensive bridge building before taking action. In Austin, the linked mobilization of networks of established business and civic leaders and emerging entrepreneurial leaders—beyond the usual organizational advocates—was instrumental in passage of major funding for regional transportation improvements.

What Success Looks Like: Common Purpose

Common purpose is what reconciles the competing values of individual and community. Although the experience varies from region to region and community to community, a point exists at which individual freedom and liberty mesh with community duty and responsibility around a common purpose that delivers mutual benefits. As this chapter has shown, there are many pathways, strategies, and techniques to forge common purpose. But what does success look like?

- People voluntarily exercise their freedom to build a community of place, believing that they will gain more in social benefits than they give up in individual liberty.

- Competing interests form working relationships based on complementary values and roles.

- Complex problems transform into manageable tasks, and independent efforts are channeled into collaborative action based on simple but elegant guiding principles.

2

Trust and Accountability
Building Webs of Responsibility

*Most residents have neither the time nor the inclination
to participate daily in the deliberations of their community. Many vote, some write letters or attend civic
meetings, but most generally trust the "system" to keep
their community moving forward. Implicit bonds of
trust provide the lubrication for the engine of government to operate. When major disturbances, such as
scandals or economic crises, or creeping problems, such
as traffic congestion or educational decline, raise questions about the system, there is a call for accountability,
but the lines of responsibility are unclear. The social
contract between residents and community breaks
down. The practical question is how to reconcile the
competing American values of trust and accountability
to rebuild the social contract.*

Trust in the American system—the people, institutions, and
processes of American civic life—is at the core of the American Experiment. Without confidence in the system, little else is possible. In America, the system is our federal arrangement of local,
state, and national governments, but it is also our private and independent sectors—all of which contribute to the web of interactions
and expectations that shape our economy and society.

As Americans, we are asked to trust that our system will provide tangible community benefits in exchange for some of our individual freedoms and resources. As individuals, we are to engage in a mutually beneficial relationship, or *social contract*, with the system. This contract is based on *implicit bonds of trust* as well as *explicit written agreements* as far-reaching as the Constitution or as specific as a driver's license. How much the social contract with the system is based on implicit trust or explicit accountability is an enduring question of the American Experiment—one faced in many ways by people and communities today.

The American Experience: Resolving the Tension Between Trust and Accountability

Thomas Paine and Patrick Henry made the case for liberty from the tyranny of the British monarchy. When Henry made his famous "give me liberty or give me death" speech at the Richmond Convention in 1775, he did not believe that it was just for the British monarch to impose its will on free people. However, neither Paine nor Henry, steeped in the tradition of limited government, was able to think beyond removing the bonds of tyranny and toward creating a civil government based on accountability.

In contrast, John Adams and James Madison, although committed to individual freedom and liberty, also understood the importance of the rule of law and explicit constitutional principles. In fact, both men were lawyers by training and had a keen sense of how to create workable political systems. Adams developed the constitution for the Commonwealth of Massachusetts, and Madison played a key role in creating the constitution for Virginia.

By 1787, both Adams and Madison knew that the Articles of Confederation would not work as a framework for the new nation because it was based too much on implicit trust (assuming that states would work together toward common ends) and not enough on explicit accountability (providing clarity about how they would work together along with the national government). Madison helped craft the great compromises that created the national Constitution, with its checks and balances and separation of powers. On one hand, Madison helped craft a federal system with a stronger national government than the one articulated in the Articles of Confederation. On the other hand, he helped protect liberty by dispersing power among different branches of the federal government and between the federal government and the states. Madison's agreement to the Bill of Rights helped ensure that the Constitution would be ratified.

In *Federalist* No. 51, Madison articulated the underlying philosophy about trust and accountability: "What is government itself but the greatest of all reflections on human nature? If men were angels, no government would be necessary." Madison continued, "You must first enable the government to control the governed; and in the next place oblige the government to control itself" (Quinn, 1993, p. 131). He was arguing that we cannot rely on trust without an explicit framework of accountability. As Quinn puts it, "The founders' view of human nature was optimistic, but vigilant" (p. 31).

In a sense, the Constitution was in keeping with an American tradition of written documents of accountability. Beginning with the Mayflower Compact of 1620, Americans have shown a preference for establishing written agreements of mutual benefits and the written rule of law to describe mutual constraints. In many countries, informal modes of conduct without written accountability are more common.

The Founders hoped that the explicit framework for accountability would actually build trust in the system, an element that was severely lacking in the Articles of Confederation and that almost destroyed the fledgling republic. They knew that trust in the system is not written down but is earned through actual governing, elections, judicial review, and other actions.

The key to resolving the tension between trust and accountability is not to overrely on either one, but rather to create a basic foundation of accountability on which to build greater and greater bonds of trust, which in turn allow a society to soar to great heights of economic and social progress, far beyond minimum expectations. For example, we need not just obey the law but can make greater ongoing improvements in public safety. We can offer guaranteed public education to all, but we can also invest in higher education, creating a burst of technological progress that allows us to send an astronaut to the moon.

With the Constitution, the Founders provided us with a foundation of accountability that protects us from the dark side of human nature and the danger of tyranny yet allows us to benefit from the optimistic side of human nature and the imagination of the American people. The Constitution provides us with a foundation on which subsequent generations can build bonds of trust that will allow them to meet the difficult challenges and reach for the compelling opportunities of their time.

The Tension Today: Practical Challenges to Address

Two of the key challenges that today's civic revolutionaries experience in balancing the issue of trust and the issue of accountability are the following:

- *The challenge of authentic participation:* from skeptical bystanders to engaged shareholders

- *The challenge of mutual accountability:* from an environment of unclear responsibility to one of mutual accountability

Today most Americans believe that some freedoms should be traded for desired community benefits, such as public safety. Although some people fear government coercion and loss of liberties, most recognize the value of clarifying responsibilities as well as rights and of pooling resources for collective benefit.

Commonly, however, people are skeptical that the system is capable of delivering desired community benefits. People do not trust that they can shape public outcomes in meaningful ways and that the system can function as a whole to deliver results. This distrust is not surprising. People see closed decision-making processes, outmoded vehicles for civic engagement, and expert-driven solutions. They see complex problems requiring collaborative solutions yet see unclear accountability and a dispersion of responsibility. The result is this: people are often reluctant to engage in civic endeavors and to be taxed or regulated even for public purposes that they value highly (such as education). Some lose hope that the public issues that matter most to them can be addressed.

This situation needs revisiting from the perspective of reconciling the tension between trust and accountability. Communities today face two practical challenges related to implicit trust and explicit accountability:

- *From skeptical bystanders to engaged shareholders:* how to create strong expectations and authentic opportunities for people to participate in civic affairs, building trust in our American system and shared accountability for results

- *From unclear responsibility to mutual accountability:* how to formalize the basic lines of accountability as a foundation for trust and confidence in the system

Both of these challenges are complicated by the fact that geographical communities today extend and overlap multiple political jurisdictions. Often people live in one jurisdiction, traveling through other jurisdictions on their way to work, shopping, or school. Residents need to participate in neighborhood and city affairs but also at times need to act as citizens of a broader metropolitan region. Local governments and institutions need to focus on their core functions but increasingly need to work together to solve pressing problems that cut across political boundaries (transportation, land use, environmental preservation).

At their essence, both of these practical challenges are about how to create a new social contract of trust and accountability between and among people and their civic institutions. Robert Reich (2002), a public philosopher who has served in two national administrations, has written about the importance of an evolving social contract: "Every society and culture possess a social contract—sometimes implicit and sometimes spelled out in detail, but usually a mix of both. The contract sets out the obligations of members of society toward one another. Indeed, a society or culture is defined by its social contract" (p. 11).

Similarly, Gardner (1990) believed that implicit trust and explicit accountability must go together in creating a social contract appropriate for our time: "We have learned through hard experience that without commitments, freedom is not possible. Something has to hold the society together. If that something is not dictatorial rule, it must be a commitment to the constitutional framework and the web of custom in an open society" (p. 192). Gardner believed that accountability must emanate from every level, from every direction: "We believe that ideas, initiative and creativity should flow both ways between the center and the periphery. We believe that social controls should not emanate solely from the top but also out of the community, neighborhood, and family— and not least out of self-discipline. We believe that individuals throughout the system should have a keen sense of responsibility— not just for their own behavior but for the larger good" (p. 89).

A real challenge, though, is how to create authentic mechanisms for people and organizations to work together and take responsibility for the common good. For individuals, Reich (2002) makes the case that "nothing happens unless citizens demand that it happen. The real reknitting of the social fabric has to be where the threads are. That requires at bottom that you and I and millions like us get involved. . . . Our strength lies not in our bombs, but in our bonds" (p. 120). The problem is that the traditional ways that our system has of engaging people—public hearings, task forces, stakeholder testimony—do not excite people, use their time effectively, or lead to tangible outcomes. Mostly, these are not authentic means of participation, but rather limited opportunities for input. Absent new forms of civic engagement, too many people will remain spectators in their region's future.

What is needed, in effect, is to *democratize* the public planning and decision-making processes. The opportunity is to give citizens access to the information, tools, and frameworks that experts have traditionally used in making decisions and to engage citizens through good process. Journalists and civic advisers Neal Peirce and Curtis Johnson see this opportunity: "Too many people are spectators in planning their regions. What's the cure? We nominate the people—citizens working to ensure a sound shared future. Regions need a shot of democracy in their planning processes" (Alliance for Regional Stewardship, 2001a, p. 8). This opportunity implies moving from the traditional closed, hierarchical, linear, authority-driven community-planning model toward a more open, self-organizing, adaptive model that is more appropriate to the complex problems that communities face today. By engaging citizens in meaningful ways, our elected and civic organizations will be more capable of governing themselves in times of change. By tapping the values, knowledge, and information that ordinary citizens possess, organizations will have more effective ways of understanding what their goals should be and identifying creative ways to reach them.

Institutions—elected bodies, civic organizations, business associations—are also challenged to work together for the common good and to be accountable to one another for results. Whereas metropolitan regions have become the place where many economic, environmental, and social issues must be addressed, our governance models are based on a nineteenth-century world of isolated independent villages and towns. The challenge for our day is how institutions can develop workable, mutually accountable ways of solving shared regional problems.

In order to build trust and accountability in the system, both individuals and institutions need to foster responsibility. Indeed the way to build trust and accountability in the system is through *webs of responsibility*. We must create mechanisms that enable authentic participation in deciding what to do and ownership or accountability in actually getting something done. Too often, neither authentic participation nor accountability is encouraged by the system, and in return little trust is created in the system. This challenge is central for American communities today.

Civic revolutionaries are reconciling the tension between trust and accountability by building new webs of responsibility. In some communities, residents are becoming engaged shareholders by participating in influential civic organizations and inclusive civic processes. In other communities, regional organizations are developing mutual accountability through regional compacts.

Promising Experiments: Building Webs of Responsibility

Civic revolutionaries can succeed in building webs of responsibility by working to achieve the following:

- Encouraging authentic participation through influential civic organizations and inclusive civic processes

- Achieving mutual accountability through regional compacts that set clear expectations

Across the country, stewards of the American Experiment are pioneering new ways to build trust and accountability in our democratic system. They are focusing on models that involve authentic participation of diverse leaders and residents and that produce explicit, written agreements of mutual accountability that are very much in the American tradition.

These models seek to rebuild trust in what have become ineffective local and regional systems of problem solving. These models include *open and influential civic organizations*, as well as *inclusive and catalytic civic processes*. Both are delivering results and building trust. They also include *new regional compacts*—mutual accountability agreements between local governments that are pioneering new forms of practical regional governance in America. What the approaches have in common is that they are building effective webs of responsibility for their communities that reconcile, for the moment, fundamental tensions between implicit trust and explicit accountability.

Encouraging Authentic Participation Through Influential Civic Organizations

A number of experiments are under way to provide an organizational channel for residents to participate in shaping the direction of their region. Of course, there are many civic organizations in the United States. Most are open to all comers, but few are truly influential in the system of problem solving in their region. This distinction is important: open access does not equal authentic participation. In fact, open access to ineffectual civic organizations can actually cause great frustration and cynicism.

Citizens League of the Minneapolis–St. Paul Region

A good example of a civic organization that provides authentic participation by being both open and influential is the Citizens League. Founded in 1952, this regional organization has been one of the most effective agents of change in the Minneapolis–St. Paul region—and has been refining its approach for almost fifty years. The league has a long and distinguished record of major, measurable impacts on public finance, education, transportation, and health care. It also helped stimulate the creation of one of the nation's most effective forms of regional government.

Beyond achieving any single accomplishment, the league has pioneered a disciplined, results-driven collaborative process that involves citizens in the framing of problems and the development of solutions that can be—and often are—implemented. The league's process is based on a set of core beliefs:

- Regular citizens are capable of developing an in-depth understanding of sophisticated policy problems.

- Information and reasoned analysis should apply to public problems.

- Ideas matter—in the sense that striving for the best ideas that can become solutions is the goal, not simply citizen participation for its own sake.

- Democracy depends on "free spaces"—places where citizens from all walks of life can assemble for uninhibited dialogue about public concerns, where people are free to agree or disagree with one another while preserving the bonds of respect and mutual obligation.

The Citizens League, through its citizen study committees, creates a vehicle for local residents to study and influence public policies. The process works as follows: league volunteers and staff conduct discussions with a wide variety of individuals and communities about potential topics, with the league's board choosing the specific issues for study and action for the upcoming year. Over the course of a year and a half, committee members learn about the issue with the help of community experts and researchers. The committee analyzes the information, evaluates options for action, and ultimately develops a proposal with workable solutions to address the issue.

The power of the citizen study committee, believes Curtis Johnson, national journalist, is in the sensible ideas that it produces:

"The committee process consistently demonstrates a rare reverence for facts and a now scarce capacity for patience, allowing competing arguments to simmer and soak until some common ground emerges." This process produces a reasoned approach to an issue that is respected widely by decision makers—and creates a climate for action. Once committee work is complete, the board, committee members, staff, and other supporters of the Citizens League interact with existing public, private, and community leaders and organizations to work toward implementation. Results are a critical part of the league's mission, says Lyle Wray, president of the Citizens League. "The ultimate attraction for participants is that they can make a tangible difference. We are not a debating society."

Sometimes recommendations are implemented through legislative or administrative action; sometimes they provide the impetus for broader civic transformation beyond government policy. As an example, in the 1960s, the Citizens League took on the tough issue of how to plan and invest regionally in housing, transportation, and land use. This task helped stimulate the creation of one of the nation's most unique forms of regional government: the Metropolitan Council. The Metropolitan Council, appointed by the governor, oversees all regional transportation and land use planning and reviews local plans for consistency with regional plans. In the 1970s, the metro council took on the difficult issue of regional equity, including the topic of tax sharing among the counties in the region. The region's fiscal disparity plan is a multicounty tax-base-sharing agreement that pools 40 percent of the growth in commercial and industrial tax revenues and redistributes it to municipalities on the basis of population and tax capacity.

The Citizens League provides a long-running example of a proven approach to authentic participation that gets results. Part of its success lies in its ability to bring both trust and accountability to the civic engagement process. According to Wray, "Trust comes from bringing diverse people together to build a common vision. Accountability comes from being here for a long time to keep the focus on results. We can be the terrier that doesn't let go of the slip-per." The organization's long history in the region also helps. "We have been here for fifty years. People know that we are credible and that we are nonpartisan. You can't build that kind of reputation in eighteen months."

Today the region is challenged to maintain civic excellence: its long tradition of social capital seems now to be under strain with the loss of traditional corporate leadership in the 1990s, changes in state political administration, and the significant time constraint faced by volunteers. In addition, finding a sustainable funding source for the Citizens League in an era of interest politics and issue-oriented giving has become increasingly difficult. According to a study by the Lincoln Land Institute, "The jury remains out on whether the region can shift gears to pursue more collaborative efforts at regionalism in the future" (Foster, 2001, p. 34).

Baltimore's Citizens Planning and Housing Association

The Citizens Planning and Housing Association (CPHA) in Balti-more is another example of an influential civic organization that fea-tures open and meaningful participation for residents. CPHA is a civic organization that has built a grassroots coalition that spans six jurisdictions in the metropolitan region and includes more than 250 other organizations representing communities, businesses, religious institutions, and environmentalists. Its history dates back to 1941, when it was formed to be an advocate for fair housing and health in the city of Baltimore. Since then, the impacts of sprawl and a deep population decline in the central city (from 736,000 in 1990 to 651,000 ten years later) have led the organization to focus on shared regional solutions. The combination of grassroots involvement and regional action makes CPHA both inclusive and influential.

For example, in June 2002, almost two thousand citizens from across the Baltimore metropolitan area, joined by the chief elected officials of nearly all the region's jurisdictions, descended on the Bal-timore Convention Center for a two-hour rally to lobby for improved public transportation, expanded drug treatment, more housing choices, revitalized communities, and open-space preservation.

As the voice and vehicle of citizens in the Baltimore region, CPHA serves as a powerful platform for issues to be aired and heard. The *Baltimore City Paper* explains the source of this power: "CPHA is stocked with enough clout and resources to get lawmakers' attention. The powerful have long known to listen when CPHA speaks. . . . But during election years such as this, politicos pay especially careful attention to what groups such as CPHA have to say because, presumably, they articulate what voters want" (Smith, 2002).

The June 2002 rally was actually the second Rally for the Region held by CPHA. The first one was in October 2000 and focused on five priority areas: transportation, community revitalization, neighborhood open space, drug treatment, workforce development. The rally included Governor Parris Glendening, the Baltimore County and Howard County executives, the Baltimore City mayor, and numerous other local and state legislative leaders. "The big-event strategy of the rally is a way to identify core issues that matter to our community and to have them raised up and affirmed. The city, county, and state leaders that take part in the event hear it directly from their constituency," reports Terri Turner, executive director of CPHA. But the event is just the beginning. "We've always recognized the need to connect the organizing work for the rally with lobbying work in the legislature. It is important to keep the momentum going and demonstrate that progress is being made. By looking for ways to move the agenda forward, we are making a commitment to people that the energy they invest in the process will pay a dividend."

Following the rally in 2000, CPHA and its partners took the issues to Annapolis, Maryland's capital, during the 2001 session of the general assembly for a Lobby for the Region day. CPHA organized for state legislators to meet with citizens in their districts. According to Turner, "At the Rally for the Region event, citizens shared their top priorities with state legislatures. With Lobby for the Region day, we were coming back to find out what they had done about it." The result was this: for each item in the 2000 Action Agenda, significant gains were made that benefited all the communities of the region. For instance, $500 million in new funds was allocated to improve transit statewide, the general assembly enacted the governor's Community Legacy Program to support neighborhood revitalization with $9 million appropriated for capital spending, and the Skills-Based Training for Employment Promotion Pilot Program was created, which encourages interjurisdictional cooperation to connect workers to jobs.

In its ongoing work, CPHA creates an important venue to connect citizens to politicians, to ensure that they are heard, and to lobby for change. Its most recent newsletter states, "The lesson for citizens: we create real power when we come together across the region to fight for a better future."

Encouraging Authentic Participation Through Inclusive Civic Processes

Like civic organizations, civic processes have proliferated in recent years. These processes do not link tightly to a single organization but are typically catalyzed and supported by many. Many civic change processes have attempted to be widely participatory, but few have actually been catalytic in influencing the system in their regions. However, some processes have managed to achieve both inclusiveness and effectiveness, making them good examples of authentic participation. At their core, effective civic processes blend participation leadership, expertise, and decision-support tools in a disciplined approach that leads to results. Gardner recognized the importance of this kind of civic innovation:

"Behind all the buzz about collaboration is a discipline. And with all due respect to the ancient arts of governing and diplomacy, the more recent art of collaboration does represent something new—maybe Copernican. If it contained a silicon chip, we'd all be excited. As it is, it is mostly tolerated as just another step in our social bumbling" (John W. Gardner, interview with National Civic League, 1996).

Envision Utah

Envision Utah provides a good example of a civic process that has been simultaneously inclusive and catalytic.

Envision Utah has found that the tension between trust and accountability heightens when communities face growth pressures. Individual actions by developers and cities can lead to unplanned sprawl—a result that ultimately undermines the confidence that the system is working to preserve and enhance the quality of life for people who live in the region. In a bold regional initiative, the leaders of the Wasatch region of Utah created a way to put the "public" back into public planning. Envision Utah, a regional public-private partnership founded in January 1997, has achieved large-scale public participation in shaping the future of their community. Through an extensive five-year process, a sense of collective interest for the region emerged through scenario planning, public engagement, and dialogue.

As Jon Huntsman, chair of Envision Utah, explains, the Envision Utah effort builds on the pioneering history of the early founders of the region: "As Utahans, we share a heritage of planning for our future. In fact, within three days of entering these valleys, Utah's founders envisioned a plan that would last for generations. These early settlers knew they were planning a community for the future." What they did not know was that this community of the future would soon exceed two million people, with the highest birthrate of any state in the country. More than 80 percent of Utah's residents live in the ten-county Greater Wasatch Area, with the region projected to grow to 2.7 million residents by 2020. With geographical constraints—the Wasatch Mountain Range, the Great Salt Lake, Utah Lake, and a desert—surrounding the region, smart-growth planning became a regional imperative.

For Envision Utah, the tension between trust and accountability is addressed through exceptional public involvement leading to regional results. The partnership has led more than 175 public meetings with more than six thousand participants, distributed more than eight hundred thousand questionnaires across the region, presented at eighty-nine city councils and eight county commissions, and provided training to more than a thousand local officials and the planning community to help them promote quality growth and development. Indeed, "Through a grass roots process of locally elected leaders and citizen involvement, Envision Utah addresses growth issues in a way that is compatible with the strong ethic of local control that is shared by many states throughout the nation" (Dolan, Godfrey, and Herbert, 2002).

Envision Utah is clearly inclusive, but it has been catalytic as well. In order to ensure that Envision Utah's Quality Growth Strategies did not become a document on a shelf, Envision Utah promoted the strategies through demonstration projects with groups of communities, cities, and towns. This work resulted in changes in local master plans and development projects. Envision Utah has trained over twenty-seven hundred mayors, city council members, developers, and realtors in its "Urban Planning Tools for Quality Growth" workbook and has done demonstration projects with several dozen communities. Further the annual Envision Utah Governors Quality Growth Awards highlight developers and local governments who are emulating smart-growth techniques, and major media campaigns help promote key concepts such as walkable communities, transit-oriented development, and mixed housing.

Tangible results have been achieved. The state legislature passed the Quality Growth Act in 1999, which created a "critical lands fund" for conservation and appointed a thirteen-member quality growth commission to advise the legislature on growth issues, administer money for open-space projects, and identify quality growth principles for local communities. In 2000, voters in Salt Lake, Davis, and Weber Counties approved an extra quarter-cent sales tax increase to raise approximately $40 million a year to fund more rail and bus service. It is in the midst of working on a land use project for western Salt Lake and Utah counties with the Utah Department of Transportation. Although great strides have been made, state support for Envision Utah is currently at risk under the weight of growing budget deficits. The challenge will be to maintain the momentum and support during difficult economic conditions.

A variety of important lessons from the Envision Utah process may have relevance in other regions, particularly those regions that want to replicate the voluntary model of coordinated regional planning:

- In a setting like Utah, quality growth cannot be created by appointing some sort of regional growth "czar." The public will not accept a top-down model. Instead quality growth must evolve from the local level, using education and common sense to promote a regional backdrop for decision making.
- Inclusion and public participation provide the foundation for Envision Utah's work. Drawing from an aphorism of Neil Peirce, Envision Utah strives to "make the table bigger and rounder." This type of framework forces a balancing of interests and a recognition of trade-offs. The Envision Utah process has demonstrated that choices have consequences, and regions cannot have it all. Moreover better decisions are made as people with diverse interests come together and find common ground. As a general guideline, the Envision Utah process has demonstrated that to make progress, one must be willing to sit in a room with people whose positions make one uncomfortable.
- Finally, the Envision Utah process has demonstrated that quality takes time. Regional visioning efforts are large undertakings that require many years of work. Vigilance is key, and change happens incrementally. Stephen Holbrook, executive director of

Envision Utah sums it up: "The key to Envision Utah's success has been its ability to involve stakeholders throughout the process. This takes extensive time, research, and patience. You must identify leaders representing a broad spectrum of interests, spend time raising their awareness of the issues, and facilitate a dialogue that promotes problem solving, rather than philosophizing."

Achieving Mutual Accountability Through Regional Compacts That Set Clear Expectations

Although regions have become the place where economic, social, and environmental issues now come together, regional governance structures have not kept pace with the progress of regions. As we enter the twenty-first century, we are stuck with nineteenth-century practices and institutions that make it difficult to address problems where they are. We face an "ingenuity gap" where our aspirations as regional citizens exceed our current capacity.

What is necessary is innovation in regional governance based on principles similar to the ideas guiding the Founders. How do we find a new balance between the interest of cities and regions; between neighborhoods and towns; between citizens, businesses, and political leaders—between all the different stakeholders in the system? Two extreme options on the continuum are a new layer of regional government and a world of weak cities without regional vision or voice.

Between these extremes, however, real regions have been experimenting, trying to develop workable, mutually accountable ways of solving problems. One promising experiment is the development of *regional compacts*, voluntary arrangements in which cities join together in cooperative efforts to solve common regional problems in innovative and often flexible ways, while holding one another accountable for results. Two current models—the Denver Mile High Compact and the New Mayflower Compact in Massachusetts—involve interjurisdictional agreements that balance implicit trust and explicit accountability.

The Denver Mile High Compact

The Denver Mile High Compact is the latest in a long series of attempts to create more rational and efficient regional governmental planning in the Denver metropolitan region. Adopted in August 2000, the Mile High Compact is an intergovernmental agreement among thirty-two local governments to help manage growth. It is essentially a self-imposed mandate, rather than one imposed by the legislature or voters, that binds these cities and counties to a comprehensive growth strategy based on the Denver Region's Metro Vision 2020.

During the economic boom of the 1990s, regional population growth skyrocketed, with more than 161,000 people moving to the area between 1990 and 1996. The composite plans of local governments showed a future urban area of over a thousand square miles, but the actual urbanized area was around five hundred square miles. A public debate began to emerge around controlling growth and development. The regional planning agency, Denver Regional Council of Governments (DRCOG), began a long-term regional planning process: Metro Vision 2020. The Metro Vision 2020 task force was formed to examine both the current and preferred pattern of development for the Denver region to the year 2020. Four growth scenarios were developed, and extensive public hearings determined residents' preferences for these options. The task force recommended a hybrid scenario, which became the Metro Vision 2020 Framework and was accepted by the board of directors in November 1995.

Four tenets guided the implementation strategy of Metro Vision 2020: voluntary, flexible, collaborative, and effective. The problem, however, was that the Metro Vision Framework was advisory, and a lack of discernible action by individual parties was evident. By 1999, it was clear to Bill Vidal, executive director of DRCOG, that the "voluntary and flexible" part of Vision 2020 was not going to be enough. He compared it with other social contracts that fostered true commitment, not just voluntary and flexible participation:

"If I went to my wife and said that our marriage was now voluntary and flexible, she wouldn't be too happy." Vidal recognized that local commitment was imperative to the success of the regional plan. DRCOG began to test the possibility of developing a stronger statement of consensus among city and county agencies.

A critical step toward the Mile High Compact was getting the support of the Metro Mayors Caucus, a voluntary collaboration of thirty-one mayors in the Denver metropolitan region. In the wake of failed legislative attempts to address growth statewide, the caucus felt it was critical to build commitment and momentum for the implementation of the region's Metro Vision 2020 growth and transportation plan. At their January 2000 annual retreat, they talked about how they always fight when the state tries to mandate growth. But then one mayor said, "I wouldn't mind so much if we bind ourselves."

Between March and May, a working group of local elected officials, city managers, and senior planners from DRCOG and the staff of the Metro Mayors Caucus began meeting to draft an intergovernmental agreement: the Mile High Compact. Elected officials then took the document back to their city councils and boards of county commissions for ratification. Twenty-nine local governments signed the Mile High Compact on August 10, 2000. By August 2002, thirty-two jurisdictions, representing 80 percent of the region's population, had signed. The agreement binds its signatories to

- Use Metro Vision as the regional planning framework

- Develop and approve comprehensive plans with a defined set of elements

- Adopt their Metro Vision 2020 Urban Growth Boundaries within their comprehensive plans

- Allow urban development only within the defined growth boundary

- Coordinate comprehensive plans with those of neighboring and overlapping entities and integrate plans at the regional level

Signatories have legal rights against one another, but they are also free to drop out of the compact as long as they provide several months' notice. Larry Mugler, planning director of DRCOG, likens the agreement to a marriage contract: "The organizations have made a commitment to work through things together. No outside entity can come and break up the relationship, but you can get out of it if you want to."

The story of the Mile High Compact is particularly important because this type of voluntary social contract, or what regional steward John Parr calls an "adhocracy," can help reconcile the tension between trust and accountability when multiple parties are involved. A key lesson in creating a regional compact is that a foundation of trust has to be established between the individual parties first. By all accounts, it took eight years to set the conditions for a compact (from the time Metro Vision 2020 began in 1992). A lot of that time was spent working collaboratively, engaging stakeholders, generating shared principles, and building trust. Not all jurisdictions have signed on—including the three largest counties in the region—but the Mile High Compact has helped establish an explicit recognition that local decisions affect regional quality of life and has helped foster trust and accountability among the region's cities and counties.

The New Mayflower Compact

The New Mayflower Compact is an echo of the first American compact. The first Mayflower Compact at Plymouth Rock in 1620 was a social contract among people who came to this new land and recognized that they needed to work together to survive. In October 2001, cities and towns in this same region signed a New Mayflower

Compact, pledging to work together to grow their communities in a unified, quality manner.

Similar to the Mile High Compact, the New Mayflower Compact arose from a multiyear effort to establish a regional framework for growth. In February 1998, three regional planning organizations representing the southeastern Massachusetts region—Southeastern Regional Planning and Economic Development District (SRPEDD) in Taunton, Old Colony Planning Council (OCPC) in Brockton, and Metropolitan Area Planning Council (MAPC) in Boston—initiated an unprecedented intraregional collaborative effort to respond to significant population growth within the region.

The southeastern Massachusetts region includes fifty-two cities and towns in three counties with one million people. It is one of the state's new growth frontiers, with population growing at 65 percent between 1960 and 2000, compared with 23 percent for the entire state. A more integrated approach to transportation, housing, and land use planning was required to keep pace with this rapid change. The Partnership for Southeastern Massachusetts: Vision 2020 became the vehicle for that planning process.

After going through a process that engaged hundreds of citizens in a series of town meetings and outreach efforts, the Task Force issued the *Agenda for the Future* in June 1999, with broad policy recommendations for the region. As the initiative moved into implementation mode, however, it soon became clear that the fiercely independent streak of New England communities would make top-down enforcement impossible. As David Soule, former executive director of MAPC, describes, "There was a strong feeling that we had to go beyond goals and principles. There had to be some fabric that kept us together, but it had to come from the individual cities. If we had pushed any harder, it would have fallen apart." The compromise was a voluntary agreement to act collectively, in the spirit of the original Mayflower Compact.

One afternoon in October 2000, more than a hundred public officials, citizens, and organizational representatives from throughout southeastern Massachusetts gathered onboard the ship Mayflower II to sign and support the New Mayflower Compact. Led by Congressman William Delahunt, officials from cities and towns across the region agreed to "voluntarily join together to implement a growth management plan that preserves the interests of each town and city yet profits from unified regional actions." The compact creates incentives to encourage growth in areas with existing and underused infrastructure. It calls for reforms in state laws and policies that promote sprawl and discourage regional cooperation, and it analyzes and addresses the full range of impacts associated with local zoning decisions. At present, forty-two of the fifty-two cities and towns have agreed to endorse the compact.

Because of its voluntary nature, Soule believes that "the compact was essential for achieving buy-in from local officials. It made the regional plan into a living document that engaged the local political community. This was the way to build both trust and accountability into the process. We are watching each other a little more carefully and are willing to hold each other accountable. It would not have worked if an outside party had tried to mandate it. This is really an exercise in self-government that reflects our uniquely independent New England culture." Following the development of the New Mayflower Compact, in December 2001, Vision 2020 established a formal board of directors to continue to drive implementation of the *Agenda for the Future*.

The tension between trust and accountability, however, continues to challenge southeastern Massachusetts. "The Achilles heel of the Mayflower Compact is the voluntary nature of it. We still struggle with some communities who make poor land use decisions in order to attract property tax. Now we are beginning to work at the state level to establish a framework for development," reports Steven Smith, executive director of SRPEDD. "What the Mayflower Compact gave us was a powerful way of saying that this region cares about smart growth. When we are lobbying at the state level, it is very effective to show that 80 percent of our local governments have pledged to work towards those goals."

In November 1620, the Mayflower landed in Plymouth Bay, outside the boundary of Virginia, which had been claimed as a colony by England. Knowing that they had no right to be there, the leaders insisted that everyone in the group sign the Mayflower Compact before they landed. By this document, they pledged to "combine ourselves together into a civil Body Politick, for our better Ordering and Preservation." This act marked the first self-government in the new land and was based on a social contract. The New Mayflower Compact, the Denver Mile High Compact, and a growing number of others like them, are based on a similar principle: that individuals or jurisdictions are willing to join together in voluntary agreements to work toward a common set of goals.

Insights from the Field

Every region and community must find its own way, its own resolution, to the creative tension between trust and accountability. Civic revolutionaries around the country have been grappling with this challenge and can offer some insights to their counterparts. As in the previous chapter, these insights are organized according to the three major roles for civic revolutionaries—to discover, decide, and then drive change.

Discover: Building a Compelling Case for Change

Assess the current climate of trust and accountability. What is the region's social contract? What are the expectations and responsibilities and the implicit bonds of trust? What is the nature of accountability in the region? Understanding the environment is important because accountability earns trust, which in turn can produce breakthrough results. Robert Putnam of Harvard University has spearheaded nationally coordinated regional surveys on *social capital,* from which information about how residents trust institutions and one another can be gleaned and compared across regions. Independently, regions such as Philadelphia, Silicon Valley, and

Orlando have been assessed through surveys and qualitative research based on interviews. National journalists Peirce and Johnson have done assessments of problems, opportunities, and the civic climates of numerous regions, which typically appear as a series of articles in the flagship newspapers of those regions—places including Miami, Phoenix, and St. Louis. Assessing the current civic climate can help energize the community and focus on the need for renewing the prevailing social contract.

Make a strong commitment to authentic participation in building the case for change. What is clear from experimentation across the country is that some kinds of participation lead to growing accountability and trust, whereas others can be exercises in futility. Authentic participation is a product of access and effectiveness. It is achievable in many ways, including through open and influential civic organizations, such as those in Minneapolis–St. Paul and Baltimore, and through inclusive and catalytic civic processes, such as those in the regions surrounding Salt Lake City and Denver. In St. Louis, civic revolutionary Christine Chadwick of Focus St. Louis launched a national award-winning initiative that builds bridges by brokering a series of informal, interracial potluck dinners, where individuals get to know one another and build bonds of trust that can serve as the foundation for future collaboration.

Another good example is Rochester, New York. Mayor William Johnson was the civic revolutionary who created an authentic opportunity for inclusive, participatory planning called Neighbors Building Neighborhoods. Residents are trained in planning processes and tools, make decisions about priorities, develop action plans, and genuinely provide much of the substance of the city's comprehensive plan—building the case for change. The effort has been particularly effective in engaging people of color and has received the Cultural Diversity Award from the National Black Caucus of the National League of Cities. According to Mayor Johnson, "We have a proud tradition of vigorous debate, followed by meaningful action. . . . Frederick Douglass and Susan B. Anthony wouldn't have gotten anywhere if they kept their mouths shut or stayed put in their living rooms" (Institute on Race and Poverty, 2002, p. 15).

Decide: Making Critical Choices in Experimentation

Focus decision making on the productive interplay between trust and accountability. The key to resolving the tension between trust and accountability is not to overrely on either one, but rather to use a basic foundation of accountability on which to build greater and greater bonds of trust. In fact, focusing new accountability mechanisms in areas where trust is weak is a good strategy. However, too much overly prescriptive accountability can be stifling and discourage flexibility. Similarly, too-high expectations for unfounded trust can produce dashed hopes and rising cynicism. A mutually supportive relationship between the two offers the best of both worlds. Clear accountability guards against the dark side of human nature and abuses of power. At the same time, earned trust in the prevailing system can give a society the confidence and security to soar to great heights of economic and social progress, achieving breakthrough results well beyond the basic standards of accountability that were originally laid out.

Design mutual accountability agreements to build confidence in new civic systems. A new wave of regional compacts—ranging from formal in structure to ad hoc in nature—is transforming the basic relationships within systems of governance. The compacts are setting the parameters for a new kind of civic system—not regional government per se, but a set of practical, mutual obligations tailored to each regional situation. This renewal of a traditional American accountability mechanism is emerging as one of the most important forces for building trust in regional problem-solving processes. The Mayflower and Mile High Compacts are two examples of the growing use of such mechanisms.

Make a series of design decisions to develop an effective compact. No one-size-fits-all model exists for regional compacts. Every region needs to go through the process of determining the most feasible approach for itself. Key choices to consider are the following:

- *Voluntary and mandatory elements.* The Denver and Boston compacts were voluntary. The Portland (see discussion in Chapter Four) and Twin Cities metro examples had more power granted by the state government to enforce regional agreements once negotiated locally. How far should a regional compact go from voluntary to mandatory, and who enforces these agreements once signed?

- *Process and structure.* One of the key lessons from Denver and Boston was the importance of a process that resulted in shared ownership by a wide range of participants. Portland and the Twin Cities have more formal structures, whereas Denver is more of an adhocracy. How much structure is needed for an effective process to reach a regional compact?

- *Trust and incentives.* The Denver and Boston examples were based on building trust among the local participants. Few incentives existed for cooperation from state government. In Portland and the Twin Cities, the state governments set the framework and provided incentives for regional plans. What is the right balance between building regional trust from the bottom up and creating incentives for cooperation from the top down?

Drive: Mobilizing Allies for Change

Build a practical infrastructure to support accountability. Just signing an agreement is an empty gesture without the infrastructure in place to stimulate and support individuals and organizations to take responsibility for delivering results. In Rochester, New York, citizen committees have worked with other key players to implement about 80 percent of their original action plans. The infrastructure of accountability has included a public-awareness campaign, a system that tracks the progress of specific initiatives, and a communications network linking responsible parties, including community participants. In San Diego, Columbus, and other regions, civic revolutionaries are using specific memorandums of understanding with clear lines of accountability among individuals and organizations that are participating in implementation.

Use accountability agreements or compacts as the core to leverage broader commitments for change. In fact, the next frontier may be the use of regional compacts in redefining federalism for our time. Although regional compacts are helping redefine regional systems for public problem solving, they could become more of a catalyst in redefining the whole set of federal relationships among local, state, and national governments. Some efforts, like the one in Portland, have important state government roles; others have tried to reach out to federal agencies on a case-by-case basis for partnerships. However, in comparison to what could be done to build a new set of mutual obligations among local, state, and national entities, very little has been accomplished thus far.

Both state and national governments need to recognize the value of this bottom-up approach as governance moves away from the top-down "mainframe" approach to a more decentralized networked model. Ideally, national and state governments should recognize the importance of regions as partners by developing performance-based relationships with regions to achieve shared goals. This recognition could create a new federal-state-regional-local partnership based on a strategic-investment approach that improves the process of regional decision making; leverages all federal, state, and local investments; and delivers results for citizens, regions, and the country as a whole.

Some specific areas could be the focus of new partnerships. The priority goals of reducing transportation congestion, producing more affordable housing, creating a productive workforce, and promoting efficient land use can be achieved when regions use effective strategies and decision-making tools. Although federal funding can help a great deal, issues such as traffic gridlock and severe housing-job imbalances often occur when regional decision making breaks down. The federal and state governments need to recognize and support a regional perspective.

A good example of recognizing the importance of regions is the Intermodal Surface Transportation Efficiency Act (ISTEA) or the Transportation Equity Act (TEA-21) program, in which federal and state government place the requirement for regional transportation planning on metropolitan planning organizations (MPOs) designated by states. Although this program has worked better in some regions than in others, it is an example of what is possible. The missing link is that some regions have multiple MPOs, and transportation planning is not connected to local land use planning.

The federal and state governments need an ongoing relationship with regions to promote performance goals in housing, transportation, and land use. This relationship should be built on a strong foundation both within the federal government and outside the government. For many important areas—from building a strong economy, to getting best use out of our infrastructure, to protecting the environment—regions are where vital decisions and actions need to be taken. A federal partnership with regions recognizes this reality and will help us move forward in meeting critical challenges across the country.

Regions could be encouraged by federal agencies to develop regional compacts that integrate housing, workforce, transportation, and land use strategies based on regional growth priorities. For example, following a "reverse-RFP" approach, regions could request federal agencies' participation in supporting the regional compacts. The federal government could challenge regional leaders from government, business, and nonprofit organizations to come together and develop regional strategies that will work for them. Regional compacts would include performance measures that will be part of the federal-regional agreements in supporting the compacts. They could be promoted on a pilot, and ongoing, basis with financial and technical assistance for building the capacity of regions to negotiate and implement regional compacts. The homeland security issue following September 11, 2001, offers an important opportunity to test this model.

What Success Looks Like: Webs of Responsibility

New webs of responsibility reconcile the competing values of trust and accountability. Although the experience varies from place to place, a point exists at which bonds of implicit trust and the foundation of explicit accountability become connected effectively through strong webs of expectation and responsibility involving people, organizations, and sectors. As this chapter has shown, there are many pathways, strategies, and techniques to build these webs of responsibility. But what does success look like?

- Both strong expectations and authentic opportunities exist to participate in civic affairs through open and influential organizations and inclusive and catalytic processes.

- Written agreements formalize the basic lines of accountability among stakeholders, creating the foundation for building trust and confidence in the system.

- People and institutions exceed the minimum requirements for accountability because they trust that the prevailing civic system is conducive to risk taking and innovation.

3

Economy and Society

Strengthening the Vital Cycle

Individual residents enjoy the benefits of the regional economy, including rising wages, improving amenities, and better public services. They also resent the impacts of the regional economy, including traffic congestion, gentrification of older neighborhoods, job displacement, and rising cost of living. Benefits and impacts are not evenly distributed, creating conflict within the region. At one end of the spectrum are advocates who feel that government must heavily regulate the economy to produce just outcomes; at the other end are advocates who feel that government must get out of the way and let the economy run its course. The practical question is how to reconcile the competing values of economy and society.

The American economic and political systems have worked both to improve and to undercut each other throughout the country's history. The free market and entrepreneurial forces of the American capitalist system have produced more wealth and opportunity for more people than exists in any other country. The liberties and laws of the American political system have provided an open society and a predictable framework in which the economy can thrive. At the same time, economic excesses (monopolies, pollution, corporate scandals) and political choices (segregation, war, poorly designed tax and regulatory policies) have put the two systems at cross-purposes.

It is inevitable—and ultimately healthy—that an ongoing tension exists between the American economy and American society. Their interests can diverge, sometimes significantly, causing economic disruption and social harm. Their interests can also converge, sometimes significantly, resulting in economic prosperity and social progress. Like the Founders, each generation must search for the right balance to help the interests of the economy and society converge and move this part of the American Experience forward.

The American Experience: Resolving the Tension Between the Economy and Society

The Founders believed that the American economy and political system were inseparable and necessary for the success of the republic. From the beginning, they focused on how the Constitution could ensure the young country's longevity by protecting both liberty and property rights. "The new American experiment in government worked both because the Constitution was a practical, workable document and because it was launched in an economically viable country" (Quinn, 1993, pp. 29–30). In fact, our Founding Fathers considered the connection between economy and society to be so self-evident that they devoted little time to make the case in *The Federalist Papers*.

The Founders disagreed, however, about the relative emphasis of economic versus societal interests. Alexander Hamilton was the strongest advocate among the Founders for the necessity of a commercial republic. He believed that economic prosperity would be an important precondition for political stability and argued for a strong national role in the economy. In *Federalist* No. 6, Hamilton described how the commercial republic would help correct political excesses: "The spirit of commerce has a tendency to soften the manners of men, and to extinguish those inflammable humors which have so often kindled into wars. Commercial republics, like ours, will never be disposed to waste themselves in ruinous contentions with each other. They will be governed by mutual interest, and will cultivate a spirit of mutual amity and concord" (Quinn, 1993, p. 51). Later, as secretary of the treasury, Hamilton helped create the basic framework for a national economic policy, including the national bank and tariffs that protected manufacturing.

Whereas Hamilton emphasized the political and societal benefits of commercial progress, such that "everything tending to establish substantial and permanent order in the affairs of a country, to increase the total mass of industry and opulence is ultimately beneficial to every part of it," Jefferson opposed the Hamiltonian economic strategy because he saw that it would speed the demise of the country's agrarian society. Jefferson's agrarian vision held that "those who labor on the earth are the chosen people of God whose breasts He has made his peculiar deposit for substantial and genuine virtue" (Blum, 1966, p. 7). He was suspicious of government's role in commercial development because he believed that the corruption of morals arose from human dependence on others for whom they worked or with whom they traded. The Jeffersonian and Hamiltonian economic visions have competed since the time of the Revolution.

Once again, the pragmatic visionaries Adams and Madison found a middle way between these two competing values. Whereas Jefferson believed in limited government and Hamilton advocated national economic policies, Adams and Madison reconciled these extremes with their pragmatic view that civic government and free markets could channel self-interest toward public good. They created a commercial republic that recognized that human nature would inevitably lead to abuses. Consequently, such a commercial system required a civil government to regulate misdeeds while also allowing enough independence for private enterprise to flourish. The modern commercial society developed from a market economy based on shared principles.

In *Federalist* No. 10, Madison described how a political system would support commercial interests by mitigating conflicts between different economic factions. As Quinn (1993) described Madison's view, it was about "the division between property owners and those without property, and between creditors and debtors. Additionally, there are landed, manufacturing, mercantile, and moneyed interests dividing different classes." (p. 69). For Madison, the political system would help temper the excesses of the economic system.

Despite their differences, the Founders joined together in the belief that a strong and stable political framework was necessary for trade and commerce. Jefferson, Madison, and other agrarian interests wanted American farmers to be able to sell their crops abroad. Not only was the Confederation unable to raise money, it lacked the commercial regulatory power necessary to compel European countries to open their markets to American goods. Other manufacturing, financial, and mercantile interests worried about the chaos and confusion of the first government, trying and failing to push through initiatives to stabilize the economy and fund the national debt. Ultimately, the Confederation was unable to effectively regulate commerce, and reforming the Articles became inevitable.

During Lincoln's time, the tension between economy and society was revisited in the struggle to establish equality, including equality of economic opportunity, for slaves. Abraham Lincoln championed the idea that economic and social mobility ought to be available to all. As John Patrick Diggins (2000) observes in *On Hallowed Ground: Abraham Lincoln and the Foundations of American History*:

> Lincoln believed that the Republic could be both explained and guided by a unifying principle. Where Jefferson's Declaration was a manifesto of separation, Lincoln reconceived it as a symbol of national unity.

> Although Jefferson praised agricultural labor, he often longed for a "natural aristocracy." Lincoln, by contrast, valued work, ambition, and those who struggled hard and took advantage of any opportunity to rise from lower to higher ranks in society [p. 31].

Lincoln reconciled the values in the Declaration of Independence and the Constitution—of liberty, equality, and opportunity—for his time. His Gettysburg Address made the case that our republic rested on the moral foundation of equality for all men. But Lincoln was also pragmatic: he promoted hard work and commitment to industry, where economic opportunity was the primary reward of the American system of equality.

Speaking in New Haven in 1860, Lincoln said, "I want every man to have a chance—and I believe that the black man is entitled to it—when he may look forward and hope to be hired as a laborer this year and next year work for himself afterward and finally hire men to work for him. This is the true system" (Diggins, 2000, p. 32).

Lincoln also understood that labor not only produced property but also created value. With wealth as a mode of exchange, one could purchase the means of nourishment and leisure and then hire others to do work that was once a matter of necessity. In this way, Lincoln's moral statements against slavery and for freedom for all men also provided an important foundation for the market ideas of Adam Smith and the importance of labor as a means of individual well-being.

Hamilton's and Jefferson's contrasting views of the role of national versus limited government in the economy take on a different meaning in the context of the moral perspectives provided by Lincoln. He helped resolve the inherent contradictions in the Constitution about the role of slaves. From this perspective, Lincoln helped create a moral foundation for our commercial society. In short, every person matters, both in our economy and in our society, and it is the duty of both government and the market to ensure that everyone has the opportunity to succeed.

The Tension Today: Practical Challenges to Address

Civic revolutionaries face the following challenges as they seek to reconcile the interests of the economy with the interests of society:

- *The challenge of business responsibility:* from free agent to long-term investor

- *The challenge of narrow ("silo") thinking:* from them to us

- *The challenge of economic opportunity:* from uneven access to universal mobility

The issues addressed by Lincoln and the Founders are still with us today. We still struggle with competing economic and societal interests, periodic market excesses, and unequal economic opportunity. But we face new challenges that our forefathers did not anticipate. In communities today, large global corporations have replaced the individual merchants of Revolutionary times. The rise of multinational corporations represents a new challenge for our time—the economic interests of distant shareholders may frequently diverge from the interests of the communities in which corporations operate.

Today we can point to clear examples of egregious corporate malfeasance, but we can also note instances of new corporate commitments to community and cases of corporate stewardship based on a new understanding of how business and government can work together to widen the circle of prosperity. To resolve the tension for our time, we must make three critical shifts:

- *From free agents to long-term investors:* how businesses can prosper as part of the fabric of communities by being both globally competitive and deeply rooted to place

- *From them to us:* how to make the economy everyone's business and ensure that it operates in a productive relationship with people and the environment

- *From uneven access to universal mobility:* how to make
  the economy an expanding source of opportunity and
  mobility for all, rather than a fixed source of opportunity for some and not for others

Despite the global scale on which modern companies operate, one can make a case that companies acting in their enlightened self-interest should concern themselves with the long-term prosperity and sustainability of their communities. The roots of this argument go all the way back to Adam Smith. As James Joseph (1995) of the Council on Foundations has said, "Adam Smith is remembered best for what he had to say about economics but he was a moral philosopher, not an economist. He wrote *The Theory of Moral Sentiments* before he wrote the *Wealth of Nations*. His economic theories are based on his ideas about moral community, especially his notion that the individual has a duty to have a regard for fellow human beings" (p. 10). In fact, in the words of Smith ([1759] 1984) himself, "He is certainly not a good citizen who does not wish to promote by every means in his power, the welfare of the whole of his fellow citizens" (p. 231).

In a foreword to David Grayson and Adrian Hodges's book, *Everybody's Business* (2002), the prince of Wales elaborates on the rationale for corporate stewardship:

> In a rapidly changing world, my own view is that glob-
> alization of opportunity for major companies is not yet
> matched by equal opportunity of responsibility. There
> are certainly some companies who genuinely seek to
> operate responsibly and demonstrate respect for the long-
> term interest and aspirations of the communities and
> localities where they base their operations. They under-
> stand that sustainable businesses can only operate prof-
> itably, over the long term, in sustainable communities,
> and they play an informed, engaged and responsible role
> in those societies [p. 8].

What is the role of business and how can business leaders set a moral example in the community? Beyond modeling responsible business practices and upholding high standards of integrity, companies can affect their communities directly by playing a *leadership* role in their region—they can catalyze important projects or initiatives, lend their credibility and resources toward compelling regional issues, and offer skilled human capital to drive these changes. This kind of corporate stewardship is special: it is a *stewardship of place*. Companies become stewards of place because they recognize that their long-term prosperity is tied to the prosperity of their community.

A second challenge of our time is to ensure that our economy and society are well integrated, not isolated or pitted against each other. The concept of a *vital cycle*—in which a robust economy creates the conditions for a strong society and a strong society supports a robust economy—describes the desired relationship between economy and society. Societal principles or rules are also essential for markets to operate effectively. John McMillan (2002) of Stanford Business School describes, in effect, how economies and societies need to be inextricably linked: "Markets do what they are supposed to do only if they are well structured. To reach their full potential, markets need help from governments. Markets and government have an uneasy relationship. Markets coordinate the economy better than any centralized alternative; government sometimes distorts and even destroys markets. But help from government is essential if the economy is to reach its full potential" (p. ix). In short, economy and society need each other to play their role to make the result beneficial to both.

Joseph Stiglitz (2002), former chief economist of the World Bank, makes a similar observation: "Old fashioned economics textbooks often talk about market economies as if it had three essential ingredients: prices, private property and profits. Together with competition, these provide incentives, coordinate economic decision-making, ensure that firms produce what individuals want at the lowest possible cost. But there has also long been a recognition of the importance of *institutions*" (p. 139). According to Stiglitz, what is required is "a balanced view of the role of government, one which recognizes the limitations and failures of markets and governments, but which sees the two as working together, in partnership, with the precise partnership differing among countries, depending on their stage of both political and economic development. But at whatever stage of development, government makes a difference" (p. 139).

A third challenge of balancing economy and society is to create conditions for everyone to succeed in the economy. Lincoln and others have defined the moral imperative of expanding opportunity for all. Today's challenge is to ensure that economic development provides upward mobility for people at all levels of socioeconomic status.

Former Cabinet Secretary Robert Reich (2002) has suggested that "to the extent there is a moral code to American capitalism, it consisted of three promises. First, as companies did better, their employees would too. . . . Second, that working people were paid enough to support themselves and their families. . . . Third, everyone has an opportunity fully to develop his or her talents and abilities through publicly supported education. . . . But now the social contract is unraveling because those who are more skilled, talented or simply wealthier are not economically dependent on the regional economy surrounding them as they once were" (pp. 12–13). If economic prosperity does not raise quality of life for all, then economic interests become pitted against societal interests. For Reich, a renewal of the social contract, based on a moral code, is necessary: "We are all in this together. Our common wealth lies not in the fatness of our wallets but in the productivity of every one of us" (p. 121).

Others have also shown that "mobility for all" is a practical, as well as a moral, imperative. It produces tremendous economic prosperity and societal progress, while also avoiding economic stagnation and social unrest. Manuel Pastor, one of the authors of *Regions That Work: How Cities and Suburbs Can Grow Together*, makes the case that "while regions are the right place for economic, environmental, and social equity issues to come together, without a broad based strategy for promoting shared prosperity and reducing inequality, regions will suffer both economically and socially" (Dreier, Grigsby, Lopez-Garza, and Pastor, 2000, p. 127). Pastor's research has shown "that low-income communities do better when their residents are connected to the region and that metropolitan economies grow faster when the poor are included" (p. 127). An analysis of seventy-four metropolitan areas showed that faster growth and poverty reduction go together. Those regions that experienced lower reductions in poverty also experienced slower rates of economic growth.

In recent years, regional economic strategies have begun to change from simply attracting new industry to a region based on low-cost land, labor, and tax incentives to more integrated strategies that recognize that high-value businesses need skilled workers and high quality of life. It is a shift based partially on the desire to foster job growth that lifts the standard of living (economic and social mobility), rather than locks a community into low wages, providing little opportunity for mobility. The strategies have moved from cost-based attraction strategies to a more sophisticated blend of quality support for homegrown entrepreneurship, retention and expansion of existing small and medium-sized firms, and attraction of firms that fit within the region's economic strengths and contribute to higher incomes and living standards.

What is important about this transition is the recognition that an economy that produces social mobility is more about people and the places where they want to live and less about physical capital and land. This recognition puts a premium on education and training of the workforce as a key economic development strategy. In this way, the economy and society are at the center for most regional strategies today.

Ultimately, to meet these challenges and reconcile the competing values of economy and society, civic revolutionaries must focus on strengthening the vital cycle. Today they are making this connection in many ways—from promoting a new corporate responsibility for place, to finding productive relationships among economy, society, and the environment, and focusing on mobility for all.

Promising Experiments: Strengthening the Vital Cycle

Civic revolutionaries can strengthen vital cycles in the following ways:

- Defining corporate responsibility to include long-term stewardship of place

- Finding productive relationships among economy, society, and environment

- Expanding the circle of mobility by connecting local and regional interests

Defining Corporate Responsibility to Include Long-Term Stewardship of Place

Where corporate responsibility is lacking, typical symptoms are lack of public trust in markets, corporate indifference, and externalities like pollution and traffic. The good news is that some firms are setting a new example for enlightened corporate responsibility focused on the long term. Some firms are focused on their business operations—making them more efficient and harmonious with the long-term health of surrounding communities and the natural environment. Others have focused their efforts on stewardship of place—the long-term improvement or revitalization of the communities in which they operate. In addition, new business coalitions are forming to redefine corporate responsibility and long-term community commitment.

Applied Materials

Applied Materials is a prime example of a company that focuses on the long-term improvement of the communities in which it operates. The world's leading manufacturer of semiconductor equipment, with operations around the globe and in major U.S. facilities in Silicon Valley and Austin, Applied Materials has played a major role in helping to build strong relationships between the economy and society in both those regions and in other communities where it has smaller operations. The Applied Materials philosophy is that community commitment is part of its role as a "total-solutions company." Corporate responsibility does not end at the company door but extends into the community. This responsibility applies to its long-term commitments to education and its support for nonprofits through an innovative initiative, Charitech, that partners with leading local companies and entrepreneurs and acts as a catalyst on regional stewardship for social change and regional economic renewal. In 2002, Charitech brought together regional leaders from Silicon Valley, Austin, Portland, and Richmond to stimulate cross-regional dialogue and action. Applied Materials is following the example of Hewlett-Packard. In the 1950s, David Packard and William Hewlett created the HP Way, which emphasized the company's responsibility to its shareholders, customers, employees, and community in order to maximize long-term shareholder value.

Chicago Metropolis 2020

In Chicago, business leaders have stepped forward to exercise responsibility for the future of their region by creating a new regional agenda called Chicago Metropolis 2020. The Commercial Club of Chicago published this plan in 1999, building on a legacy of civic leadership that it initiated in 1909 when it sponsored Daniel Burnham's *Plan of Chicago*, which established the basis for Chicago's downtown development. This tradition of civic leadership continues through the Chicago Metropolis 2020 organization.

An important component of Chicago Metropolis 2020 is the promotion of clustered development, integrated public transit, pedestrian-oriented neighborhoods, mixed-income zoning, and areawide land use planning—the kind of growth pattern advocated more commonly by environmentalists, smart-growth advocates, and "new urbanist" planners and advocated less commonly by business leaders. According to Frank Beal, executive director of Chicago Metropolis 2020, the case for business involvement is clear: "Long-term, business leaders know that creating a region that is attractive, that has amenities, and that functions well is the greatest economic development program that you can have. Better transit systems are good for business, period. Better-trained kids are good for business. The other thing that we often forget is that business leaders are also citizens; they reap the benefits for the region as well as the rest of us."

The Chicago Metropolis 2020 program has multiple initiatives, but the following example illustrates the philosophy that community and business leaders are interconnected and interdependent. King Harris, a member of the Commercial Club, a senior executive at Metropolis 2020, and former president and CEO of the Pittway Corporation, quickly got interested in Employer Assisted Housing (EAH) programs after being presented the concept by Chicago's Metropolitan Planning Council. Harris knew that Pittway's System Sensor Division, a major manufacturer of commercial-grade smoke detectors, was having difficulty recruiting and keeping quality workers at its manufacturing plant located in Chicago's western suburbs. He saw an EAH program as a way to improve worker retention by giving System Sensor employees the opportunity to live nearer their workplace, to reduce their commuting times and related stress, and to own their own homes. Pittway ended up investing over $200,000 in the program over a two-year period and helping thirty-five employees purchase their own homes. A follow-up study by the Metropolitan Planning Council showed that Pittway got an excellent return on its investment via reduced turnover and recruiting costs. Eventually, Harris began to work with other business and not-for-profit institutional leaders on expanding EAH programs in the metropolitan Chicago area.

Harris and his colleagues also developed a unique social and economic compact, the Metropolis Principles, which committed a supporter to carefully consider the availability of affordable housing, especially affordable housing near mass transit lines, when making decisions regarding facility construction or expansion. By August of 2001, more than a hundred Chicago-area businesses—including Allstate Insurance, United Airlines, and of course Pittway—had signed on to the Metropolis Principles. Chicago Metropolis 2020 leadership hoped that once the American economy improved, the principles would lead to the creation of more jobs in communities with an ample supply of affordable housing near transit lines.

What the Metropolis Principles demonstrate is how business leaders can define corporate responsibility as long-term stewardship of place. In Chicago, business recognized that its collective location decisions could be at odds with shared public interests and that by banding together business leaders could influence one another and collectively make an impact on land use decision making. A strong business voice can also influence the very real decisions of elected leaders in Chicago-area communities.

Looking ahead, there are two challenges that Chicago Metropolis 2020 will continue to face. One is to address ongoing regional issues related to transportation, land use, education, and the economy with new commitments from business leaders. According to Frank Beal, although interest groups in Chicago have tried to address important regional questions before, "We have never been there with a strong business voice." Driven by business leadership from the Chicago Commercial Club, this strong business voice is the value that Chicago Metropolis 2020 brings to the table. The second challenge is in securing the ongoing participation of business leaders at the intersection of economy and society. Chicago Metropolis 2020 is "wedded to structural change, rather than tactical or incremental change. People's patience runs thin with that; you don't get a lot of quick, easy victories when you are taking on the scale and scope of issues we take on, and having to constantly explain that is a challenge." Exhibit 3.1, the Metropolis Principles, bears out this philosophy.

The Metropolis Principles draw upon other corporate code of conduct models implemented by numerous American companies working overseas. The Sullivan Principles, created in 1977 by the Reverend Leon H. Sullivan, were developed for U.S. companies with operations in South Africa. They helped put economic pressure on the South African government and helped contribute to the fall of apartheid. Less widely known but equally effective, the MacBride Principles of 1984 outlined nine fair-employment principles to bring fair and equal treatment to Catholics working in Northern Ireland. More than forty-five U.S.-based multinationals are signatories (including at least ten companies that have also signed the Metropolis Principles). In a similar spirit, the Metropolis Principles are meant to encourage fair access to affordable housing and transit for U.S.-based employees.

Exhibit 3.1. Metropolis Principles.

In making decisions relating to the expansion of an existing facility or the location of a new facility in a given community, we will give substantial weight to whether

(1) A community has zoning, building, and land use policies that allow the construction of housing that is affordable to working people

(2) A community is served by reliable mass transit, especially mass transit near work sites

Source: The Metropolis Principles, 2003. Reprinted with the permission of Chicago Metropolis 2020.

Austin, Texas

Austin has one of the strongest track records of long-term corporate stewardship of any region. In the early 1980s, Austin was still a sleepy state capital and college town torn by town-gown growth versus no-growth debates that blocked progress on any economic, social, or environmental objective. The University of Texas at Austin was a state university that did not see itself connected either to the region or to local businesses. The state government was more attuned to traditional pillars of the Texas economy: oil and real estate. Then came an opportunity—and a group of regional leaders who knew how to seize it—that would fundamentally transform Austin.

Austin's business leaders, the university, and the state joined forces in 1983 to recruit Microelectronics and Computer Technology Corporation (MCC), the first major U.S. technology consortium assembled to meet the competitive challenge from the Japanese. However, they did not stop there. They set their sights on becoming a major regional player in technology by not only investing in thirty-two new faculty chairs in engineering at the university to attract the second major consortium, SEMATECH, in 1986 but also creating entrepreneurial support networks through incubators, seed capital funds, and active mentoring. Between 1989 and 1999, the number of jobs in the region grew by more than 5 percent a year, and per capita income increased from 85 percent of the U.S. average to 107 percent.

Guiding this effort was an underlying strategy crafted by the Austin Chamber of Commerce in cooperation with public and civic leaders. This plan—Creating an Opportunity Economy—developed in 1985. This strategy made the case that Austin could become a magnet for high-wage information companies and the creative talent associated with those companies by focusing on quality of life because knowledge workers had great choices in where to live. Austin had to become a great place to live if it were to become a vital regional economy. The plan also made the case that whereas attraction within growing information industry clusters would be important initially, homegrown entrepreneurship would ultimately determine the level of Austin's success.

With a strategic plan in place, Austin created an ever-expanding body of regional stewards who built and extended a collaborative leadership network, an informal set of relationships that has provided the real foundation for the region's results. As one of the longtime leaders in Austin, Pike Powers, said, "We went beyond any normal economic development effort. We created ways to contribute to the large sense of mission or purpose. It was pretty magical. From the start, we told them how much we needed them and valued them. We planned events and training to integrate new managers into our community. Most responded well."

Austin's leaders did not stop with their first round of success. Many continued to work together in informal and formal ways to mentor the next generation of leaders in the 1990s. George Kozmetsky, the founder of Teledyne and a former dean of the University of Texas Graduate School of Business, created the Innovation, Creativity and Capital Institute, which provided assistance to entrepreneurs through its incubators and seed capital funds.

Pike Powers and other Austin regional stewards began to mentor young entrepreneurs from the new economy during a time when it seemed that growth was undermining the very quality of life that attracted talent to the region in the first place. Faced with some of the same concerns as Silicon Valley during the Internet boom, these young entrepreneurs organized the Austin 360 Summit to connect the emerging technology community and encourage greater participation in Austin's future. More than three hundred high-level executives joined in an active day of dialogue and debate at the first 360 summit.

The initial meeting was followed up in 2000, and what has emerged is the Austin Idea Network. Using the language of regional stewardship and the new economy, the network is based on a "declaration of interdependence." This adopted declaration recognized that "we are interdependent on resources, institutions, assets, and people of the community." The stated purpose of the network is to build collaboration among and beyond individual interests to preserve the positive lifestyle for the entire community. The network has initially focused on transportation, education, and social inclusion while working toward a longer-term vision of connecting the technology and cultural assets of the broader region to promote Austin as a "creative community."

According to its charter, the network does not see itself as a "new organization but instead a network of networks, a connector of people, institutions, and resources." It facilitates the collaboration of teams of stewards to do serious work on serious issues. Cochaired initially by Tom Meredith, managing director of Dell Ventures, and Lee Walker, a venture capitalist who chairs the board of Capital Metro, the network wants to be a platform to engage civic entrepreneurs and connect them to address the complex issues facing Austin.

In recent decades, Austin has had a tradition as a leader in regional collaboration, starting from the time the business community, the university, and the city decided to join forces to create one of the most dynamic regions in the nation. Whereas earlier efforts focused on attracting and growing high-tech manufacturing based on talent and quality of life (as well as cost advantages), in recent years the profile of the Austin region has changed, with a shift toward more entrepreneurial software and media firms locating downtown. As Austin grows, however, it has faced the same traffic congestion as other major cities, including Silicon Valley, and concerns about the growing disparities between the rich and poor.

With mentorship from some of Austin's established leaders from a long-standing informal organization—the Austin Area Research Organization—younger leaders are taking up their positions as regional stewards based on a sense of responsibility for improving Austin as both a good place to live and a good place to work. While Austin continues to work through its issues—including a recent economic downturn because of the bursting of the dot-com bubble—it is a good example of the merging of regional and corporate stewardship as well as the power of mentoring.

Finding Productive Relationships Among Economy, Society, and Environment

When regions polarize into economic, environmental, and social equity interests, the symptoms are apparent: a widespread lack of understanding about the economy and how it operates, a lack of participation by economic leaders in community affairs, a tendency to define problems and solutions narrowly, and an overemphasis on some aspects of community success (like the environment or poverty) over others (like broad-based and sustainable prosperity). However, in promising experiments across the country, regions are trying to integrate the economic, environmental, and social equity interests (the three E's of development) and strategies.

Sierra Business Council

The Sierra Business Council is a nationally recognized regional group that has worked with an unusual cross section of business, environmental, and community interests to monitor and build the social, financial, and natural "capital" of the Sierra Nevada region. In fact, the first major project of the council, the Sierra Nevada Wealth Index, looked at the entire region and developed an innovative framework for evaluating the region's three forms of capital. The wealth index provides a new lens for helping business leaders and local decision makers understand the importance of quality of life as a core regional attraction for business and tourism. Sierra Business Council members realized that if they destroyed their unique environmental and social assets, they would undermine their own economic future.

What makes the group so unusual is both its geographical and its organizational scope—it is made up of more than five hundred business agencies and individuals across four hundred miles of California's Sierra Nevada mountain range. It represents a mix of ranchers, timber executives, small business owners, tourism businesses, developers, and environmentalists. The Sierra Business Council works in a variety of communities spread along the Sierra Nevada; one of the key challenges for the group is to develop a diverse set of tools to assist these communities that range in size, complexity, and experience of working together. What holds the council together is a shared belief that preserving environmental quality is key to the region's economic prosperity and that natural resource conservation is essential to building regional wealth. The group explicitly rejects the notion that Sierra communities must choose between economic and environmental health.

One of the best examples of the impact of the Sierra Business Council is Placer Legacy. Placer County is the second fastest-growing county in California; its population increased 44 percent during the 1990s. During this time, developers, environmentalists, and proponents of the region's agricultural heritage began to come into conflict. In 1998, Placer's board of supervisors recognized that the county's growth patterns were consuming open space at an unprecedented rate. The supervisors realized that a loss of open space threatened not only endangered species and farmland but also the region's economy; if too many species became endangered, federal and state regulations would block new construction. In 1998, the board launched Placer Legacy by partnering with the Sierra Business Council to plan for different kinds of open space—agriculture, working landscapes, scenic vistas, biological diversity, recreation, and public safety.

The board of supervisors appointed a Citizen Advisory Committee (CAC) to take primary responsibility for developing the plan. In the two-year process of working on Placer Legacy, CAC members interacted with a wide array of stakeholders, including environmentalists, business leaders, ranchers, farmers, and a few "good citizens." Ultimately, CAC presented a plan to the board to protect seventy-five thousand acres over the next thirty years. The board of supervisors passed the plan unanimously and then Placer

County voters also approved the plan. However, the citizens of Placer County were not willing to pay additional taxes to fund acquisition. Despite this setback, the supervisors and citizens who had created Placer Legacy were not willing to give up on securing funds for the program. As a result, the county has creatively pulled together more than $8 million in funding, primarily through grants but also through the use of general funds. This dedication to the program was a direct result of the collaborative process undertaken by hundreds of citizens and dozens of diverse stakeholders.

Another major contribution of the Sierra Business Council was the creation of *Planning for Prosperity*—a document that provided guidelines for local communities on how to plan wisely and effectively for the future. This guide won the prestigious Daniel Burnham Award from the American Planning Association and has been used widely in different communities across the region and the rural West.

The Sierra Business Council is now promoting leadership development for the Sierra's local elected officials and business leaders, incorporating best practices and principles for developing natural, financial, and social capital in an integrated way. In a large, rural region where individuals are so spread out, the competitive politics of environmentalists, ranchers, conservatives, and liberals can stand in the way of the success of some projects. The Sierra Business Council still struggles to adapt the right tools to work in such a wide range of communities and to apply those tools at the appropriate level so that good projects do not lose their potential for economic, social, and environmental change.

Although much of the credit for the initial success of the Sierra Business Council goes to its original founder and regional steward, Lucy Blake, winner of a MacArthur Genius fellowship, the continued progress of the council is a good example of how an organization can help a polarized region work together and build social, financial, and natural capital for a sustainable future. This role is particularly important now that the Sierra is in the midst of so many profound changes—with the shift from traditional extractive industries to tourism, the rise of second-home ownership, and the political and social impact of so many newcomers on the region. Although conflicts between developers and conservationists still occur, the council has provided an important new framework and set of tools for moving the discussion to a win-win dialogue rather than the more traditional win-lose debates.

South Florida

South Florida presents another example of how a region can pursue complementary economic and environmental goals. The three core counties of the South Florida Region—Dade, Broward, and Palm Beach—are a good example of how regions are attempting to look at the three E's (environment, economy, and equity) in a more integrated way. Regional collaboration began in the 1990s, when a focus on preserving the Everglades led to an innovative regional initiative—Eastward Ho—that promoted compact urban development along the coast as a way to prevent further encroachment into the threatened natural environment at the urban edge. This new environmental consciousness began to promote a greater sense of regional identity based on shared natural resources and common challenges.

With the support of the John D. and Catherine T. MacArthur Foundation, a series of initiatives followed, which built on and further developed South Florida's emerging regional identity. These initiatives include a regional report on critical challenges and opportunities prepared by journalists Peirce and Johnson and the development of regional scenarios prepared by the Global Business Network, both funded by the Collins Center for Public Policy. Florida Atlantic University's Catanese Center for Urban and Environmental Solutions published *Imaging the Region*, a comprehensive set of regional indicators that examined the South Florida region through the intersection of three region-binding forces: place, economy, and people. At the same time, the Urban Land Institute's Southeast Florida/Caribbean District Council began sponsoring a series of meetings focused on the importance of regionalism.

Concurrent with these initiatives, regional leaders began to work with one another to develop a vision for the region that connected the three E's: economy, equity, and environment. Business leaders recognized that South Florida, with its proximity to Central and South America, was a hub for Latin America in international trade and tourism. South Florida branded itself as a hub for Internet services, through the efforts of an initiative called the Internet Coast, led by technology business leaders. A group of business leaders, known as the Regional Business Alliance, formed to move forward an initiative to transform the regional commuter rail agency into a more comprehensive regional transportation authority. As a multicultural region, South Florida is on the leading edge of diversity, which is an increasingly important asset in attracting and retaining creative talent. As a sustainable region, it was demonstrating how water, land, and transportation challenges could stimulate innovative regional thinking and action. In short, South Florida understood that it was changing rapidly—economically, culturally, and environmentally—into what national journalist Johnson has called "America's most fascinating, fastest-changing urban laboratory."

With ongoing support from the MacArthur Foundation, a small group of regional leaders who believe in this vision are now taking action as members of the South Florida Regional Resource Center. Partners include the Catanese Center at Florida Atlantic University, the Collins Center for Public Policy, Inc., and the South Florida and Treasure Coast Regional Planning Councils. The resource center intends to fulfill three main goals: use the resources of the individual partners to assist both public and private projects, serve as a catalyst for the training and education of community and business leaders, and organize groups such as the Internet Coast and the Regional Business Alliance around a broader, more comprehensive regional focus. Acting as regional stewards on behalf of the long-term well-being of the region, these committed leaders are developing the networks that are essential for building a regional agenda for South Florida. Their core beliefs are expressed in Exhibit 3.2.

Exhibit 3.2. South Florida Regional Resource Center Core Beliefs.

One of South Florida's strengths is that it is a constellation of communities, each unique in its own way.

To preserve and enhance who we are, we need to recognize that we all have a shared stake in the region's future.

We share serious challenges: water, transportation, growth.

We share some incredible opportunities:

- To become the economic hub of the Americas

- To connect globally through the Internet Coast

- To lead in environmental innovation

- To leverage and blend diversity as an economic and social asset

As leaders, we need to recognize our shared future and work together in new ways as one region. In this manner, we can sustain our communities and become a model for other regions nationally and globally.

Source: South Florida Regional Resource Center, 2003. Printed with permission.

Although South Florida's leaders have just started to embark on their common journey, the first step in recognizing their common interests and developing a shared regional identity around the three E's has begun.

Expanding the Circle of Mobility by Connecting Local and Regional Interests

The most powerful force for upward mobility in contemporary society is education and skills. Access is important too, in terms of removing racial, language, and other barriers to the acquisition of education and skills that the economy will reward with higher wages and in terms of tapping networks that lead to jobs. In some cases, labor unions and government policies can succeed in setting minimum or livable wages, but sustainable upward mobility requires possessing the knowledge and skills that the economy values more than others.

In this vein, a number of promising experiments have emerged that focus on connecting disadvantaged people to regional job and career opportunities. The Annie E. Casey Foundation, through its Jobs Initiative, has sponsored a series of projects across the country—including in Denver, Milwaukee, New Orleans, Philadelphia, St. Louis, and Seattle—creating coalitions of employers, education and training institutions, local community groups, and others to prepare and support disadvantaged residents for jobs that offer the potential of upward mobility.

The James Irvine Foundation is pursuing a similar strategy, sponsoring career-progression partnerships across California. In Fresno, for example, the partnership links the growing water-flow technology industry with local community colleges and other community groups to recruit, train, and place disadvantaged individuals in the initial positions in a career progression and to put into place additional opportunities of upgrade training as individuals gain experience.

San Antonio's Project QUEST

In 1990, a large manufacturing plant closure in San Antonio put hundreds of Latino workers out of work. The region had already lost fourteen thousand manufacturing jobs over the previous decade. During the same period, the economy gained nineteen thousand high-paying jobs in growth industries like health care, but they were inaccessible to low-income residents, who had little formal education and lacked appropriate job training. What could have been a traditional appeal to address an immediate economic crisis became a partnership for long-term progress in San Antonio.

Two long-standing community organizations—Communities Organized for Public Service (COPS) and Metro Alliance—swung into action. Drawing on their significant experience in organizing congregations, schools, and civic associations, leaders from COPS and Metro Alliance invited neighbors and community members to house meetings, where they listened to the obstacles faced by unemployed workers and identified gaps in the current workforce-training system. From this process, Project QUEST was born. Rather than seek short-term assistance or training, Project QUEST reached out to the city government, business leaders, and community colleges to fundamentally change long-term job training services for disadvantaged workers in the region. Project QUEST acts as an employment broker, connecting workers to high-demand occupations through up-to-date training.

Four key principles guided the formation of Project QUEST (Bear, Conway, and Rademacher, 2001). First, the program used a market-based approach that targeted the occupations that were most in demand by the local labor market. Second, the program encouraged economic mobility by training individuals for high-skilled jobs that offered good pay and advancement opportunities. Third, the program provided intensive client services to help people make the transition into a new job or career. Fourth, the program sought to leverage resources that already existed in the community.

From the beginning, Project QUEST understood the importance of connecting economic demands with social goals. Private sector leaders were integrally involved in identifying high-skilled occupations with the greatest growth potential, such as health care workers, electrical technicians, and aircraft mechanics. Rigorous labor market research and employer-driven training ensured that the skills of new trainees were demanded in the marketplace. Further, COPS and Metro Alliance secured early job commitments from area employers before participants began training. From the perspective of local businesses, Project QUEST helped them meet their labor needs while reducing the cost of recruitment and turnover. As one report put it, "A growing number of employers in San Antonio think of QUEST as a valuable extension of their human resource capabilities" (Bear, Conway, and Rademacher, 2001).

Because of its strong partnership with the business community and its industry knowledge, QUEST has helped reshape some occupations to the mutual benefit of both employers and employees. For instance, QUEST was able to convince hospitals to combine and modify the duties of two low-paying jobs into one job with higher skills and better pay. It helped design and implement training programs specifically for the new position and created a new sustainable occupation.

The city government and local community colleges also played significant roles in making Project QUEST successful. Nearly half of QUEST's $3.5 million budget is funded by the city of San Antonio. The significant level of flexible funding allows the organization to focus on long-term program priorities. Project QUEST has also formed alliances with the Alamo Community College District to create a tiered training program that accommodated the different skills and educational levels of QUEST participants while being responsive to employer needs.

Since its founding, QUEST has served more than fourteen hundred people. Project QUEST graduates from fiscal year 2001–02 averaged a 186 percent increase in annual earnings. This group of 187 students earned a total of $1.5 million in the year before entering QUEST and will earn a total of $4.3 million in their first year at their new jobs. With proven results, Project QUEST represents a new social compact between employers, workers, and the community to mutually serve economic and social interests that reinforces the vital cycle.

Tupelo, Mississippi

Tupelo, Mississippi, offers one of the most dramatic examples of widely shared upward mobility, as illustrated by the following facts, taken from a 2001 Economic Development Administration guidebook on innovation-led development.

According to the U.S. Census of 1940, Lee County, in which Tupelo is located, was one of the poorest counties in the poorest state in the United States. Lee County and Tupelo, its main town, possessed almost no competitive advantages. The agricultural land was depleted and eroded. The people were mostly illiterate. The physical infrastructure connecting town and rural areas was abysmal. The county was geographically isolated, and there was little industry.

Yet by the 1990s, Lee County was the second-wealthiest county in Mississippi, after Hinds County, the home of the state capital. Today it has a diverse manufacturing base, it is home to the largest non-metropolitan medical center in the country, and it has a public school system consistently rated as one of the best in the nation. Its manufacturing sector has been growing approximately a thousand jobs per year over the past thirteen years, while its services sector has been growing fifteen hundred jobs per year over the same period.

The seeds of change were planted as early as the 1930s. Having convinced local businesses that the future of the town's prosperity was tied to the future of its poorest rural farmers, George A. McLean, owner of the local newspaper, ignited a seventy-year process of developing economic interdependence—integral links between the city and rural areas, between the poorest and the most affluent, and between community health and economic growth. McLean introduced a rationale, which held that the reversal of failing farms to export-oriented successes would, in turn, stimulate the local economy of this rural region. He persuaded the local hardware store owner that he would never do well as a local-serving business unless those who shipped goods and services outside the region were successful in bringing revenue back to the region, thereby increasing their purchasing power. With this approach, he convinced local businesses to invest in a dairy technology program.

This first effort built trust, a momentum of success, and credibility for an integrated approach to economic development. Programs and initiatives alone, however, do not have staying power—another important lesson of the Tupelo region's economic development. Economic development is unsustainable without collaborative institutions and organizations that provide a forum and structure for ongoing discussion, mobilization, and action. Individual champions and leaders are very important, but institutions and organizations provide structure and sustainability. In response to this need, rural development councils were formed as part of the web of networks facilitating the dairy program in rural areas. Not long after, community leaders in Tupelo formed the Community Development Foundation (CDF). It is noteworthy that this organization supplanted the chamber of commerce, which was thought not to be broadly representative of the region and to be guided by business interests, disconnected from community concerns. Membership in the dues-based CDF was and still is based on a sliding scale. Anyone can participate, so many do. One local leader commented that newcomers to Tupelo often remark about both the diversity and the numbers of participants, from local farmers to heads of corporations.

Over time, the CDF became the network of networks in northeast Mississippi, creating and spinning out many organizations and networks focused on an integrated approach to economic and community development. Examples include the Community Relations Agency, Itawamba Community College, the University of Mississippi at Tupelo, the Lee County Council of Governments, the PALS literacy program, the National Model for Technical Career Development, the Entrepreneurs Forum, the Inventors Forum, the Natchez Trace Parkway Association, the Northeast Mississippi Economic Symposium, and Leadership Lee.

The CDF, under McLean's leadership, made an important decision to reject a model of economic development that swept the

South starting in the 1930s. This model, Balance Agriculture with Industry (BAWI), focused on providing tax exemptions and other subsidies and advertised cheap and abundant labor. CDF recognized that economic diversification was needed and that industrial development was promising. But it also understood that quality, higher-paying jobs could only be brought to Tupelo if there were skilled workers—and a quality of life in which those workers and companies would want to locate. For these reasons, education was the key to economic development in the philosophy of this region. A "strong community, strong economy" approach led to the creation of more community-oriented organizations that would help develop the region's assets, its "raw material"—its people. This form of indigenous development was opposite in approach to that of BAWI, and it resulted in the retention and attraction of value-added industry.

The region's choices of development tools were aligned with their commitment to upward mobility for all. Tupelo developed incubators, it carefully located industrial parks, it developed programs for upgrading existing businesses, it created technical training programs for incumbent workers, and—very important—it made long-term investments in its human assets. This commitment is evident in the creation of a worker-training program that evolved into a community college, as well as in the addition of a University of Mississippi campus to the region. The university was a critical ingredient in the creation of the future of well-paying, quality jobs and economic growth in an increasingly knowledge-based economy.

The University of Mississippi at Tupelo was sited next to the Itawamba Community College and linked by a resource center, funded by Christian Research Education, Action, Technical Expertise (CREATE), a community foundation founded by George McLean. CREATE developed specifically to collect and administer the large funds that would be necessary to invest properly in an educational system for the next century.

Tupelo's success would not have been enduring had it not been the result of broad-based participation. Civic engagement has been the linchpin for Tupelo's successful economic transformation. Its premise has been that the vitality and strength of the economy links directly to the strength and vitality of the community. "Economic development is a process, not a product," one Tupelo leader has said. Another local leader said, "The consensus-building process is vital and must arise from the citizenry for it to take root. The public sector is an important partner, but it listens and acts as a partner for the initiatives that bubble up from the private sector." Many people in Tupelo increasingly recognize the fundamental truths of interdependence and how they are prerequisites for regional vitality. A continued focus is on increasing awareness of the shared destiny that the well-off communities in the region have with those still not flourishing.

In 1994, CREATE began an effort to build and strengthen ties in northeast Mississippi that takes regional planning to the next level, following the same philosophy that motivated George McLean to seek funding from a local hardware store for his dairy program. Mike Clayborne, the director of CREATE, has developed an endowment strategy based on community matching to fund the development of regional leadership and strategic planning.

It is important to note that CREATE's "strategy" lies in building a model for working together—a process. It does not need or want a master or comprehensive plan; the process itself changes plans. The important point is to cultivate resource and leadership capacity. A strong model or successful demonstration project can be illustrative and stimulate other such models—one effort begets another. This approach captures the Tupelo region's institutional richness and flexibility. It explains why Tupelo continues to be able to anticipate, respond, and regularly reinvent itself.

Insights from the Field

Communities and regions across the country are constantly wrestling with the creative tension between the economy and society, including the natural environment. There exists no single blueprint for how to mesh the two, but some insights from the field are provided here. They are discussed according to the major roles played by civic revolutionaries—to discover, decide, and drive change.

Discover: Building a Compelling Case for Change

Document and promote regional role models of long-term corporate stewardship—and recruit these natural allies for change. The best examples of corporate stewardship today are companies that make a practical and tangible commitment to the long-term stewardship of the regions in which they operate. None of them have had to compromise their ability to compete at a high level in the global economy. At a minimum, they pursue a business model that is sustainable—ethical, efficient, and productive, with little waste and impact on the surrounding environment. Even more powerful, they seek out opportunities to leverage long-term improvements in their regions—through strategic investments, collaborative initiatives, and capacity-building efforts to improve the region's problem-solving environment (including leadership development, open and influential civic organizations, and inclusive and catalytic civic processes). Applied Materials has played such roles in Silicon Valley and Austin, as well as in Richmond, Virginia, and Portland, Oregon. Every major metropolitan area has role models to showcase and engage—although they may not be the largest and most visible companies.

Diagnose the health of your vital cycle—the system of interactions between economic, social, and environmental processes in your community or region. Many regions collect indicators, data that show various trends. Some focus on economic, social, or environmental measures. Others collect data from all three categories. But the key is to make the linkages and propose implications. Even though causality can seldom be proved in an academic sense, a case for interdependence can be made in a practical sense. Good examples of this approach are found in community index reports from Silicon Valley, Chicago, and the Sierra Nevada region of California. Some, including South Florida, Salt Lake City, and Austin, have tried to imagine how the economic, social, and environmental relationships might change in the future by developing scenarios. Whatever means is chosen, focusing on the concept of the vital cycle is key to reconciling the important values of economy and society (including the environment). It offers a positive possibility that resonates with people, not to mention a widely accepted view that is supported by both research and experience.

Decide: Making Critical Choices in Experimentation

Identify specific opportunities for the productive integration of economic, social, and environmental interests. Natural tensions, different perspectives, and at times incompatible values exist among these interests. Knowing that sometimes interests will clash, seek out specific opportunities for productive integration of economic, social, and environmental interests to build mutual understanding, trust, and a long-term relationship that can weather the inevitable periods of conflict (resulting in a Madisonian "regulation" of excesses). For example, economic and equity interests can find common ground on workforce development; environmental and equity interests might naturally work on revitalization of urban neighborhoods as both a social equity and a smart-growth strategy. Chicago's business community and affordable housing and public transportation advocates find common ground through the Metropolis Principles on the need for workforce housing and public transit near workplaces. A business coalition, the San Francisco Bay Area Council, connects with equity and environmental interests in a partnership to promote investment in disadvantaged neighborhoods in the inner core of the region as an integrated strategy for smart growth, environmental preservation, and community revitalization. (See Chapter Four for further discussion of the council.)

Explore a ripe opportunity for collaboration working for Lincoln's vision of a "true system" of mobility. Lincoln challenged America to be a country of equal treatment and opportunity, but he believed further in a true system of economic and social mobility in return for hard work. Earned mobility is a widely shared American value on which practical regional strategies can be based. It provides a natural opening for connecting neighborhood residents and regional economic interests in a mutually beneficial relationship—and provides a strong justification for removing obstacles to earned mobility (such as child care, transportation, language, and racial discrimination).

Examples of mobility strategies include education improvement initiatives. Efforts that have linked regional economic and societal interests include Project Grad, which is helping implement proven literacy and mathematics improvement models into sets of schools in Houston and Los Angeles's San Fernando Valley. Other regions, from Boston to Cincinnati to Baltimore to San Jose, have experimented with educational improvement efforts, such as compacts and venture capital investment models that at their core are about opening up avenues to economic and social mobility for young people.

Other regions have focused on workforce development. Examples include career-progression partnerships in California regions such as Santa Cruz, Fresno, Orange County, and the Gateway Cities region of Los Angeles, as well as efforts supported by the Annie E. Casey Foundation in Denver, Milwaukee, New Orleans, Philadelphia, St. Louis, and Seattle. These examples create coalitions of employers, education and training institutions, local community groups, and others to prepare and support disadvantaged residents to gain access to career ladders providing the promise of upward mobility in return for hard work. Other examples include labor-led *high-road partnerships* in regions such as Philadelphia and San Jose, in those cases working with employers and other community stakeholders to define opportunities for entry and career advancement in the health care and hotel industries and to help people access those opportunities.

Drive: Mobilizing Allies for Change

Mobilize through a focused campaign of education and influence. General advocacy for better relations between the economy and society is not likely to produce many tangible results, especially in the short term. However, a focused campaign of education and influence can mobilize people and institutions for action. The Sierra Business Council has followed a multifaceted approach to mobilizing civic revolutionaries in communities across a multicounty region. The council provides information on economic, social, and environmental trends (the vital cycle) to help change mind-sets about the region; guidebooks with vivid and practical examples of how to reconcile business vitality and environmental preservation in community settings through new patterns of development; technical assistance on how to change city and county general plans; and leadership development to prepare more and more civic revolutionaries for action in their communities. The civic revolutionaries driving the Austin Area Research Organization form teams, select targets, and influence those making decisions about how the economy and society (including the environment) can productively support one another. More established leaders have developed mentoring relationships with younger, emerging leaders, often as team chairs and vice chairs, educating new civic revolutionaries as they influence the relationship between the economy and society in Austin.

Drive collaboration among regional and local interests. One way to find common ground is through *inclusive stewardship*, a process by which regional and community leaders take shared responsibility for the long-term *commitment to place*. In practical terms, inclusive stewards codefine challenges, codevelop strategies, and coimplement actions to address common issues facing both regions and communities—including economic development, community revitalization, housing, transportation, education and workforce, and a host of other issues. They are teams of local and regional leaders that share compatible interests and must play complementary roles to move the region and local areas forward.

In addition to Chicago and the San Francisco Bay Area, good examples of this kind of collaboration are found in Atlanta through the leadership of the Atlanta Neighborhood Development

Partnership in building a local-regional coalition for affordable, mixed housing (discussed in Chapter Four); in Detroit and Denver in building alliances of regional and local interests for transit improvements; and in Baltimore where regional and local interests are uniting to advocate for a series of improvements in transportation, community revitalization, open-space preservation, drug treatment, and workforce development whose benefits are spread across the region.

In many places, regional and community leaders operate in separate worlds. In these places, community development is about grassroots capacity building or community organizing, whereas regional organizations are often expert driven and focused on planning and infrastructure projects. In some places, regional and community leaders come in contact with one another, but as adversaries. In other places, regional and community leaders interact with one another, but as unequal partners. Inclusive stewardship is a good fit for those instances where local leaders are willing to work with regional leaders and regional leaders are willing to open up what has often been closed regional decision-making processes to local leaders. In this sense, inclusive stewardship is distinct from both bottom-up community advocacy and top-down regional decision making—both of which involve imposing one's agenda on another.

Use practicality and public morality together as a powerful motivator for change. The Founders deeply believed that a moral foundation was important for the long-term health of the republic. As realists, they acknowledged the dark side of human nature and set up a system of checks and balances. They were also ruthlessly practical and used the instability of the Articles of Confederation to build support for the Constitution—and strategically integrate the American economy and society. They turned concern about the crisis into support for a practical and far-reaching strategy for systemic reform. At the same time, they used the language and symbols of public morality as a foundation for the new republic and in *The*

Federalist Papers to advocate for the ratification of the Constitution, giving it a deeper sense of meaning than the political document represented by the Articles of Confederation. As civic revolutionaries think about how to best resolve the tensions between economy and society today, the experience of the Founders and subsequent stewards, such as Abraham Lincoln, Theodore Roosevelt, and Franklin Roosevelt, is still relevant: a moral foundation combined with a practical course of action provides lasting power for change.

What Success Looks Like: The Vital Cycle

The vital cycle is what reconciles the competing values of economy and society. Although the experience varies from region to region and community to community, a point exists at which economy and society exist together in a mutually beneficial relationship. But what does success look like?

- Businesses prosper as part of the fabric of communities by being both globally competitive and deeply rooted to place.

- The economy is considered an essential part of the community and operates in a productive relationship with people and the environment.

- The economy is an expanding source of opportunity and mobility for all, rather than a fixed source of opportunity for some and not for others.

4

People and Place
Making the Creative Connection

*In a major metropolitan area, several neighborhoods
are in decline, with housing stock crumbling, commercial districts suffering, and residents still living
in poverty. Other neighborhoods have experienced a
boom not only in commercial and residential development but also in gentrification, as established residents
(mostly renters) fail to benefit from the rise in home-
owner equity and are squeezed out of a housing market by more educated, higher-paid residents. Elsewhere
in this metropolitan area, economic growth has spread
to the suburbs, with the central core losing its vitality
and relevance. What seems to be missing is a buzz,
an excitement about being in a distinctive, creative
place that is the source of new ideas and businesses—
one that benefits established residents and attracts
new people who can contribute to the area's economic
prosperity. The practical question is how to reconcile
the competing American values of people and place.*

The rights of people and the rights of places are both important
in the American tradition. People have liberty and freedom of
mobility. Places have the property rights and local government
powers as defined in the context of the American federalist system.

People obviously live in places, but the interests of the two can diverge.

Whenever the development of people and place is out of balance, individuals leave voluntarily or are displaced involuntarily, and communities are disrupted. People sometimes leave voluntarily when the quality of place declines or when they gain education and other means to live in different, better places. But people sometimes are forced to leave when places suddenly change and become unaffordable (gentrification) or unlivable (through urban renewal, environmental contamination, or other forces).

In the past, the tension between people and place often has been resolved through migration. For example, people left East Coast cities to settle in land made available to them under the Homestead Act of 1862. After World War II, the interstate highway system and prevailing policies promoting racial segregation helped stimulate the development of suburban America. Beginning largely in the 1960s, new educational access and the gains of some African Americans led to their departure from inner-city ghettos as they entered the middle class and had greater choice of places to live. When the country had plenty of room to grow, migration was an effective release for tensions between people and places.

Today, with the effects of suburban expansion and inner-city decline, resolving these tensions is more complicated. But new opportunities also exist for connecting the interests of people and place in creative ways—helping people prosper in vital places.

The American Experience: Resolving the Tension Between People and Place

The American story is about both people and place. The idea of America is of an open society that has welcomed people from around the world to freedom, equality, and opportunity. The diversity of our people has been a constant source of our creative energy. That diversity keeps changing, and the ability of America to change its face has been an important part of its story. America has been and will continue to be about people on the move.

America is also about place. Its communities mean something to the people who live in them, and their many traditions are important to those people. Increasingly, however, population mobility and growing diversity have meant that traditional notions of community have given way to new definitions of community. Today we talk about communities of culture (for example, the Vietnamese community) or communities of interest (for example, the eBay community) in addition to neighborhoods, cities, and regions. Concerns about the loss of social capital and trust have created a growing sense that the American people have lost their connection to particular geographical places.

One of the most interesting aspects of our country's Founders was that each was a leader in his own community before he connected on a national stage to create the new America. Adams was a leader in Massachusetts, Franklin in Philadelphia, Hamilton in New York, and Jefferson and Madison in Virginia. They had the opportunity to be creative "in their own backyard" by creating their own state constitutions and developing their own innovative designs for governing. Adams, in Massachusetts, developed his ideas about separation of powers to constrain the executive; Jefferson was proud of his work in Virginia protecting the right to religious freedom, as well as his work on the constitution of Virginia and the University of Virginia. (In fact, he chose to have the latter two accomplishments along with having written the Declaration of Independence listed on his tombstone, rather than his presidency.)

A sense of connection between people and place was important to the Revolutionary leaders. James Madison in *Federalist* No. 51 emphasized that "the interest of the man must be connected with the constitutional rights of the place," and worried in *Federalist* No. 10 that "the most common and durable source of factions has been the various and unequal distribution of property" (Quinn, 1993, p. 23, p. 131).

Only after they had become leaders in their colonies did they begin to connect through committees of correspondence and later the Continental Congress. This bottom-up evolution was important for the development of the nation. Rather than a single design providing a model for the country, as France attempted with the Napoleonic code or with many other failed constitutions, the development of the American "civic DNA" was more organic, coming from the ground up.

Furthermore the concept of federalism itself embodied the idea that Americans could be citizens of the nation and of their states at the same time. The Articles of Confederation, which focused on allegiance to the states and built the nation from states' rights, proved unworkable. The federal system of allegiance to both national and state government was a major innovation.

The key concept of "We the People" in the Constitution has proved, however, to be critical in interpreting the Constitution. John Marshall, the Supreme Court chief justice, understood that the federal government had a direct responsibility to the people and was empowered by them to act on behalf of the Union. Marshall and Jefferson had different views of the Constitution, with Jefferson preferring a more limited, states' rights view. However, the federal perspective prevailed in a series of major cases, including *Marbury* v. *Madison*, which established the prerogative of judicial review. Lincoln's view of the Union finally settled the matter of states' rights during the Civil War, and the increasing industrialization of the nation in the late nineteenth century led to a growing power of the national government to regulate industry.

Lincoln once again was the pivotal figure in interpreting the Founders' views of liberty (people's rights) and property (place rights) across a number of domains. He was a proponent of the Union and of the further development of the nation along the lines of Henry Clay's original American Plan, including investments in internal improvements. He was a lifelong supporter of railroads and helped promote the completion of the transcontinental railroad that was so critical to the development of the national economy. He was also a proponent of the 1862 Homestead Act that made land available for settlers as well as the land-grant college system that made education available to more people. Lincoln understood the importance of investing in both people and place to create a dynamic economy and an equitable society.

The Tension Today: Practical Challenges to Address

To resolve the tension between people and place, civic revolutionaries must address the following challenges:

- *The challenge of divergence:* from separate paths to shared destiny

- *The challenge of distinctiveness:* from common places to creative environments

Mobility in American society clearly has its advantages—bringing new people, ideas, and energy to communities across the country and offering individuals the opportunity to find a place that best fits their desired lifestyle. However, when mobility is due to reluctant migration or involuntary displacement, it is disruptive to people and places alike.

Regions have an important role to play in meeting the practical challenges of people and place. As a broader concept than a locality, the region offers more options for finding a match between people and place and for providing more opportunities for limited mobility, so if residents are displaced they might be able to relocate within the region. Regions are likely to offer more varied housing choices than can single cities.

If a region wants to avoid significant disruption, the challenge is to shift

- *From separate paths to shared destiny:* how to put people and places on a shared pathway to better living standards

- *From common places to creative environments:* how to create an environment where people and places feed off each other in a creative interaction that fuels economic and community vitality

If a region wants to have both stability and progress, the challenge becomes how to ensure that people and place advance together—linking the upward mobility of people and the quality of neighborhoods in which they live. This approach offers the opportunity to avoid the mass migrations and displacements of the past, which have often hurt or destroyed the vitality and even the basic safety of neighborhoods. Manuel Pastor of the University of California-Santa Cruz has described this challenge well:

> Previous efforts have tended to break down into either place- or people-based approaches. In the place-based approach, real estate development and the elimination of physical blight are seen as key; attention is therefore focused on "bricks and mortar" in the neighborhood. In the people-based approach, connections to employment are essential and therefore more attention is paid to individual skills and opportunities. The risk in the place-based approach is that it may affect the physical but not the social landscape. The risk in the people-based approach is that economically successful individuals may exit the neighborhood, leaving even more concentrated poverty and worsened social problems as they depart. . . . The challenge is to creatively combine place- and people-based approaches, stressing both neighborhood livability and regional job connections [Dreier, Grigsby, Lopez-Garza, and Pastor, 2000, pp. 7, 174].

If a region also wants to have places that will attract innovative people who are critical to driving their economy—then it must develop creative centers in which diverse people and their ideas can mingle. A welcoming and distinctive place can fuel the social interactions that lead to creativity and innovation in the economy and the community.

Balancing the needs of people and place today requires redefining community for our times. Gardner (1990) describes this social challenge: "Stories of the traditional communities of nineteenth century America or Europe evoke nostalgia, but we can never bring them back, and if we could they would prove hopelessly anachronistic. The traditional community was relatively homogenous. We live with heterogeneity and must design communities to handle it" (p. 114).

Today we face the challenge of creating quality communities that are appropriate to human scale. The large industrial economy created at the turn of the nineteenth century contrasts with today's economy, in which many people want to earn their living from the new economy of ideas. Much of today's discussion is about how to create communities that work better for the economic and social life of people. Writer and public philosopher Wendell Berry (2000) observes that "planners are now trying to reinvigorate the idea of communal spaces, places where people can gather around common concerns. . . . The hope of the community finds its strongest support in the development of local economies, for it is here on the level of long-term face-to-face exchange, that the work of cooperation and mutual help can find its most honest expression" (p. xix). Places that provide rich opportunities for human interaction are places that enjoy long-term economic and community vitality.

The companies and communities that will thrive in the coming years are those that can generate new ideas (creativity) and apply them effectively (innovation). Ideas will drive economic growth, in marked contrast to the "raw material" of our previous industrial economy: access to natural resources, low-cost labor, mass-production abilities. Prize-winning Stanford economist Paul Romer makes the case that in advanced economies ideas are the primary catalyst for economic growth. New ideas generate growth by reorganizing physical resources (natural, human, capital) in more efficient and productive ways. What is valuable in a floppy disk, a grande latte, or a bag of salad is not merely the ingredients (iron oxide, coffee beans, lettuce), which have been around forever, but how the ingredients are combined and presented to the customer.

There is evidence of the growing economic power of ideas. The U.S. Patent and Trademark Office hands out 70 percent more patents than it did ten years ago. Fewer and fewer of us earn our living producing food and physical goods; most of us provide services or produce abstract goods, such as data, analysis, software, and entertainment. McKinsey & Company measures the growing marketplace for intellectual property: the total estimated royalty revenue among all companies is $100 billion and growing rapidly.

In an economy based on ideas, creativity and innovation are the ultimate competitive advantage. As researcher Shira White notes, "Creativity and innovation have always been important, but because of technological advances, speed of communications, growth of information, and the rapid changes of the last decades, the need for creativity has never been greater" (Henton and Walesh, 2002). This reality makes quality of place matter more than ever. Talented, mobile people are attracted to places that are hubs of creativity, environments essential for success in today's economy. Creative people want to live in creative places, as Richard Florida of Carnegie Mellon University has shown in a number of measures in his book *The Rise of the Creative Class* (Florida, 2002). Creative people want to congregate in "cool" places where there is a creative "buzz."

Why is this happening? For one thing, it is clear that *innovation is a social process*. It rarely occurs because a single individual or firm generates an idea and takes it to market. Instead innovation involves many people playing different roles in a dynamic, collaborative process built around creative teams and face-to-face interaction. Creative work, as opposed to routine production, requires close geographical proximity that encourages human interaction.

Innovation is not a linear process, but an active process of learning through trial and error. Relationships speed up the innovation process by connecting people across boundaries and accelerating learning. All of this happens in real places, sometimes via telephone or Internet, but more commonly in face-to-face interactions.

How does innovation occur? Research and experience suggest that the process seems to have the following characteristics:

- *Interactive process.* Innovation does not occur in straight-line, chain-link fashion from research lab to development to commercialization. In fact, British historian James Burke (1999) points out that "innovation is often surprising and unexpected because the process by which new ideas emerge is serendipitous and interactive" (p. 11).

- *Tacit knowledge.* The original work of Michael Polanyi in *Personal Knowledge* (1974) and later observations by Ikujiro Nonaka and Hirotaka Takeuchi about innovative firms in *The Knowledge-Creating Company* (1995) both point out the importance of tacit or personal knowledge to the innovation process. Theoretical or explicit knowledge is important for establishing a base of information for innovators. It is, however, the know-how gained through personal experience and interaction that leads to innovations. The innovation process is a trial-and-error learning process that takes place primarily through creative face-to-face exchange. As sociologist Francis Fukuyama (1995) points out, "A great deal of knowledge is tacit and cannot be easily reduced to a commodity that can be bought and sold in the intellectual property market" (p. 11).

- *Trust networks.* Innovation takes place in trust networks that link university researchers, entrepreneurs, financiers, lawyers, and accountants to markets. The unit of innovation has become the network, not simply the firm or the sector. The process of innovation is not conducted simply within an individual company but through knowledge-creating networks of individuals with ideas in companies, universities, and other institutions. The key is the sharing of tacit knowledge through interactive processes based on trust, willingness to share, and exchange over time. Networks are, in effect, markets with memory.

- *Porous boundaries*. In the traditional economy, ideas were held tightly within institutions; in the new economy, ideas flow freely within networks. The walls that once separated public and private institutions, education and business, large and small firms, are coming down much like the Berlin Wall. Why? The end of the Cold War helped foster a closer relationship between defense and nondefense sectors around the concept of *dual use*. Furthermore the fast pace of competition has forced companies to speed up the commercialization process by creating new forms of strategic alliances and partnerships. Universities are opening up their research to more commercial applications. A new model of collaborative research has become more accepted in the past decade. More is on the way as economic forces demand greater cooperation.

- *Competition-collaboration*. The new hybrid model— sometimes called "coopetition"—means that individuals and companies can compete ferociously but collaborate at the same time to create knowledge. Networks distribute know-how and ideas among a community of professionals that can transcend their particular companies (for example, loyalty to Java programming). The networks organize the sharing and distribution of knowledge through a wide variety of formal and informal relationships. An early model of precompetitive collaboration developed by MCC and SEMATECH has evolved into a rapid sharing of information and ideas in a more open systems environment.

If innovation in the new economy is a social, iterative process, and face-to-face tacit knowledge is important, then innovation is also place based. Place matters in the new economy because people and their interactions spark innovation. Ideas essential to innovation are generated and shared by talented people who choose to work and live in close proximity to one another.

Increasingly, civic revolutionaries are reconciling the values of people and place by growing the *creative connection* between them—from positioning people to grow with their neighborhoods to promoting synergy among creative people, industries, and centers.

Promising Experiments: Making the Creative Connection

For civic revolutionaries to resolve the tension between people and place, they must focus creatively on developing workable connections:

- Growing people and place together

- Growing interactions among creative people, industries, and centers

Growing People and Place Together

A growing number of regions are experimenting with connecting people-centered and place-centered development. For example, if neighborhoods are physically revitalized and property values rise, people's incomes or equity must rise too if they are to remain.

People can be educated and trained or can be helped to acquire equity in their homes or purchase a home, so that they can prosper as property values rise. In this way, people want to remain and can afford to do so because they are prospering along with their place.

Community Capital Investment Initiative

The San Francisco Bay Area's Community Capital Investment Initiative (CCII) is an example of a regional effort to direct strategic capital investments into low-income communities across a metropolitan area. Despite the overall wealth of the San Francisco Bay Area, a 1997 study by the Bay Area Partnership identified forty-six high-priority neighborhoods that had concentrated, persistent, and in many cases increasing levels of poverty. These neighborhoods offered large markets, a strong potential workforce, and strategic locations—but lack of capital prevented large-scale business development from taking place. The rationale for CCII, a project of the Bay Area Council, and its sister organization, the Bay Area Alliance for Sustainable Communities, came from recognizing the mutual benefit that could accrue from encouraging investment in these communities: impoverished neighborhoods need outside investment for revitalization, and the broader region needs vital neighborhoods and developed urban centers to reduce the pressures of sprawling growth at the periphery.

CCII's objectives are explicitly based on the three E's of sustainable development: economic prosperity, environmental quality, and social equity. It is deeply committed to the notion that social and environmental benefits can be achieved through market-based investments, creating a powerful "double bottom line." Toward this end, the Bay Area Council and CCII helped launch three investment funds to finance investments that fulfill a combination of economic and social equity criteria: the Bay Area Smart Growth Fund will invest in real estate developments such as mixed-use, mixed-income projects; the Bay Area Community Equity Fund will invest in profitable growing businesses that can bring substantial job and wealth creation to the forty-six target neighborhoods; and the Bay Area Community Equity Fund will invest in the cleanup of brownfields throughout the entire state of California. In particular, CCII hopes to invest in a few *keystone developments*—large-scale projects that have the potential to catalyze additional investment in older urban areas without displacing the people that live there.

The most important breakthrough that CCII has helped spur is the adoption of a comprehensive set of financial, social equity, and environmental investment criteria. The stakeholders were represented through three governing councils—business, community, and government advisory. Each council developed a set of investment criteria based on its own interests and then shared them with the other members. Facilitated by CCII, the councils spent more than six months working through their differences. Getting business leaders and community leaders to agree on a set of shared criteria posed a significant challenge, explains Andrew Michael, vice president of the Bay Area Council: "The hardest part was, and still is, helping people from different perspectives speak a common language. Each group had to answer to a different constituency, and they faced different types of risk. The nonprofit side had to think on a larger scale than they were used to, which caused some tension and discomfort. From the business side, there was concern about the possibility of overly burdensome social criteria that could kill deals. We had to work through a lot of trust issues."

The three funds have raised $140 million of private equity and are now closed and moving on to their second round of fundraising. Independent fund managers are now working with CCII and community leaders to identify projects that meet the economic and social criteria and are ripe for investment. The Business Council, Community Council, and Government Advisory Council will advise the process and help generate deal flow. Beyond the integrated economic and social criteria that have been established for future investments, CCII has also helped bridge some of the divides and misunderstandings between business and community leaders in the Bay Area. "There is noticeably more trust now between the Business Council and Community Council. A year ago, people were more hesitant and more likely to block something because they didn't want to take the risk. Some trust issues remain, but we are able to walk further together," says Michael. "The most important thing is to keep your eye on the prize—hold steadfast to the vision that double bottom-line benefits can be met through market-based mechanisms, and make sure that this belief is represented at every level." By building bonds of trust between local and regional leaders, CCII is helping strengthen the bonds between residents and their neighborhoods.

Westside Industrial Retention and Expansion Network

Cleveland's Westside Industrial Retention and Expansion Network (WIRE-Net) is an effort to improve the economic prospects of a specific place, while explicitly positioning people who live there to participate in the new prosperity. WIRE-Net formed in 1988 as a partnership between three community development corporations and a local trade school to stem the loss of manufacturing companies in Cleveland's Westside. The Westside is an industrial area with a population of more than one hundred thousand people and six hundred manufacturing companies. At the time, manufacturing jobs accounted for approximately half of the local employment base. The neighborhood's health and the companies' economic survival were therefore intimately intertwined.

Even though the primary goal of WIRE-Net is to encourage the growth and retention of companies in the region, it has taken a balanced approach to meeting both people and place needs by strengthening linkages among residents, firms, and neighborhoods. In one of its first major initiatives, WIRE-Net visited more than two hundred local manufacturers to understand their perspectives on the Westside as a place to do business. According to John Colm, founding director of WIRE-Net, "The first two years were spent listening and learning and finding out how the neighborhood was perceived by the employers and companies." These conversations led to the creation of valuable services, such as manufacturing and technology assistance programs, a peer-learning network, and a database of available industrial sites. In 2000, WIRE-Net initiated a project to revitalize two industrial corridors, which has since generated $8 million in redevelopment funds.

WIRE-Net also plays an important role in helping local residents access good manufacturing jobs while helping companies reduce the cost of turnover and recruitment. It devotes half of its budget to adult workforce education and has formed a number of innovative partnerships to train the local workforce. In 1999, it began a partnership with the NASA Glenn Research Center to create the thirty-two-week Pre-Apprentice Machining Program that trains low-income individuals for a career in the metalworking trade. It also helped form the Northeastern Ohio Metalworking Association Consortium with other industry associations, created to forge better links between schools and industry and improve metalworking training programs. Now in its fifteenth year, WIRE-Net has helped spur the revitalization of a community that everyone had all but written off. It not only has helped revitalize a place but also has helped provide opportunities for development for the people who inhabit that place.

Atlanta Neighborhood Development Partnership

The Atlanta Neighborhood Development Partnership (ANDP) is working on housing in a way that avoids displacement of people while also encouraging neighborhood revitalization and better linkage to transit and jobs. Hattie Dorsey, president of ANDP, recognizes the tension between development and displacement: "Our mission has become more complicated. In-town areas that once were neglected are now magnets for gentrification, putting low-income residents at risk as property values escalate and predatory lenders enter the scene. We are working aggressively for public policy changes to protect these residents from being forced from their homes."

ANDP, through the creation of a new regional initiative in 1998, developed an approach that focuses not on affordable housing per se, but on mixed-income housing in the context of developing vital neighborhoods. "We started out as the Mixed Income Housing Initiative, but we know that housing is only one part of building a successful neighborhood. We changed our name to the Mixed Income Community Initiative (MICI) to reflect the importance of other community factors like transportation, education, and proximity to jobs," explains M. von Nkosi, director of the MICI. Their strategy is to create vibrant communities that blend mixed-income housing options, thereby ensuring that people at all income levels can be close to their jobs, remain in their community as their housing needs change, and put less strain on an already overburdened transportation system.

With this approach, MICI seeks to serve people's housing needs, while also improving the livability of urban and suburban places within the region. A critical part of the effort has been a significant public education campaign to make the case that lack of affordable housing affects everyone—not just poor people—by contributing to regional problems such as gridlock, congestion, and air pollution. MICI used spatial analysis to show how lack of mixed-income housing affects local employers and the regional workforce. Working with two local employers, MICI plotted the zip codes of where employees lived, overlaid that with average rents in the zip code, and compared it with employees' salaries. The analysis helped make the link between jobs-housing imbalance and commuting distances, which affect transportation congestion and regional quality of life.

In a decade, ANDP has stimulated the development of more than six thousand mixed-income housing units in the region, has succeeded in having the Atlanta Regional Commission make inclusion of mixed-income housing a condition for localities to receive certain transportation-related funding, and has developed the capacity of local community development organizations to drive the mixed-income housing agenda with leadership development and capital skills training.

Perhaps ANDP's biggest contribution is a fresh approach to reversing the effects of a long history of racial segregation that has been reinforced by housing, transportation, land use, and other local and regional policies and programs. This approach shows that "advocates for racial justice need not accept the 'either-or' solutions put forward in the past. The proposition that families of color can either gain access to affordable housing in middle-class areas or sustain community strength is unacceptable" (Institute on Race and Poverty, 2002, p. 27). ANDP is an example of advancing people and place together and leaving both better off.

Growing Interactions Among Creative People, Industries, and Centers

Some regions are focusing on growing the interactions among creative people, industries, and centers—such that these elements feed off one another and fuel economic and community vitality. At a basic level, the increased importance of creativity to the economy is an argument for increased emphasis on arts education and participation. Arts education and participation develop the very skills that will be required of the twenty-first-century workforce as a whole—analysis, synthesis, imagination, teamwork, and appreciation for diversity. C. J. Van Pelt, executive director of the Cisco Systems Foundation, explained why her company gave $1.2 million to arts and cultural groups in 2001: "We hire very creative people, and the arts encourage that creativity." Today creativity is fundamental to devising new products, services, technologies, business models, and ways of earning a living.

From a community perspective, economic development today is about competing for talent. A region's economic success depends on attracting and retaining entrepreneurial, technical, and creative people. These people are mobile, have many choices, and have become sophisticated consumers of place. So quality of life has become a competitive economic asset.

Professor Richard Florida (2002) of Carnegie Mellon University has identified the increasing share of workers whose livelihood depends on regularly engaging in the creative process—some 30 percent of the U.S. workforce. He shows that the higher a worker's education level and creative orientation, the more the worker values cultural offerings and the diversity and openness of a community. And once workers have made a location decision, arts and cultural participation can help bind people to one another and to place (p. 130).

Leading regions are recognizing the growing role of the commercial creative sector—companies and free agents who produce and distribute products and services rooted in art and culture. They are broadening their definition of the *creative sector* beyond nonprofit arts and cultural organizations to include the commercial creative sector: professions and industries such as design, digital arts, advertising, interactive media, film-video, and on-line publishing. Two trends are driving this shift.

First, the creative services industries are growing rapidly. The core "copyright" industries alone (film, music, media, advertising) are already 6 percent to 7 percent of the global economy, are generating $2 trillion in revenue, and are growing faster than the world economy. This growth is impressive enough, but it excludes the creative element in other industries, including technology sectors such as software, new media, and computing.

The second trend is that the development, production, marketing, and sales of technology products increasingly involve people trained in artistic skills. As companies race to make their products engaging, exciting, and pleasing, regions are starting to see graphic designers, creative writers, animators, photographers, and music producers taking their place in the "technology" workforce. The first wave of technology featured large companies producing computers, semiconductors, and communications equipment ("hard" technology). The emerging second wave ("soft" technology) emphasizes smaller-scale activities that incorporate artistic and creative skills, such as media, design, animation, advertising, and software. Over time, as technology becomes more prevalent, use of the creative element in product or service may be one of the few ways of sustaining competitive advantage.

Portland, Oregon

Portland, Oregon, has launched the Creative Services Alliance to nurture the growth of creative-services companies and freelancers. With initial support from the city, entrepreneurs and artists involved in software, graphic design, interactive media, film and video, and advertising are working together to build effective networks and create support infrastructure. For example, company leaders are working with educators to prepare local people for jobs that integrate technical savvy and creative talent. They are branding and marketing the region's capabilities and creating a creative-services center with meeting, product demonstration, and office facilities. The alliance estimates that the Portland region's cluster of commercial creative activity includes eight hundred small firms, fifteen thousand employees and freelancers, and an annual payroll of $600 million.

Downtowns are emerging as important physical centers of the creative economy and community, because interaction is a driving force behind creativity. For this reason, a premium is put on places where diverse ideas and people can circulate and interact with great velocity. In several key regions, business and civic leaders are intentionally trying to transform their downtowns into creative hotbeds of the next new thing—adding a twist to downtown's traditional role as a retail and entertainment center. They are thinking strategically about their downtown as a creative nexus where arts, technology, and entrepreneurship come together. They are building bridges, soft and hard, between districts that are emphasizing arts and culture, business, and education.

Portland is a place that has, through a period of years, put all the pieces together—creative people, industries, and centers. Today

Portland is known for having one of the most vibrant, livable downtowns in the country. But the case was not always so. In the 1960s and early 1970s, Portland had many of the same problems as other cities in the era of urban crisis. The downtown emptied out daily at 5 P.M., the Rose City Transit Company was bankrupt, and the new Washington Square super regional mall in the affluent western suburbs threatened the end of downtown retailing (Langdon, 1992).

To turn the tide, Portland's leadership sketched out an integrated strategy that involved the coordination of land use and transportation. Preservation of a user-friendly downtown was the strategy's cornerstone. Neil Goldschmidt, Portland's mayor from 1972 to 1979, led Portland to develop new parks and plazas; high-density retail and office corridors crossing in the center of downtown; better transit, including a light-rail system—Metropolitan Area Express (MAX)—to serve the corridors; middle-income housing in the central city; and pedestrian-oriented design.

The result of such comprehensive planning is a strong and viable central core that anchors the metropolitan region. Downtown has the largest single concentration of the Portland area's jobs. Nearly 40 percent of downtown employees travel to work on light rail or buses—one of the highest rates of public transit use in the United States. At the same time, visitors to the city nearly always start at the center. They come to see the downtown square and streetcar-era shopping districts, fountains and parks, coffeehouses and microbrewers, bookstores and bike paths, and neighborhoods such as St. Johns and Brooklyn that have a modest but firm sense of self.

To make downtown the place where Portlanders go for fun and entertainment, officials have placed in the central city nearly all the metropolitan institutions and gathering places: art, history, and science museums; performing arts center and civic auditorium; the Oregon Convention Center; Microsoft billionaire Paul Allen's new privately funded arena for the Trail Blazers; and the Pioneer Courthouse Square and Tom McCall Waterfront Park, which are both places for food-and-fun festivals and community events.

Critics have noted that even as the "entertainment face" was added to Portland's downtown in the 1980s and 1990s, it managed to hold on to its individuality and distinction and thus skirt the "planet downtown" phenomenon. *Time* and *Atlantic Monthly,* the *Los Angeles Times,* and *Architecture* have all reported on the strength of downtown design, the careful conservation of a sense of place, the friendliness to pedestrians, and the enhancement of the downtown with public art. Downtown design earned a City Livability Award from the U.S. Conference of Mayors in 1988 and an Award for Urban Excellence from the Bruner Foundation in 1989. Portland's leaders were praised for closely controlling new buildings, carefully monitoring rehabilitation of worthy buildings, and vigorously creating open space so as to create a city of distinction, diversity, and compatibility.

Turning a corner in a new century, Portland's leaders are once again making deliberate choices for downtown. Taking notice of initial information about the great promise of creative-services industries for Portland's central core, Mayor Katz hosted a luncheon in 1997 for industry leaders to learn more about the industry. Creative-services firms, ranging from software to advertising and public relations to film and video and encompassing new media and e-commerce, told the mayor that they all share a strong propensity to locate in the central city and that they are characterized by good wages and rapid growth. The mayor asked the Portland Development Commission (PDC) to explore this industry further as a way to achieve the region's vision (Metro 2040 Plan) for a distinctive, economically vibrant central city.

In June 1999, the PDC released a report recommending that the city and region pursue a four-part strategy to build the creative-services industry. One recommendation is for the creation of a creative-services center—a centrally located physical facility providing space for a range of industry associations and trade groups; a hub for training activities and vendor demonstrations; a location for shared meeting space, computer labs, and other specialized equipment; and a site for flexible space tailored specifically to creative-services firms (Abbott, 2001). Opened in September 2001, the Creative Services Center is an eighty-thousand-square-foot, seven-story brick-and-timbered historical building in Portland's Old Town. Home to the Oregon Creative Services Alliance and a number of firms, the Creative Services Center is a dynamic hub for creative-services activities in downtown.

Austin, Texas

Austin has experienced the same ups and downs in recent years as other technology communities as a result of the dot-com implosion and the national recession. Most agree that Austin's resurgence will be tied to factors that drove growth in the recent past—a highly capable workforce, innovation and entrepreneurship, clusters of knowledge industries, the presence of a world-class research university and several other institutions of higher education, strong community assets, and an excellent quality of life. In many ways, Austin is blessed with an unusual interrelationship between creativity, innovation, and quality of life

Long billed as the Live Music Capital of the World, Austin is home to an unusually large number of musicians and music support industries. At the same time, film and digital entertainment are establishing a growing presence in the community. Applying Richard Florida's occupation-based definition of the creative segment of the economy, the data from the Bureau of Labor Statistics indicate that 242,000 Austin metropolitan statistical area residents were working in creative jobs during 2000, or 36 percent of the total workforce.

The city of Austin is now encouraging the growth of the creative sector through its support of small business and entrepreneurship, city ordinances and codes, and community development strategies. The tag line for these efforts has become "keep Austin weird." To continue to foster local cultural vitality, the city is developing an inventory of social and cultural assets in the community and evaluating existing and potentially new programs that would leverage the region's emerging strengths in this area (*Austin's Economic Future*, 2002).

Burlington, Vermont

Whereas Portland and Austin are well-known examples of regions creatively linking people and place, smaller communities like Burlington are also making the creative connection. The community has been recognized repeatedly in recent years: in 1999, the Arts and Entertainment Network rated Burlington, Vermont, as the number one city in the United States that "has it all." It is one of the most livable cities with a population under one hundred thousand according to the U.S. Conference of Mayors, the fourth most "enlightened" town according to the *Utne Reader,* the seventh "hippest arts town" in the country according to a survey of the Hundred Best Arts Towns in America, one of the seven best retirement locations, and the second-best place to raise children.

Part of Burlington's success is clearly a function of its location along beautiful Lake Champlain between the Adirondack and Green Mountains and the fact that it is home to the University of Vermont, one of the nation's oldest state universities, founded in 1791. But the real story of Burlington is the foresight of its leaders during the 1970s in preserving its historical business district— originally built in the early 1880s when the city was an important port—by converting it into the Church Street Marketplace, a thriving social center with sidewalk cafes as well as mixed-use commercial, retail, and residential development. The marketplace became the heart and soul of Burlington.

Earlier than most cities, Burlington realized that a good downtown core is important to a vibrant community and economy. Rather than let the historical downtown decline while suburban shopping centers grew to take its place, Burlington took an early stand. The historical districts of the city, with more than two hundred rehabilitated housing units, are now well connected to the

University Green Historic District and the city's historical water-front. Burlington created walkable compact development based on historical preservation.

"Downtown Burlington is a place of commerce, conviviality, and chance encounters(the commercial, cultural, and social center for an entire region(because of a sustained, collaborative effort by an activist municipal government, engaged citizens, businesses, and a network of municipally supported nonprofit organizations," says Burlington Mayor Peter Clavelle, who began his seventh term as mayor in 2003. Some of the visionary regional leaders who made the difference include Lisa Steel and Melinda Moulton, who in the early 1980s formed the Main Street Landing Company to promote environmentally and socially responsible redevelopment of the Burlington waterfront. The result is a nationally recognized exam-ple of concentrated development within the city core. It includes mixed-use structures for housing, office, and retail; reduced depen-dence on automobiles; support for arts and culture; and incubator space to grow local businesses.

In Burlington, creative places and creative people grow together. According to Mayor Clavelle, "Together we've invested in public amenities and services, and we've consistently tried to balance eco-nomic development, sound environmental policy, and practices that share the benefits of growth." In addition to being a vibrant and liv-able community, Burlington has been the home to socially progres-sive businesses such as Ben & Jerry's ice cream, as well as a habitat for environmental activism. What seems to make Burlington work is a deep sense of civic responsibility and a commitment to com-munity improvement. A typical Web site posting on its community bulletin board provides notices for a parade celebrating the Old North End neighborhood, a community forum on civic responsi-bility, a conference on "downtowns in the twenty-first-century econ-omy," and a town meeting on affordable housing—all in one week.

The success of Burlington suggests that climate is not destiny. Here is a thriving small community in the upper Northeast that has

learned to create warmth in terms of its social capital and a creative
interaction among people and place.

Insights from the Field

Every region and community must find its own way, its own reconciliation to the competing values of people and place. Although
there is no standard formula to follow, civic revolutionaries can benefit from the experimentation of others. Insights from the field are
organized in the following discussion according to the major roles
that civic revolutionaries play—they build a compelling case for
change (discover), make critical choices in experimentation
(decide), and mobilize allies for change (drive).

Discover: Building a Compelling Case for Change

*Explore the existing, emerging, and potential connections between
people and place in the region.* Discovering and describing the nature
and potential of such connections can produce breakthroughs in
thinking about how the two can move forward together. Atlanta's
ANDP is building a case for change by doing research on where
people live and work to show how mixed-income communities can
help reconnect people and place, bringing people closer to where
they work, which in turn could help improve that region's transportation flows and air quality. In the Los Angeles region, the Gateway Cities Partnership has assessed and connected the local need
for skilled workers (in particular, machinists and logistics technicians) and the lack of education of the local population and has
used this information to drive change in the way local educational
institutions and employers collaborate to help people and place
grow together. Portland examined the nature and scope of its
creative-services sectors and the regional assets that together helped
shift thinking about the purposes and value of the urban core.

Some regions have used an index to showcase the connections between people and place. Pittsburgh developed an index on

entrepreneurship, which examined key trends, attitudes, and assets, introducing a new way of thinking about a place that many people inside and outside the region associate with severe population and job loss. Massachusetts developed an index that described its innovation assets, process, and outcomes—and showed how they were connected. In the San Jose region, an organization called Cultural Initiatives: Silicon Valley publishes *Creative Community Index*, which measures creative assets and highlights opportunities for new connections among assets and new initiatives to spark creativity. Also in San Jose, local leaders from the Mayfair neighborhood, in partnership with Community Foundation Silicon Valley, assembled a neighborhood index that among other things examined how well residents connected with their neighborhood, one another, and others in the broader region. Even though the exploration process can take many forms, it is likely to uncover existing, emerging, or potential connections that can help a region rethink how to creatively reconcile competing values of people and place.

Expand the definition of what's possible by experiencing other communities. Leaders from Columbus, Ohio, have drawn inspiration from visits to Austin and other places and are working collaboratively to build the creative core of their region. Pittsburgh has brought in innovators from Chattanooga, Portland, and elsewhere to provide insights and has sponsored research on innovative regions across the country to fuel creative thinking regionally. Seattle has one of the nation's strongest traditions of intercity visits, which continuously stimulates the imagination of leaders about how their region might creatively link people and place.

Decide: Making Critical Choices in Experimentation

Focus on strengthening specific connections that appeal to multiple partners. Atlanta's ANDP chose the focus of mixed-income communities, drawing in both local and regional interests from housing advocates to employers, and has succeeded in getting thousands of units of housing built. The Gateway Cities Partnership in the Los

Angeles region chose the focus of local participation in regional economic opportunities, appealing to residents, elected officials, employers, and educational institutions, and has succeeded in getting new education and training programs launched. The San Francisco Bay Area's Community Capital Investment Initiative chose neighborhood revitalization as a focal point, uniting economic, equity, and environmental interests, and will help broker more than $100 million into the region's most disadvantaged communities over the next few years.

Some regions are choosing to focus on the natural linkage between creative people, industries, and centers, experimenting with *creative industry corridors* or *creative zones* similar to those in Portland, Louisville, and now under consideration in Columbus and other regions. Mary Jo Waits of Arizona State University has found in her research on downtowns that creativity comes at the nexus of *expertise* (cosmopolitan workers in dynamic places doing interesting work), *diversity* (ethnic and social diversity, mixed uses and amenities), and *interaction* (downtown advantages including compact, dense venues). Describing the evolving roles of downtowns from industrial (1940–1960s) to retail (1960s–1970s) to entertainment (1980s–1990s), she found that cities today should adopt strategies for their downtowns that reinforce their evolving, creative role in the regional economy and build on the distinctive urban assets that are valued by knowledge workers. Focusing on the nexus of expertise, diversity, and interaction is the key, which means making livability a hallmark of downtown development, along with mixed-use real estate that fits with small, fast-changing companies and the design of public and private spaces that promote social interaction (Alliance for Regional Stewardship, 2001b).

Define the terms of engagement for strengthening the connection between people and place. In the San Francisco Bay Area, economic, equity, and environmental interests came together around a set of criteria that would ensure investments in the region's disadvantaged neighborhoods in ways that produced a reasonable economic return and helped the region revitalize its inner core as an alternative to development at the outer edge of the metropolitan area. In the development of alliances in places such as Detroit, Indianapolis, and Denver, allies agreed to a set of shared objectives for transportation improvements that would help strengthen the connection between people and place.

Drive: Mobilizing Allies for Change

Launch a "bonding-and-bridging" organizing effort. Traditionally, community development has been either a top-down process (shaped by federal government guidelines, programs, and funding) or a bottom-up effort to pool the energies of a neighborhood for action. Both have demonstrated their limitations in practice. Top-down efforts are too often insensitive to community needs and ineffective in producing sustained positive change; bottom-up initiatives often lack the capacity to carry out significant change. Growing people and places together requires both regional and local partners working together—with each party bringing unique assets to the table. Regional partners have the access to resources, expertise, and networks of employers, education and training institutions, and other sources of support. Local partners have knowledge of the problems and opportunities for change, access to local people and institutions, and the incentive to keep at it over a period of years.

Manuel Pastor has said that "while community-based organizing can create 'bonding' social capital within a neighborhood, equally important is the construction of 'bridging' social capital that can connect the poor and their advocates to new sources of employment and arenas of decision-making" (Dreier, Grigsby, Lopez-Garza, and Pastor, 2000, p. 14). Both bonding and bridging strategies are necessary to make the creative connection between people and places. MOSES in Detroit pursued a metropolitan organizing approach to link urban and suburban allies in a regional effort to transform the transportation planning and implementation process. Atlanta's ANDP has mobilized change in housing by encouraging bonding within neighborhoods through community development organizations, while also bridging with regional allies, including the business community, around a practical, shared vision of mixed-income communities. Baltimore's regional Citizens Planning and Housing Association, local neighborhood groups, and others came together to advocate for better regional approaches in transportation, housing, community revitalization, drug treatment, and open-space preservation—visibly making their case at a Rally for the Region in 2000 and 2002, which has helped influence the state legislature to increase their financial commitment to these priorities by millions of dollars.

Mobilize an innovation coalition. Although creativity (the *generation* of new ideas) is important, it is not the same as innovation (the *application* of new ideas). Creative ideas that are not used do not contribute to economic prosperity. They may be valuable to the culture or society, but the process of turning ideas into commercial products and services is a different and difficult process. Some regions, such as Silicon Valley, Austin, and Boston, have developed natural innovation networks that help speed up this process; other regions, such as Columbus and Pittsburgh, are purposely trying to strengthen or build new networks. A good example is biotechnology, in which only a few regions seem to be successful today in commercializing new ideas. Creative thinking and new ideas are not enough; a dense network of institutions, scientists, large and small biotechnology companies, specialized law and financial expertise, and other networked resources are necessary to turn ideas into economic benefits.

Leaders from the arts, business, government, and civic community must recognize their vested stake in working together to sustain an innovative economy and community. They must develop a shared framework for thinking about potential leverage points and how to recognize, cultivate, and capitalize on a region's innovation assets. To start down this path, start by recognizing and understanding the economic and demographic changes under way in a community. Identify individuals who are passionate about how integral innovation is to where the economy is heading. Explore the special cultural and creative assets that can be connected and channeled in new ways. Most important, start building a team of boundary-crossing leaders from the arts, business, and community who are committed to learning and acting together for the long term. Today few communities succeed through destiny; most succeed through vision and determination.

If your region is not known for its creative buzz, where do you start? It is important to realize that Portland took years, but regional stewards put the initial pieces in place, even though they themselves were not "creative types." Seattle (see discussion in Chapter Six) may have had some natural advantages (port and international tourism destination) and some good fortune (location of Boeing and Microsoft), but again, regional stewards started the process moving. What such stewards are creative about is finding hidden assets, learning about potential opportunities for their region to prosper, and executing collaborative efforts that deliver results. Innovative stewards seem to come first; then innovative places and people follow.

What Success Looks Like: The Creative Connection

The creative connection is what reconciles the competing values of people and place. At some point, as some regions have discovered, the destinies of people and places become better, more creatively connected in a mutually reinforcing cycle of progress. But what does success look like?

- People and places are on a shared pathway to better living standards.

- People and places feed off one another in a creative interaction that fuels economic and community vitality.

5

Change and Continuity

Creating Vigilance for Renewal

*In one region, economic crisis has overwhelmed all
other issues. Many residents have lost their jobs;
many more fear losing them. The newspaper reports
daily on layoffs, home foreclosures, and dire predic-
tions about the future. A second region has a different
problem. Residents expect change and move into and
out of the region in great numbers. Although they do
not fear change, they do not strongly value continuity. They do not put down roots, reach out to other
residents, or participate in the community. A third
region does not seem to have any problems—until
you look closer. The practical question for each region
is how to reconcile the competing values of change
and continuity.*

The problem in the first region is that change is needed, but people resist it, clinging to old ways and hoping that the good old
days will return. The region is in a cycle of decline, triggered by economic crisis but extended by a mind-set that holds back renewal,
one that resists opportunities for fundamental change, which often
appears in troubled times.

The second region is subject to boom-and-bust cycles because
so many of its residents rush in during the good times and leave

quickly during the bad times. This pattern has eroded regional vitality over time and gradually has undermined community institutions that are critical to the quality of life of the area.

As to the third region, it appears there are no problems: it has a major state-funded facility, so it can expect a stabilizing inflow of tax revenue, even during private sector economic downturns that hurt other places more severely. With a stable population, there is no great urge to change the status quo. Residents participate in community affairs in large numbers and are generally pleased with the quality of life of the region. However, there are signs that something is wrong. Young people are leaving. The economy is slipping, slowly losing competitiveness to more innovative, aggressive regions. The old guard that has led the region for decades is retiring, leaving a leadership void in its wake.

All of these regions actually face the same challenge: too much of what can be a good thing. Change can bring new ideas, new people, and renewal out of crisis, but too much change can discourage long-term commitments to the community. Continuity can create strong communities, but too much continuity can undermine community vitality by resisting new people and ideas. It is not an either-or question.

Although not unique to the American experience, the tension between the forces of change and continuity explains much about American history. The Founders seriously weighed these competing values and designed a political framework that would provide enough stability and continuity to enable productive risk taking and change.

The Founders worried that a system of extreme continuity would produce stagnation and concentration of power, just as one that allowed extreme change would produce chaos and ineffective dispersion of power. In fact, the Articles of Confederation embodied the worst aspects of continuity and change, creating a political system marked by continuous chaos. The question of change and continuity has been at the core of the American Experiment ever since.

The American Experience: Resolving the Tension Between Change and Continuity

Although American revolutionaries were united in their desire for independence and individual freedom, some, such as Patrick Henry and Thomas Paine, believed in maximizing liberty and democracy. This strain of American revolutionary thinking favored large and egalitarian town meetings and elected bodies. In this view, government is a mirror, rather than a filter, of the popular will. The political system should be a vehicle for change in keeping with the shifting popular mood, not a rock of stability run by and for a small group of elites distant from the general population. The latter excess was at the root of the American Revolutionary War with England— and therefore a real concern for Americans.

Opposing this strain of thinking, however, were those revolutionaries who became founders of and contributors to the Constitution. They wrestled with the real-life challenges of a rapidly changing country, with many different, often competing, interests. In *The Federalist Papers*, they articulated an important resolution to the question of change and continuity. They focused on the difference between pure democracy, in which a free people decide all questions, and republican government, in which a free people choose through elections who among them will decide all questions within a system of checks and balances. Throughout *The Federalist Papers*, authors James Madison, Alexander Hamilton, and John Jay echoed similar sentiments: "Wisdom, regularity, coolness, temperate, reasonable, and deliberate were words the three authors used to describe the leadership the national government would attract through its filtered and refined selection process. This protected the country against impulsive decisions by uninformed mobs who would put self-interest first" (Quinn, 1993, pp. 20–21).

From 1776 to 1787, the question had shifted from how to achieve freedom to how to restore order within the context of freedom. The Founders were leery of pure democracy as a formula for chaos. Even Jefferson, who so eloquently argued for the ideal of widespread democratic participation, was more comfortable with the guiding hand of a natural aristocracy. As Madison explained in *Federalist* No. 37, the Founders wanted both "energy" and "stability" to characterize the political system:

> Stability in government is essential to national character . . . as well as to the repose and confidence in the minds of the people, which are among the chief blessings of civil society. On comparing, however, these valuable ingredients with the vital principles of liberty, we must perceive at once the difficulty of mingling them together in their due proportions. The genius of republican liberty seems to demand on one side not only that all power should be derived from the people, but that those intrusted with it should be kept in dependence on the people . . . whilst energy in government requires not only a certain duration of power, but the execution of it by a single hand [Quinn, 1993, p. 100].

To the Founders, the formula of "republican liberty" was how change and continuity would be "mingled" to achieve an energetic and stable system of self-government. They created a framework that established some change processes to be practiced often (like elections) and some to be invoked rarely (like constitutional amendments).

They also created a framework that provided a stabilizing separation of powers between the national and state governments and clear powers for the national government. These national powers would offer a secure and predictable environment for both the turbulent economy and the complex society of the new country— through the ability to raise revenue, pay debts, provide for the common defense, and create a legal and regulatory framework for trade and commerce.

It was Jefferson who famously said that America would need a revolution every thirty years or so to survive: "Some men look at Constitutions with sanctimonious reverence and deem them the Ark of the Covenant: too sacred to be touched. Laws and institutions must go hand and hand with the progress of the human mind" (Jefferson, 1816). Throughout American history, civic revolutionaries have understood that when conditions change, it is necessary to pursue perennial goals by new means, that revolution is conservation by means of innovation.

The Tension Today: Practical Challenges to Address

To resolve the tensions between change and continuity, civic revolutionaries must meet the following challenges:

- *The challenge of disruption:* from stability as an expectation to change as a given

- *The challenge of turnover:* from leadership roulette to leadership renewal

The modern-day tension between change and continuity has taken on dimensions that the Founders could have scarcely imagined. Massive technological, economic, and demographic changes are challenging the stability of our communities and institutions. These forces can be stalled or diverted temporarily but are too complex and ingrained in human ambition to be stopped. In fact, it is these kinds of forces that have led to economic and social progress in the long term.

The modern-day question, then, is not a choice between change or continuity, but rather what kind of disruption will inevitably take place and how will the people and institutions in communities respond? Will crisis precipitate a disruption that shocks, and will this shock lead to decline or transformation? Or will complacency in a turbulent world inevitably result in disruption, and will this disruption lead to decline or transformation? Or can we avoid both choices offered by crisis and complacency through a commitment to continuous renewal, especially of leadership? Two practical challenges face modern-day civic revolutionaries as they try to reconcile the competing values of change and continuity as part of their role in the continuing American Experiment. These include the following shifts:

- *From stability as an expectation to change as a given:* how to anticipate constant, dynamic change to lessen the negative impacts and leverage the positive benefits, while preserving core values

- *From leadership roulette to leadership renewal:* how to be purposeful about filling their leadership pipelines, expanding the sources of leaders and excusing no one from service

These challenges are heightened today by the unprecedented acceleration of technological innovation and globalization of markets. The sociologist Francis Fukuyama makes the case in *The Great Disruption* (2000) that the emergence of new technologies and global markets is constantly disrupting communities, undermining elements of trust that girded communities in the past. Fukuyama's view is a modern-day echo of Karl Polyani's *Great Transformation* ([1944] 1980), which described how the nineteenth-century free market and global trading system collapsed in the face of a new economy of industrialization in the early twentieth century. During this time, and others like it in the past, rapid economic and technology change has destabilized communities and undermined traditional institutions.

The Austrian economist Joseph Schumpeter (1942) made this point most forcefully when he coined the famous phrase *creative destruction*. Today communities are in a period of intense creative destruction as a rapidly changing economy creates opportunities for some people and places and leaves others further behind. Unlike our traditional models of continuous change along predictable paths (tomorrow will be an extension of today), creative destruction occurs along a discontinuous path.

Creative destruction comes in waves that disrupt existing relationships. It could be driven by a new technology, a war or world event, or a change in social values and demographics. The invention of electricity, the integrated circuit, and the Internet are clear examples of technology change that prompted creative destruction. Whole industries and communities were transformed as the structure of economy changed. Wars, in contrast, can change economies and societies fundamentally, as we saw with the Civil War, World Wars I and II, and Vietnam. Sudden events such as September 11, 2001, can have transforming impacts as well. Demographic changes such as the shift in racial composition, maturation of baby boomers, or increased in-migration prompt fundamental change in where communities search for leadership and where they invest their resources.

Whatever its source, the change creates a ripple effect that disturbs the temporary equilibrium. The first change will require other changes—economic change, for example, will require social change—but a lag in response is usual. If leadership steps in to help transform institutions to keep pace with change, then communities can experience progress. Although this process is inherently difficult, it is important to recognize that in complex systems, equilibrium (no change) means death. No living thing can stay in equilibrium; it must be constantly changing to survive.

New technologies and events not only create new opportunities, they also destroy the old. Preparing for the next waves of innovation becomes harder as the last waves tend to undermine the strengths of existing institutions and values. Schumpeter's solution was to focus on the role of innovation and the entrepreneur.

Entrepreneurs understand that creative destruction has a unique ability to take advantage of this "punctuated" state of equilibrium. In fact, entrepreneurs dislike stability and equilibrium and instead seek opportunities presented by change to create an advantage.

Strategic transformation of regions, and many organizations, happens in intermittent, quantum leaps. The traditional view claims that change is continuous: organizations should be adapting all the time. What this view fails to address is how and when to promote significant change. A fundamental dilemma of strategy is the need to reconcile the forces for stability and the forces for change—to focus efforts on gaining operational efficiency on the one hand and yet adapt and maintain currency with the changing external environment on the other.

The enemy of creative destruction and the innovation that follows is *conventional wisdom*. Fixed mental maps create a cultural "lock-in," which resists change or even the ability to see change. The old ways of doing things become a blockage to future success. Examples abound, including the railroads' inability to see air and automobile transportation clearly, or IBM's inability to anticipate the impact of the personal computer. These new technologies or events force a change in mind-set, but people are often slow to change, and society always lags in response to major economic and technology revolutions. The results create a challenge for civic revolutionaries during times of significant change.

As we move beyond the dot-com implosion of 2000, many regions are now asking what is next. If we are living in a world of creative destruction, what can we expect the next creative wave of innovation to be that will shape our communities? Though it is impossible to predict the future, it is important for leaders to look at coming technologies and try to anticipate how to prepare both people and places for the next economy. For example, regions across the world are trying to understand the implications of advances and convergence of information, biological, and atomic-level nanotechnologies for industrial processes, communities, workforces, and societies. The revolutionary nature of these changes is summarized by Stan Williams (2000) of Hewlett-Packard Laboratories:

> We are actually watching the birth of three great new technologies, all simultaneously. "Bio" is the utilization of chemistry in life to not only understand living organisms but to manufacture all types of things that we have in our environment. "Info" is the harvesting, storage, and transmission of information of all sorts that we want about our environment. And "nano" is the control of matter at the scale where basic material properties are determined.
>
> All three of these areas are completing the transition from applied science into technology right now. And during the next twenty years, all three of these are going to see exponential types of increases, or we'll see factors of ten thousand improvements in the capabilities of each of these.
>
> Any one of these areas by itself would be classified as an industrial revolution. But having all three of them progressing simultaneously, sometimes competing with each other, but very often interacting and reinforcing each other is going to be completely beyond anything we've ever experienced.

We have entered an era of accelerating, continuous innovation. Because waves of innovation are likely to disrupt people, institutions, and place, it is important that civic revolutionaries work together to help their regions become more resilient. Economic, social, and civic innovation must go together.

Further complicating this unsettling situation in most communities is leadership turnover. In addition to generational shifts, many communities are feeling the effects of sudden corporate departures or the decline of once-powerful institutions. Some places have grown so fast that they no longer can be managed like a small town by a room full of civic leaders. Many communities are undergoing significant demographic transformation, with the rise of new ethnic groups who want a voice in civic affairs. In many places, leaders do exist, but they are too often working in silos, unaware of one another and the broader need for collaboration across boundaries. This *anonymity of leadership* can prevent communities from effectively addressing the complex issues of today. Some communities simply have lost their way, as they once relied on a few top leaders who have now passed from the scene. These communities have done little to fill the leadership pipeline and now find themselves without people prepared to take charge in a more challenging era.

In an environment full of disruption and turnover, civic revolutionaries are hard pressed to maintain a commitment to core values. But that is exactly what is necessary to navigate in these waters. As Gardner (1990) observed:

> Particularly important to a society's continuity are its long-term purposes and values. Those purposes and values also evolve in the long run; but by being relatively durable, they enable a society to absorb change without losing its distinctive character and style. Purposes and values do much to determine the direction of change. They ensure that a society is not buffeted in all directions by every wind that blows [p. 124].

Some observers, such as Peter Drucker, see the opportunity for the creation of new institutions to cope with challenging times. In his most recent book, *Managing the Next Society* (2002), Drucker sees a future with new social institutions involved in major changes for corporations, the workplace, and the rise of the social sector. Echoing these themes, Gardner (1970) reminds us that "such redesign is not new to us. In our history as a nation, we have done a great deal of social inventing and innovating. Among the consequences are the land-grant college, the county agent, antitrust legislation, the Federal Reserve System, the Social Security System" (p. 12).

It is clear that many of our current institutions and arrangements are ill suited to an environment of disruption and turnover. J. F. Rischard (2002), the World Bank's vice president for Europe, finds that "the main reason that human institutions are struggling to meet the momentous changes afoot is that they are not designed for these changes." He too argues for "flatter, more networked organizations that are smarter, more adaptable and flexible at turning around than traditional hierarchies." "Forget about government—federal, regional or local—being able to solve tomorrow's complex problems *alone* without major help from the other two sectors of society. All this leads to a new important reality: it will take partnerships among the government, business, and civil society to solve intractable problems" (p. 51). Renewal is a team sport.

In the struggle between change and continuity, Gardner's guidance (1970) is useful: we should not be "infatuated with everything new and reject everything old. We have seen change that does senseless damage to significant continuities—natural neighborhoods destroyed by the highway bulldozer, historic landmarks razed to make way for commercial development. In all growth there is a complex interweaving of continuity and change. One purpose of social change is to find new solutions that will preserve old values" (p. 8). Reconciling the competing values of change and continuity for our time will likely require new solutions. It will require creating transformation out of crisis, shaking ourselves out of complacency, and making a new commitment to continuous leadership renewal.

Promising Experiments: Creating Vigilance for Renewal

Civic revolutionaries can resolve the tension between the need for change and the need for continuity in the following ways:

- Turning crisis into transformation

- Breaking through complacency by revealing problems and raising ambitions

- Making leadership renewal a priority

Turning Crisis into Transformation

Sudden disruptions bring too much change too quickly for people and institutions to adapt without significant pain. But where there is great pain, there is great motivation for change. Lincoln used the crisis of the Civil War to reinvent the nation, just as Franklin Roosevelt used the crisis of the Great Depression to create a new social safety net. Theodore Roosevelt turned the crisis of confidence in the trust-based economic system into a progressive expansion of government that propelled both the economy and society forward. Rachel Carson focused attention on a growing environmental crisis and helped launch a lasting environmental movement. Martin Luther King and Cesar Chavez made injustice visible for many Americans and helped create momentum for major legislative and social change.

The story does not always have a happy ending. Some communities give up, accepting crisis as a "new normal." They lose hope and eventually suffer visible decline and loss of population. Some communities implode, with factions fighting over a shrinking pie. They adopt a mind-set of scarcity that leads them into a downward spiral of conflict. Some communities, however, do fight crisis, turning it into an opportunity for transformation. A number of regions across the country, forced into crisis, have responded positively. Two of these regions are Akron, Ohio, and Greater Washington, D.C.

Akron, Ohio

Like many industrial regions, Akron has gone through a dramatic economic transformation in the past two decades. It suffered significant loss of industry and population but has utterly transformed itself from a dying "rubber capital" of the world to a diversified and successful "polymer valley." Rather than denying or fighting global economic forces, Akron's leaders proactively evolved their community from an industrial base in raw natural rubber production to one that, today, develops and processes advanced synthetic polymer for a wide range of high-end applications. It is an excellent example of transformation from commodity to higher-value-added economic activity.

From the 1970s to the 1980s, intense global competition, automation, the commoditization of plastics, and the restructuring of the automobile industry caused low-value-added, hand-skilled jobs to move offshore and brought a major recession to the region. The transformation was painful but long overdue, and it resulted in a restructuring process that made the plastics cluster more competitive by eliminating inefficient enterprises. The remaining firms are diversified processors and manufacturers focused on process and product innovation in various niche markets.

Akron's plastics cluster is now an important site for both low- and high-value-added polymer processing, manufacturing, research, design, and development. The cluster's core competencies are both product and process innovations in plastics. The cluster's extensive supplier base, distribution networks, and R&D capabilities are unsurpassed anywhere. Global competition continues to force many firms to move upmarket and to place a premium on product innovation, manufacturing-process upgrades, and speed to market. Expensive R&D and product development functions are becoming critical, effectively forcing many plastics firms to consolidate and to form joint ventures.

At the center of this economic transformation has been a committed group of regional business, education, and government leaders who first issued a wake-up call to the region with the Akron Plus Campaign in 1985. The campaign, initiated by then General Tire CEO, Jerry O'Neill, and city of Akron Mayor, Don Plusquellic, and others, rallied business and government leaders to address the challenge of lost jobs in the traditional rubber industry and the headquarters of tire companies. The program met its goal of adding thirty thousand jobs to the region in 1998.

The Akron Plus Campaign set the stage for the cooperative efforts led by the Akron Regional Development Board (now the Greater Akron Chamber) in the 1990s. The regional development board was looking for a better way to attract and retain businesses to the region. According to Bob Bowman, senior vice president of the Greater Akron Chamber, "We had been through the economic base studies in the past, but we found that didn't work. . . . We became fascinated with the idea of economic clusters and that's how we got into it." The idea of *economic clustering* began to drive a process that led to a coordinated effort to link the University of Akron with the private sector around three economic clusters: advanced polymers, metalworking, and electronics.

Throughout this entire transformation process, regional leaders promoted new university-industry relationships that encouraged the application of new technologies and innovation within traditional industries. The university had a strong interest in ensuring that its highly trained polymer scientists could find employment in the local economy. Visionary leaders from the University of Akron (for example, Luis Proenza) and from business (for example, Thomas Waltermire of PolyOne), among others, were important in driving the process forward. But regional collaboration around clusters was not an easy process, according to Bob Bowman: "It took a lot of communication, grunt work, and explaining the importance of collaboration around issues such as workforce and technology before we had the full attention of businesses that serve global markets. It was hard for these companies to grasp how they could be connected to the region at first."

As a result of this process, Akron has become a leader in creating institutions to support applied R&D that is based on cooperation between universities and industry. University research centers such as the University of Akron's College of Polymer Science and Polymer Engineering and Case Western Reserve University's

Center for Applied Polymer Research have cooperated with business and government to create public-private partnerships such as the Edison Polymer Innovation Corporation, the Ohio Polymers Strategic Council, Polymer Ohio Incorporated, and the Ohio Polymer Enterprise Development Corporation. These efforts are part of the brain trust to advance the polymer cluster, serving collectively as intellectual, advocacy, and commercialization engines for the cluster's process and product innovation.

Greater Washington, D.C.

Greater Washington is a region that built some trust in responding to a creeping crisis, which helped in dealing with a subsequent, sudden crisis. Efforts began in the 1990s to develop regional cooperation across multiple jurisdictions as business and civic leaders convened to address common regional challenges. New-economy business leaders such as Steve Case of America Online began to join with established business leaders and with civic leaders to support regionwide efforts focused on "creating a world-class connected community." Although the region's largest industry had become information and communications services, its educational and transportation infrastructure had not kept pace with the growth in the regional economy or the new patterns of development. Traffic congestion had become a major quality-of-life issue, and disparities in income and capacity of educational facilities across the three jurisdictions had become real problems.

Established by the Board of Trade, the Potomac Conference identified common issues, such as workforce and transportation, that required attention on a more regional basis. Several conferences were held to develop a shared vision and common goals with quantitative indicators. The Potomac Index was developed in 2001; it focused on measuring regional progress in education, equity, mobility, and regional governance.

What the business and civic leaders came to understand was that leadership in the region was extremely fragmented by political jurisdictions (District of Columbia, northern Virginia, suburban Maryland, and the federal government); between public, business, and civic sectors; and between the new-economy companies in Northern Virginia and suburban Maryland and the traditional-economy companies in the District. The former head of the Greater Washington Board of Trade once remarked that the "Potomac River is more like an ocean," because of historical and emerging political, economic, and sectoral boundaries.

In addition to the Potomac Conference, several programs and projects were under way to bring the region together. The Meyer and the Fannie Mae Foundations played an important role in regional community building in Greater Washington. Business, civic, and government leaders led specific initiatives to help prepare people for the new economy focused on education, equity, and e-government. At a basic level, just "connecting" these efforts to increase awareness and promote success regionally was an important step.

Although modest progress was achieved through these kinds of collaborative efforts, political jurisdictions and the business leaders within them continued to see more barriers than commonalities. A major division remained on transportation issues, with prodevelopment interests in Virginia focused on building more roads and environmental interests, largely in suburban Maryland and the District, opposed to roads and in favor of more transit. There was more deadlock than progress on the key issue of transportation. Although the need for regional cooperation was clear, no galvanizing issue had yet developed to bring the region together.

Then came September 11, 2001, and the attack on the Pentagon. Regional collaboration became a life-and-death issue. A lack of coordinated decision making between federal and local officials and across sectoral boundaries had hindered emergency response during and after the terrorist attack. The public and private sectors both took action and then joined forces in a unique regional partnership that may be a model for the nation in preparedness and homeland security.

"September 11 produced an extraordinary amount of new boundary crossing," recalls George Vradenburg, chair of the Potomac Conference. "A crisis gives existing regional efforts a little rocket fuel. It raises public expectations that officials are going to work together and generates more political will. We had to come together to design effective response systems to prepare for other crises." First, the Metropolitan Washington Council of Governments (COG), which represents eighteen local jurisdictions in the region, took the lead in developing a regional emergency response plan. It built on the efforts of its local governments, each of which already had individual emergency response strategies. The council also built on its own efforts to foster regional cooperation—working with regional committees of public safety officials, public health officers, communications officers, utilities, and chief administrative officers—to strengthen mutual-aid agreements.

Building on the initial steps of regional cooperation through the Potomac Conference process, the Greater Washington Board of Trade's Potomac Conference created a task force to explore how private businesses and nonprofit organizations across the region should organize their resources and assets to prepare for, respond to, and recover from threats. The Potomac Conference and key federal and state agencies agreed to participate in the COG's process to develop a coordinated public-private strategy for addressing terrorist threats in the National Capitol Region.

The COG Task Force on Homeland Security and Emergency Preparedness for the National Capitol Region was formed to enhance regional preparedness and ensure a coordinated regional response to future public safety challenges. The task force was initially composed of representatives from the federal Office of Homeland Security and key federal offices; the District of Columbia, Maryland, and Virginia emergency management and transportation agencies; and public and private first providers across the region. The task force was organized into six working groups—public safety, health, waste and debris management, water and energy, transportation, and communications.

The mission of the Potomac Conference Regional Preparedness and Recovery Task Force was to bring the business and nonprofit sectors to the emergency preparedness table. Its efforts were launched at a meeting of the Potomac Conference in November 2001, bringing together public, private, and civic leaders across the region to endorse creating the task force and coordinating its activities with the COG. The Potomac Conference private sector group consisted of four work groups: emergency preparedness, business and nonprofit continuity, economic recovery, and communications. The COG and the Potomac Conference integrated their efforts and over the course of a year jointly developed the Regional Emergency Coordination Plan (RECP) to foster regional coordination and communications in regional emergency situations.

The centerpiece of the RECP was the Regional Incident Communications and Coordination System, hosted by the District of Columbia and managed by the COG, to facilitate real-time emergency communications and coordination among federal and local public officials and critical private sector service providers. Explains Vradenburg, "One powerful but simple rule we developed is an incident command system, where the first person/organization at the scene of a crisis is the one in charge. It democratizes regional leadership because it saves us from having to choose a leader among many people; the event chooses the leader." Public and private sector leaders also worked together to ensure the inclusion of the Office of National Capitol Region Coordination in the Department of Homeland Security so that the federal government would have a simple point of coordination with local officials and business and nonprofit leaders.

On August 6, 2002, the governors of Virginia and Maryland and the mayor of the District of Columbia signed a historic eight-point regional compact that pledges the governments and the private sector to work together to coordinate decisions, public statements, and emergency procedures in case of a regionwide disaster. Greater Washington has demonstrated that in the face of a sudden crisis such as terrorism, regional cooperation can achieve results that cannot be achieved by either local jurisdictions or individual businesses acting alone. As Tom Ridge, then director of the Office of Homeland Security, said in January 2002 to the National Governors Association, "We hope to change the old relationship—cities-state-federal model—into one based on mutual cooperation, collaboration, and partnership."

Breaking Through Complacency by Revealing Problems and Raising Ambitions

Complacency is the challenge of too much continuity for too long a period, which in an ever-changing world inevitably leads to crisis. The problem is that it is often a creeping crisis, in which the gathering threat is subtle or unable to be seen by the community. When a community or region is mired in complacency, the following symptoms can become apparent: festering problems being addressed with Band-Aid solutions, leaders acting as guardians of the status quo, low expectations for economic and social progress, and a slowly slipping standard of living.

Some regions have, however, broken the trance of complacency. They have done it by effectively framing and communicating problems or inspiring higher ambitions. These regions are in the middle of promising but very difficult experiments in finding a new balance between continuity and change.

Louisville, Kentucky

Louisville is an example of a place that has avoided complacency and has sought ever more ambitious goals: economic diversification in the late 1980s, increased entrepreneurship in the late 1990s, and a consolidated regional government in the new century. After weathering a 1981–82 recession that eliminated thirty thousand manufacturing jobs, the Louisville Area Chamber of Commerce sought to diversify the region's economy to include two new activities that fit its competitive strengths: air freight and back-office–call-center operations. In 1988, a new seven-county economic development group, the Greater Louisville Economic Development Partnership, was formed to coordinate business attraction. By all accounts, the region succeeded quite well with its aims. A large number of back-office processing and call-center facilities moved to the region, and the region's per capita income jumped from 95 percent of the national figure in 1982 to 102 percent in 1995.

But Louisville's leadership did not become complacent. In mid-1996, the Greater Louisville Economic Development Partnership and the Louisville Area Chamber of Commerce joined forces to reassess the direction of the region's economy. They convened a regionwide collaborative visioning process, involving several hundred local executives from the private and public sectors. The visioning process effectively created a challenge for the community—it raised aspirations for Louisville to move from being a "nice, average city" to become an entrepreneurial "hot spot." Rather than maintaining the status quo, the report warned that "trying to stay the same can result in our gradually slipping backwards."

The final report of the Visioning Task Force was published in August 1997, with a few principal recommendations. First, the region chose to intensely focus on two target industries in which it could excel—logistics-distribution and biomedical. Second, the plan called for a "community permeated with a culture of entrepreneurialism" (Economic Development Administration, 2001, p. 17). Special emphasis was placed on ensuring African American participation in economic growth and entrepreneurship. Investing in assets—including the region's workforce, physical infrastructure, and the University of Louisville—was recognized explicitly as key to success. In its implementation, the visioning document called for accountability and benchmarking: "We must continually place the community and its economy under a microscope" (p. 17). In addition, the report called for the creation of one organization to manage all aspects of the implementation process, not the three that existed at the time.

Implementation moved forward quickly and aggressively. Within weeks of the publication of the report, the partnership and the chamber merged to form Greater Louisville, Inc. (GLI). Now the region has one single voice for development. Doug Cobb, a local entrepreneur and venture capitalist, became the new CEO of the merged organization. Cobb was particularly interested in stimulating entrepreneurship as an economic development strategy: "Louisville needed to be more focused on growing our own jobs rather than on attracting them from the outside" (Economic Development Administration, 2001, p. 17).

In a few short years, Louisville has made great strides in promoting entrepreneurship. GLI created the Enterprise Corporation as a subsidiary to encourage entrepreneurship in general and stimulate advanced-technology business development in particular. In 1999, the Enterprise Corporation worked with fifty-one new firms that opened in the region, creating 5,650 jobs. The University of Louisville College of Business now has the second-ranked entrepreneurship program in the country (after that of the University of Texas at Austin). Between 1996 and 1999, the region's local supply of venture capital climbed from $9 million to $150 million. The Enterprise Corporation, the city, and other players have created eMainUSA, a high-tech development district downtown. Louisville is also actively promoting its two target industries: logistics-distribution and biomedical. Louisville International Airport is now the sixth-largest cargo airport worldwide. UPS has completed its new $1 billion sorting hub in Louisville, bringing thousands of new jobs to the region. The Louisville Medical Center Development Corporation—now in operation for well over a decade—is continuing to develop a health-science business park and incubator downtown.

Recently, the citizens and leaders of Louisville set their sights on the most audacious goal yet—to catapult from the sixty-seventh to the sixteenth largest city in the United States. In 2000, residents of the city of Louisville and Jefferson County voted to merge their governments. The proposal won 54 percent of the votes after being defeated three times before, in 1956, 1982, and 1983. What made the critical difference this time? According to Joan Riehm, deputy mayor of the new Louisville–Jefferson County metro government, "It was a unique combination of bipartisan leadership, a feeling among the citizens that it was time to put behind us the divisiveness of the past, and a real yearning for a more efficient, effective, unified government." The campaign had significant support from current and past public officials, including the then Democratic mayor and Republican county executive. Former Mayor Jerry Abramson, the longest-serving mayor in the history of Louisville, endorsed the campaign, as did every living former mayor and county executive (both Republican and Democrat). Says Riehm, "Each leader appealed to different constituents and brought diverse groups together around the unity campaign."

The new Louisville–Jefferson County metro government, which began operation in January 2003, is the first major U.S. city-county merger to take place in more than thirty years. Proponents of the merger envisioned benefits not only to efficiency of government services but also to the region's economic development efforts. Louisville's population doubled from the merger, now making it the nation's sixteenth-largest city. "There was a lot of talk during the merger campaign about not being content with being a second-tier city. We wanted to be in that category of top twenty-five cities," says Riehm. "But we not only wanted to be there in terms of our population, we wanted to be there in mind-set, in the way that we thought about ourselves. The merger was a way to say to people that we are serious and to prove that we can reach as high as we want." As their history shows, Louisville has reconciled the forces of change and continuity through a process of ongoing appraisal and rising ambitions.

The Pittsburgh Region

The Pittsburgh region, like many industrial regions, has gone through a dramatic economic transformation in the past decade.

Once known primarily for its steel industry, Pittsburgh today has a diversified economy that is driven increasingly by entrepreneurial firms in software, bioscience, robotics, and materials, with a strong intellectual foundation in world-class universities such as Carnegie Mellon and the University of Pittsburgh. Pittsburgh is also richly endowed with major foundations, including the Heinz Endowments and the R. K. Mellon Foundation.

Pittsburgh's business community, its civic and political leadership, and its citizens are beginning to fully appreciate—and respond to—the economic and social changes taking place. "One of the most important things we've done is change our civic structure to be more regional, inclusive, collaborative, and cost-effective," says Richard Stafford, CEO of the Alleghany Conference on Community Development. The Allegheny Conference, a long-standing regional organization, has been the traditional source of business and civic leadership in the Pittsburgh region. Over the years, it has played a major role in two Pittsburgh renaissances (one in the late 1940s and another in the late 1970s) that created a more vital downtown and addressed critical pollution problems.

A significant change to the civic structure came in 1998, when the citizens of Allegheny County voted to enact a Home Rule Charter for the county, to take effect in 2000. The new government abolished the three-commissioner system in favor of an elected chief executive, a fifteen-member county council, and an appointed county manager. According to Stafford, "People were ready for change. The old form of government was inefficient and unresponsive." Today the county CEO is the third most powerful public official in the state of Pennsylvania.

In addition to changing the governmental structure, Pittsburgh regional leaders recognized that they had to become more inclusive toward emerging entrepreneurial leaders, who had not been part of traditional leadership circles. In 2000, the Heinz Endowments embarked on an active effort to increase awareness of Pittsburgh's entrepreneurial economy. It issued the Pittsburgh Entrepreneurial

Metrics, created a "hot team" of young entrepreneurs to develop a strategy to retain top talent, and helped form Innovation Works, a public-private initiative to bring venture capital and support to innovative businesses. A cadre of leaders from entrepreneurial firms has now emerged and is beginning to play a more important role in Pittsburgh's regional leadership, working side by side with the traditional business leadership from larger companies.

At the same time, the Allegheny Conference expanded its focus from Pittsburgh city-centered initiatives (for example, downtown revitalization) to regionally focused efforts. It helped create the Allegheny Regional Asset District (which raises and invests funds in regional parks, libraries, civic auditoriums, and the like), the Strategic Investment Fund (a $70 million private fund to encourage regional economic development), and the Southwestern Pennsylvania Growth Alliance (a public-private effort that has helped spur brownfield remediation legislation and increases in state capital improvement funding).

In December 2002, a major announcement was made that four major regional organizations—the Allegheny Conference, Pennsylvania Economy League/Western Division, the Greater Pittsburgh Chamber of Commerce, and the Pittsburgh Regional Alliance—would work together in a new partnership to improve and market the ten-county Pittsburgh region. Entitled *Three Rivers: One Future*, the plan hopes to influence growth across the region of fifty thousand new jobs and $1 billion of new public and private investment by the end of 2005. Further, to strengthen their ability to realize the plan, the leadership of these four regional development organizations formalized a strategic affiliation by uniting as a single entity.

With a new county government system, emerging entrepreneurial leaders, and a consolidated regional organization to support growth, the Pittsburgh region is poised to take off. As Stafford says, "We are taking regionalism seriously by building a nexus of regional organizations that are effective, that are more inclusive, and that emphasize collaboration over competition. It's a combination of necessity, a feeling that we have to innovate to survive, and new opportunities that are available to us." Among those opportunities are innovative public-private initiatives such as the Life Sciences Greenhouse, the Digital Greenhouse, and a Robotics Foundry. In addition, a new branding campaign began to address the "image gap" that exists between the perception of Pittsburgh as a smoky industrial town and the new reality of its increasingly diversified economy.

Although clearly still a work in progress, Pittsburgh is a region that has recognized the need to make a transition to a different kind of economy, one that will need to attract talent and entrepreneurial leadership. Rich in university and foundation assets as well as history, Pittsburgh is creating a new civic structure that connects traditional and emerging leaders, links an innovative economy to a vibrant community, and reconciles the tension between change and continuity.

Making Leadership Renewal a Priority

The challenge of leadership renewal is universal. Every region faces inevitable transitions in leadership and maturing of institutions. Most regions, however, give continuous renewal little attention, focusing on immediate problems and solutions. The results: rigid institutions, uneven leadership transitions, or dramatic loss of leadership as one generation passes from the scene. Some regions, however, are trying to break from this common pattern.

Richmond, Virginia

The story of Richmond is filled with tension between continuity and change—and offers a promising experiment in a new initiative for civic renewal. In the next decade, leaders there will determine whether this dynamic tension sparks creativity and forward motion or whether it produces divisiveness and fragmentation. As one Richmond leader has observed, "An interracial group of one hundred leaders from business, the public sector, and the nonprofit sector could save this metropolis. That is how simple it is. That is how open this situation is for leadership."

As the center for manufacturing of commodity products such as tobacco, Richmond prospered economically through the 1940s, 1950s, and 1960s. By 1970, Richmond was the leader among southern cities in *Fortune* 500 headquarters. But in the early 1970s, two forces set Richmond on a path of pulling apart and falling behind—at the same time that other southern peers were aggressively pulled together and moving ahead.

On the social front, Richmond's white leaders fought to defend their way of life, and black activists fought for change and new standing. In the wake, white residents and businesses moved to the outlying counties, most of them abdicating their sense of responsibility or connection to the city. The black residents of Richmond were left with concentrated poverty, a severely diminished tax base, and few allies in the region or state to upgrade the city and its people. "The mistrust and hatred at that time was palpable," one leader notes. Over time, the disparity of opportunity and outcome grew markedly within the region.

On the economic front, globalization started chipping at the low-cost advantages that had become so important to Richmond's traditional manufacturers. The regional economy began to lose its high-paying jobs and headquarters operations to other regions that offered intellectual and quality-of-life amenities, including progressive civic initiatives and partnerships and a sense of shared destiny. Between 1970 and 2000, Richmond—once an undisputed leader among southeastern cities—lost fourteen major headquarters. By 2002, the region's economic performance fell to 112 out of 200 metropolitan areas ranked by *Forbes* in a survey of the growth of high-wage jobs.

In 2000, a small team of people who cared about the Richmond region started coming together to talk about how to reverse these trends. The handful of corporate and civic leaders included an unusual threesome: T. J. Daly, a young venture capitalist; Jim Ukrop, the well-established leader of a successful, homegrown grocery chain; and John Crews, the thirty-nine-year-old general manager of Applied Materials' new operation in Richmond. They started by learning firsthand, along with a team of ten others, about the long-term civic and economic revival efforts in Austin and Portland. According to Daly, "What became clear to us very quickly was that we needed to build a team that included people with backgrounds and perspectives dramatically different than ours. To act effectively, we had to connect people and networks in nontraditional ways and then channel new energy to help move forward on priorities as a region, rather than as a series of disjointed communities, interests, and networks. This would have to be done in ways that reflected who Richmond was today as a community, not where the leadership came from in the past."

With economic change had come dramatic diminution in the traditional sources of civic leadership. Many of the industrial-age patriarchs and related "first families" of Richmond were less active in the community because of other priorities, asset diminution, and loss of influence in a changing world. The CEOs of large companies, if the companies still existed, were less available and reliable, needing to respond to out-of-town headquarters and national and international markets. The emerging growth was in new areas such as technology, biotech, software, and high-quality service businesses. The people running these companies were younger and were relative newcomers. Typically, they were not connected to the traditional business organizations, civic organizations, and social structure. And immigration and mobility were diversifying the region's population beyond the black-white lens. Asians of all sorts, and Hispanics of all sorts, were becoming part of the region's social and economic fabric.

What economic change did not undo, generational change did. The once-dominant power generation simply was not there anymore, was tired, or had moved on to other pursuits. These people included the senior black leaders, mostly activists and politicians and small business owners, as well as the senior white leaders, mostly big businessmen and patriarchs of wealthy, old-line families. As one senior partner of a law firm explained, "My generation fought the good fight. It is time for the next generation to step up, but I have no idea who these people are. Perhaps we should have been thinking about this more; perhaps some of us have been holding them back. It is time for us, the elders of both races, to move over and get out of the way."

It became clear that any serious change initiative must identify, recruit, and retain community leaders in new ways. A central theme is to steer the transition from the generation of leaders now in their sixties and seventies to the next generation of leaders. From an organizing perspective, the key opportunity is to connect and tap new sources of leadership. In particular, interviews showed that five types of people, many of them in their thirties and forties, seemed particularly ready to step up:

- Leaders of homegrown, entrepreneurial firms, many of them in technology fields

- A new generation of executives and professionals, black as well as white, many of whom were born or educated outside Richmond—and who therefore are considered newcomers

- Social entrepreneurs—new leaders of civic organizations and initiatives with a collaborative perspective

- Public sector executives who have developed practical working relationships with one another

- Grassroots leaders, especially faith leaders

A team of leaders with these and other backgrounds is working on this new approach. The team is taking a big-tent approach but is focusing especially on these priority groups. It is connecting with select leaders from the older generation who have access to important networks, resources, and perspectives. Together they are walking a fine line between change and continuity.

These leaders call the new initiative taking form the "Richmond Revolution." This name indicates both the need for a significant departure from the past ways of operating (a revolution) and the need to build on the positive, and often overlooked, identity of Richmond as an important birthplace of and contributor to the American Experiment. In a similar vein, the tag line "still making history" has great appeal to this group because it both acknowledges the past and sets a standard for the future.

The process will involve forming some action teams to work on innovative strategies and solutions to a set of interrelated challenges that are ultimately regional in nature. These strategies include creating a more inclusive, innovative economy that builds on the assets of local universities and new technology companies, building a creative downtown core that can attract and retain highly mobile talent, promoting a new framework for growth that encourages more compact development, and supporting development of the next-generation workforce through efforts that help children prepare for school and adults train for better jobs.

The experiment launched recently in Richmond is reflected in regions throughout America. Such regions are finding that a traditional civic leadership model that worked in the past is no longer effective or possible. In its place, leaders are struggling to create new platforms for strategic leadership and new processes for involving people who have something important to contribute. But seldom do they invent such platforms de novo. Rather, they bridge to some traditional leaders, they work with some long-standing organizations, and they build on cherished or defining cultural characteristics, even as they pull aggressively in some new directions.

Two Richmond leaders summed it up: "We need a better way for more people with good ideas to have access to the change momentum. For too long, the need for the 'right people' to validate you has been a little thick." And, "We need a future that is more representative of the perspectives and energies of the twenty-four to forty-five-year-olds. Younger people provide the social energy for change and culture shift."

Richmond is trying to shift from a static leadership model from the past to a continuous-renewal leadership model for the future, as Exhibit 5.1 shows.

Fresno, California

On the opposite end of the country, the community of Fresno in California's Central Valley provides an example of a gradual approach to leadership renewal. Fresno is the economic capital of the Central Valley—the agricultural "breadbasket" of the world. More agricultural value is created in Fresno County than in any county in the United States. But like the comedian Rodney Dangerfield, Fresno and the Central Valley of California for years "got no respect."

Exhibit 5.1. Renewing Civic Leadership.

Shifting Model in Richmond, Virginia

Past	Future
Concentrated	Dispersed
A few people lead the way	Many people contribute differently
Biracial, lifelong residents	Multicultural, lifelong residents, and newcomers
Closed system, hierarchy	Open systems, network
Represent particular "community"	Stewards of the region
The parts	The whole

Part of the problem was that leaders from the region saw little about their place that they were proud of. They had a high unemployment rate, a high crime rate, drug problems, and a declining commodity agricultural base. What's more, because of the low cost of housing, the region had become one of the fastest-growing parts of the state, and people from the coast as well as immigrants flooded in, in search of affordable housing.

Fresno and the Central Valley faced a crisis of confidence as well as an economic crisis. Then something happened, as leaders began to face up to harsh realities and take action in the best American spirit of visionary pragmatism. The story has two parts.

First, a group of regional leaders made the case that the Great Valley needed more capacity to solve its many social, environmental, and economic challenges. Former mayor of Modesto, Carol Whiteside, went to several foundations—including Hewlett, Packard, and Irvine—and secured significant funding to create the Great Valley Center to help revitalize the region. The center has undertaken major research projects to learn more about the economic potential of the valley and to plan for the environmental, housing, and land use future that will be driven by the population growth that is coming. The center also created a leadership institute to train the next generation of leaders for the valley. Most of all, the center created a sense of regional identity. It helped create a vision of how the region could participate in the new economy by diversifying within its agricultural base to higher-value food products and across its economic base into new economic clusters such as advanced logistics, agile manufacturing, and water technology.

Among the efforts that the Great Valley Center has seeded is the Highway 99 Task Force. Leaders from cities and counties along the state highway (the traditional backbone of the valley, connecting the region that people originally called the "Golden State highway") are working together with the California Transportation Department, foundations, and others to create a scenic highway that will stimulate economic development and environmental improvement along the corridor.

The second part of the story takes place in Fresno, once rated by Rand McNally's *Best Places Almanac* as the worst place to live in the nation. The mayor of Fresno, Dan Whitehurst, went on the David Letterman show to make fun of the designation. Although his doing so showed both moxie and a sense of humor, the truth in the designation was also painful. Fresno was not doing well in the mid-1990s: its downtown declined, crime rose, unemployment grew, and people lacked hope. Many people were in leadership positions because of the city's legacy system, but they were not performing. They contributed to a civic culture of dysfunction, degradation, and in some cases outright impropriety and abuse of power. The best and the brightest in the community were not engaged in civic affairs, much less leading them.

Leadership started to come from the business community as the Fresno Business Council, its activist CEO, Deborah Nankivell, and three "lions"—older, credible businessmen who were in many ways symbols of continuity—decided that they wanted to be part of fundamental change and to bring others along. They rallied members of the business council around the idea of civic entrepreneurship. Working with The James Irvine Foundation and the Great Valley Center, Nankivell and others, including Ashley Swearingen of Fresno State University and Ken Newby of Deloitte & Touche, developed the Collaborative Regional Initiative, involving business, civic, and government leaders to attack some of the most pressing issues facing the region, including economic development, education, and reform of the human services system.

As Deborah Nankivell has observed, "Together, we realized that we needed to build a new civic infrastructure, a place where potential leaders could work together to lead in a new way." They started by inviting in some people who were the "natural" leaders in the community, rather than those who claimed to be leaders by title or tradition. They decided to start with values: to articulate how they were going to exercise leadership in a new way. They decided to use this values statement not just as their own operating principles but also as an assertion that these values needed to become the community values of the entire Fresno region (see Exhibit 5.2).

They circulated initial drafts widely, took in comments, recirculated, and revised. According to Nankivell:

> There was tremendous value in putting how we wanted to live and work together into words. It made it clear that we were about a departure from business as usual. It set a transparent standard that we could hold ourselves and others to. We identified the "five dominoes" in our community. We knew that if they tipped over, things would really start to change. We started drip-irrigation-style consciousness raising. Weekly, we issued bullet-point messages among our group and the broader community. These messages provided inspiration, celebrated success, drew people to our Web site, or announced upcoming meetings and events. Ultimately, it is the responsibility of a steward to change what is wrong.

Fresno and the Central Valley are setting up an infrastructure of continuous renewal in the face of seemingly insurmountable challenges, overcoming adversity, and taking on new tasks to make their place a better place.

Insights from the Field

Every region and community must find its own approach to reconciling the competing values of change and continuity. There is no single road map for navigating between them. But much can be learned about how civic revolutionaries are grappling with the challenge. Practical insights from the field are described in the following discussion according to the major roles that civic revolutionaries play—to discover, decide, and drive change.

Exhibit 5.2. Community Values of the Fresno Region.

Stewardship. We will lead and follow as stewards of our region, caring responsibly for our community assets. We will work together to achieve the greatest, long-term benefit for the community as a whole.

Boundary crossing and collaboration. We are willing to cross political, social, ethnic, and economic boundaries and partner with others to achieve community outcomes. We will lead "beyond the walls" to create an inclusive, cohesive community through partnership and collaboration.

Commitment to outcomes. We are willing to take responsibility for tasks and achieving specific outcomes. We are committed to staying involved until the tasks are completed.

"Art of the possible" thinking. We believe that anything is possible in the Fresno Region. We will envision "success without limitations" and then backward map a specific, attainable strategy for achieving that vision.

Fact-based decision making. To the greatest extent possible, we will base decisions and action plans on objective data, thereby avoiding distortion of issues by personal feelings or agendas.

Truth telling. We value the empowerment of everyone involved, along with all community stakeholders, to honestly and forthrightly share all knowledge, experiences, and insights relative to the work at hand. We take responsibility for ensuring that our "truth" is current, not historical. We all share responsibility for maintaining the truth-telling standard.

Power parity. We respect all persons and recognize that there are diverse viewpoints. Positional power will not determine a strategy or preferred outcome, merit will. Viewpoints from diverse constituencies will be proactively sought to ensure the best possible outcomes for the community.

Commitment to resolving conflict. Conflict is inevitable and is sometimes required in order to achieve the best outcomes possible. Healthy conflict involves valuing every individual regardless of his or her stance on a specific issue and an unwavering commitment to working through the conflict in a positive manner despite its severity.

Asset-based approach. We are focused on using a strengths-based, asset-oriented approach to people and issues. We believe that positive change occurs when we appreciate, value, and invest in what is best in our people and community.

Conflict of interest. We agree to disclose any personal or professional conflict of interest that may affect our objectivity before engaging in work that will impact the community. We seek to avoid even the appearance of impropriety.

Source: Fresno Area Collaborative Regional Initiative, 2003. Printed with permission

Discover: Building a Compelling Case for Change

Take the mystery and fear out of change. The idea of change is often enough to discourage many regions: it seems too difficult, dangerous, or distant from local circumstances. Civic revolutionaries must help other leaders move beyond the idea of change and feel the benefits of purposeful change. Information and secondhand accounts of positive change in other communities are not enough. Leaders need to talk with peers, ask questions, see the results for themselves, and be part of a change network of individuals who can be supportive over time. Columbus was able to take the mystery out of change and inspire its leadership to take the region to the next level of development. Recent intercity visits by large numbers of Columbus leaders were a way to give many leaders a shared experience of inspiration and practical, just-in-time learning.

Deliver a wake-up call. Whether it be crisis or complacency, civic revolutionaries are often among the first to give their region a strong wake-up call. In Hampton Roads, Virginia, they focused attention on declining per capita income and showed how a continuing slide would have devastating effects on their region. In San Diego, civic revolutionaries at different times have called attention to the strong cross-border connections and urban-suburban educational disparities to force leaders and residents to deal with regional realities. In one of the most dramatic examples, one of Cleveland's leading banks actually forced the city into bankruptcy to force leaders to face reality and take action.

Decide: Making Critical Choices in Experimentation

Creative destruction is inevitable, so choose a course that preserves your core values. Creative destruction may be inevitable, but a region's preparation and response can vary widely. The longer that a region and its leaders hold on to a false sense of stability in the face of rapid and disruptive economic and technological change, the more likely it is that they will not fare well when the inevitable crisis arrives. Planning for constant and disruptive change can be creative in ways that preserve (or even advance) a region's core values. Fresno's civic revolutionaries identified operating principles to preserve their core values while guiding their collective action to address their region's ever-changing set of issues. Akron embraced the very technology (advanced polymers) that had decimated its economy, turning disruption into transformation.

The bigger the crisis, the bolder you can be. Although it might seem that in the face of crisis or disaster, people and institutions would tend to hold tight to familiar patterns, experience is showing the opposite to be true. Certainly, the desire for stability in the wake of crisis is strong, but a crisis in confidence also tends to develop with existing institutions and approaches. If leaders can put forth an alternative approach that is more likely to deliver stability, then change can happen quickly. A case in point is Greater Washington's regional homeland security compact. But a region need not suffer a terrorist attack to take bold action. It can target areas for bold action where disruptive change and a crisis of confidence exist.

Choose a target that embodies a "big idea." Louisville organized itself to pursue an entrepreneurial revolution, to transform the mind-set of the community, but in bite-sized, practical ways through a series of projects. San Diego took on educational equity and cross-border integration as two enormous ideas, but ones that could produce immediate progress (for example, driving a new education reform agenda, creating new cross-border infrastructure to improve the flow of goods and people). With its Metropolis 2020 effort, Chicago is looking back to the beginning of the last century for inspiration in the first Burnham Plan, which created the blueprint for the transformation of the city into a more beautiful and pleasant place to live. The current effort seeks to recapture the spirit of that original plan, this time encompassing the larger metropolitan area and focusing on key issues such as housing and transportation that will transform the region in this era.

Drive: Mobilizing Allies for Change

Mobilization can take the form of a unified campaign or a dispersed seeding of change. Civic revolutionaries have used the power of a focused campaign to unify people around visible crisis (as in the case of Akron) as well as complacency (as in the case of Louisville). They have also seeded change in a more dispersed fashion, as in the case of Pittsburgh. The Heinz Endowments has been a major catalyst in that region, not as the leader of a unified campaign, but rather as an investor in a number of experiments with new and existing organizations to encourage entrepreneurship (for example, networking among new technology-based firms, an index describing the regional climate for entrepreneurship), technological innovation (for example, commercialization of life science innovations), and improvements in quality-of-life amenities (for example, riverfront development). This seeding of dispersed experiments is being done in an effort to transform how Pittsburgh views itself and invests in its future as an innovative place with a mix of networks, institutions, and amenities that are attractive to those who would drive the region's emerging economy.

To mobilize for change, make civic revolutionaries and their relationships, not organizations, the priority. If you make civic revolutionaries and their relationships the priority, then organizations will follow. If these leaders exercise influence over the organizations as board members in most cases and staff leaders in some instances, then a region can embrace change. If a region gives organizations the priority over civic revolutionaries and their relationships, it has a formula for sustaining the status quo. In contrast, if a region makes civic revolutionaries and their relationships a priority, a coalition of established and emerging leaders can mobilize existing organizations (and create new ones if necessary) around an agenda for change. This is the general formula for success in regions from Austin to Cleveland to Louisville to Phoenix, where a core group of individual innovators (not organizations) worked together to design and implement a process that succeeded in redefining how Arizona approached economic development, shifting from a population-based growth model to an export-based, industry-cluster driven model that now has been in place for more than a decade.

In some regions, civic revolutionaries have defined a new system of relationships, rather than new organizations, to drive a flexible and decentralized approach to implementation. Civic revolutionaries in Louisville set up a decentralized system of implementation of its ambitious vision for change. Those in Silicon Valley used written memorandums of understanding among implementation partners to drive a decentralized set of projects forward. Those in Washington, D.C., created a new "incident command" system following September 11, a clear organizing rule in which the first person or organization at a scene of a crisis is the one in charge and is effectively connected to all other first-responders in the region, calling in whatever additional assistance is required. It democratizes regional leadership because it prevents having to choose a leader among many people for political or other reasons—the event chooses the leader. No new organization is required, only a new system of relationships. By decentralizing decision making, it also creates a widely shared as opposed to narrowly held leadership capacity that can be flexible and responsive to change in unpredictable situations.

Put continuous leadership renewal on the real agenda. In most regions, continuous leadership is not even on the real agenda, the one that established leaders make their top priority. Too often, leadership recruitment and development is a worthwhile goal but is in practice a low priority. Regions that put continuous renewal on their real agenda, as Fresno, Richmond, and other places are trying to do, can launch experiments that really expand the leadership pool and knit together existing organizations, established leaders, and emerging leaders in a new kind of coalition for ongoing renewal. Gardner (1990) observed:

> Leaders discover that the great systems over which they preside require continuous renewal. Organizations and societies age. Historians tell of the decline of Greece and Rome. Business journals recount the growth and decay of commercial enterprises. It is not a question of excellence. A society that has reached heights of excellence may already be caught in the rigidities that will bring it down. An institution may hold itself to the highest standards and yet already be doomed by the complacency that foreshadows decline. . . . The processes involved in the rise and fall of human institutions are universal. But the cycle of birth, maturity and death is not inexorable in organizations and societies as it is in living things. Renewal is possible, and an organization or society may go through a number of waves of decay and renewal before its story ends [p. 121].

In the long run, a region's commitment to renewal will determine its destiny. Civic revolutionaries have a central role to play to instill a *vigilance for renewal* in the face of crisis or complacency.

What Success Looks Like: Vigilance for Renewal

Maintaining a vigilance for renewal is the means by which competing values of change and continuity can be reconciled. Civic revolutionaries work against the grain in times of both crisis and complacency, understanding that being vigilant and committed to ongoing renewal is the only way out of rigidity and inevitable decline. Although the approaches vary from place to place, at some point the forces of change and continuity can coexist and energize each other through a commitment to vigilant renewal. But what does success look like?

- The community expects constant, dynamic change, seeking to leaven the negative impacts and leverage the positive benefits while preserving core values.

- The community is purposeful about filling its leadership pipeline, expanding the sources of leaders and excusing no one from service.

6

Idealism and Pragmatism
Building Resilience of Place

Everyone was excited at the summit meeting following a visioning process that defined bold aspirations for the region's future. Residents from every jurisdiction, leaders from all sectors, had their say. And consultants wrote up the results in a glossy, inspiring report. But none of it panned out. In the region next door, a group of local leaders known for their can-do attitude opted for practical projects to promote economic prosperity. Within a year, they had recruited new firms, upgraded the convention center, and raised record funding for United Way. But then, more intractable problems arose. The practical question for both regions is how to reconcile the competing values of idealism and pragmatism.

What happened to the first region following the rosy optimism generated by the summit meeting? Even though their effort captured the best of the American spirit of idealism, a year later, reality set in. All the soaring words and ambitious goals remain on the shelf. Not much is happening or likely to happen. In the aftermath of the summit meeting, it was not clear what to do next. People fell into the old ways, and soon familiar gridlock reappeared.

In criticizing the effort, a local leader has said, "We should have been pragmatic about the present instead of dreaming about the future. Just look at the approach of the region next door."

And what about the region next door? What happened after their initial successes? Unfortunately, during this time, it became clear that many firms were losing jobs or leaving, and few firms were starting up. The region finished in the top ten—in traffic congestion and poor air quality. And long-festering social and racial tensions flared in the form of disputes over public funding and accusations of unfair treatment. In criticizing their effort, one of the local leaders has said, "We should have been bold about charting a new future for our region, rather than settle for a series of projects that together didn't make much of a difference in ways that really mattered. Just look at the vision of the region next door."

The challenge for these regions and many more just like them is reconciling the competing values of idealism and pragmatism to meet the challenges of today while setting a bold course for the future.

The tension that influences all other tensions of the American Experiment is that of idealism and pragmatism. From the beginning of the republic, much of the struggle among revolutionaries was between the idealism of freedom and direct democracy and the pragmatism of community and republican government. Although the latter prevailed as the form of government, much of the former was incorporated into the new political system.

Without the idealism of the Declaration of Independence, together with the pragmatism of the Constitution, America could easily have failed as an experiment. The nation needed Lincoln to invoke the idealism of the Declaration to lift the Constitution to a more *visionary pragmatism*. Subsequent generations have used our founding ideals to help raise the level of what is possible to achieve over time. America is at its best when guided by a visionary pragmatism.

The American Experience: Resolving the Tension Between Idealism and Pragmatism

What we learn from the American Experience is that too much idealism or too much pragmatism simply does not work. Pragmatism reigned supreme in the decades before the Civil War, as compromise after compromise delayed the inevitable. Too much idealism and too little pragmatism have also stalled or stopped numerous social and economic reform efforts over time. Although some of these efforts were no doubt premature, others might have had more impact sooner with a more pragmatic approach and might have helped change America for the better.

The purpose of idealism is to inspire. Idealism in leaders is crucial. Without inspiration, only incrementalism is possible. Idealism offers hope, a constant reminder that we stand for something bigger than what we are today. Gardner correctly observed, "That we have failed and fumbled in some of our attempts to achieve our ideals is obvious. But the great ideas still beckon—freedom, equality, justice, the release of human possibilities. And we have an uncelebrated capacity to counter disintegration with new integrations" (O'Connell, 1999, p. xv). The integration of idealism and pragmatism is the defining and never-ending process of the American Experiment.

Strong strains of both idealism and pragmatism have been part of the American makeup from the founding of the republic. In fact, as Yale President Richard Levin (2001) pointed out in an address to the university's entering class of 2001, "Our Founding Fathers might be thought of as 'visionary pragmatists.' They saw the opportunity to create a new nation based on fundamental values of liberty, freedom, and equality, but they achieved those goals through hard-headed realism, a willingness to fight and die for a cause and a pragmatic ability to forge institutions that would endure."

Levin (2001) recalls that near the end of his life, Jefferson, the eternal optimist and idealist, responded in a September 12, 1821, letter to the ever-pragmatic John Adams, who was skeptical that "free government was well comprehended by the people," by saying, "I will not believe that our labors are lost. I shall not die without a hope that light and liberty are on a steady advance. And even should the cloud of barbarism and despotism again obscure the science and liberties of Europe, this country remains to preserve and restore light and liberty to them. In short, the flames kindled on the 4th of July 1776 have spread over too much of the globe to be extinguished by the feeble engines of despotism."

The influence of the Scottish Enlightenment thinkers on Adams and Madison is evident at the roots of this visionary pragmatism. It recognizes that human beings are self-interested and that human nature has a dark side. Building on the lessons from David Hume, Madison said that "if men were angels, there would be no need for government." However, men are not angels, and civil government with checks and balances on power is necessary to achieve common goals. The process always will be messy.

In *Federalist* No. 85, Alexander Hamilton concluded the series with a plea not to let a fruitless pursuit of perfection undermine a principled and practical course of action: "I never expect to see a perfect work from imperfect man. The result of the deliberations of all collective bodies must necessarily be a compound, as well of the errors and prejudices as of the good sense and wisdom of the individuals of whom they are composed. . . . The judgments of many must unite in the work; experience must guide their labor; time must bring it to perfection; and the feeling of inconveniences must correct the mistakes which they inevitably fall into in their first trials and experiments" (Quinn, 1993, pp. 185, 188).

In a similar vein, the elderly and ailing Benjamin Franklin famously arose at the end of the Constitutional Convention in Philadelphia to assure the delegates that they had succeeded in putting together a workable plan: "I consent to this Constitution because I expect no better, and because I am not sure that this is not the best." Franklin was a visionary pragmatist who knew when the time was right for America to take a revolutionary, yet practical, step. Initially, Franklin had been a representative of Pennsylvania to England and had counseled caution, arguing that the colonies were still a part of England and that stability was the best course. However, the course of events—both in the colonies as they grew more independent economically and politically and in England with King George's rise to power—led Franklin into the revolutionary camp. He became one of the leaders in developing the Declaration of Independence as well as the Constitution, while also helping to create many of the first civic institutions in America, including the University of Pennsylvania and the first public library, hospital, and volunteer fire department.

In fact, Franklin has become a symbol for the American tradition of visionary pragmatism. In *The Promise of America* (1966), historian John Morton Blum describes Franklin this way:

> [He was] the spokesman and emblem of American possibilities and the importance of protecting them. His example heartened all men who sought to excel. The artisan, the child of generations of artisans, his career fixed on centuries of local traditions, could best break through those limits by striking out on his own by practicing—with Poor Richard—the "diligence" that overcame difficulties by becoming American. He could thus avail himself of the chance, the revolutionary chance to achieve success through talent and character. . . . His life with its homely yet heroic message, dramatized American opportunity and its dependence on a free society and individual responsibility [p. 6].

Outside the political realm, Franklin also pioneered a visionary pragmatism. He was an inventor who made major contributions in the fields of printing, newspaper publishing, and electricity. All of these practical inventions helped lay the groundwork for the later development of our mass media.

The Founders actually embodied, as a team, the guiding philosophy of visionary pragmatism. The idealism of Jefferson is evident in the Declaration of Independence—the rallying cry for a new nation—which is followed by the practicality of Adams and Madison's careful crafting of the compromises necessary for achieving the enduring Constitution. What seemed to make the entire process work was the credibility of Washington and the wisdom of Franklin, which created confidence in what was a very risky experiment at the time.

Under the influence of Washington's presence and under the scrutiny of Franklin's intelligence, the representatives of the thirteen colonies found themselves drawn into a process of communal exchange that opened them to a wisdom that not one of them and no separate group of them could have reached alone. As a symbol of the kind of communal relationship that is necessary in the search for truth, the Constitutional Convention stands for us at the very root of the American story (Needleman, 2002, p. 352).

Something happened among those delegates to the Constitutional Convention that launched a new public philosophy based on visionary pragmatism. The Founders left an unfinished story: the compromises around the issue of slavery almost led to the destruction of the Union during the Civil War. The wise Franklin saw this problem coming and gave his last speech on the need to abolish slavery. But it remained to Lincoln and his generation of visionary pragmatists to resolve the issue.

In the post–Civil War era, a series of American philosophers, including William James, Charles Pierce, and John Dewey, helped articulate the pragmatic philosophy of experimentation and learning by doing, in contrast to the clash of ideals that led to the Civil War. Pragmatists rejected idealism and bigness in favor of trial-by-error learning. Reflecting on the horrors of war, William James said: "I am against bigness and greatness of all forms and I am with individual molecular forces that work from individual to individual. The bigger the unit you deal with, the hollower, the more brutal, the more mendacious is life displayed. So I am against the big success and big results, in favor of the external forces of truth that always work in the individual" (Menand, 2002, p. 372).

At the root of the American pragmatic tradition is this faith in the individual and a rejection of externally imposed authority or dogma from government, business, or religion. Self-government is a decentralized self-correcting system based on individual freedom. It is the basis for rejecting big-government solutions in favor of community approaches closer to the individual, but on a scale that can make a difference.

At its core, pragmatism reflects Karl Popper's idea of the *open society,* where ideas are constantly tested against experience. What is necessary is a constant testing of the ideas of liberty, fraternity, and equality in the context of experimentation and learning in communities. This necessity argues against model building in favor of a learn-by-doing adaptive strategy for building trust and relationships within communities that balances freedom with responsibility around specific issues and opportunities.

Gardner (1970) was a visionary pragmatist. On the one hand, he firmly believed in the necessity of idealism: "A nation is held together by shared values, shared beliefs, shared attitudes. That is what enables a people to maintain a cohesive society despite the tensions of daily life. That is what gives a nation its tone, its fiber, its integrity, its moral style, its capacity to endure. If a society believes in nothing, if it cannot generate a sense of moral purpose, there is no possibility that it will develop the level of motivation essential to renewal" (p. 93). He was an irrepressible optimist, who, in the midst of the turbulence of the late 1960s, said, "What we have before us are some breathtaking opportunities disguised as insoluble problems."

At the same time, Gardner was a clear-eyed realist. Recognizing the need for organization in the change process, he helped form Common Cause, the Independent Sector, and other initiatives during his lifetime. He recognized that "the heroic task" is to make values live through action. "When ideals are torn loose from the earnest effort to approximate them, the words swirl endlessly and no one is enriched, no one is bettered, no one is saved" (1970, p. 96). True to his visionary pragmatism, Gardner reflected in the final year of his life on the emergence of regional stewardship: "No more regionalism for its own sake. We need pragmatic regional solutions for a purpose" (John W. Gardner, personal conversation, 2001).

The Tension Today: Practical Challenges to Address

To resolve the enduring tension between idealism and pragmatism, civic revolutions must meet the following challenges head-on:

- *The challenge of powerful ideas:* from wishful thinking to visionary pragmatism

- *The challenge of perseverance:* from diverse leaders to regional stewards

Leaders today continue to face the tension between vision and reality. Without optimism, it is not possible to move forward, but a lack of realism or a willingness to follow any new idea can hold back real progress. What is necessary is a set of core values that allow leaders to make realistic choices among many good ideas and then persevere in the face of challenges.

Many communities veer too far in one direction or another. They are susceptible to the following:

- *Dreaming too much.* Some places create a vision but fail to identify practical steps toward that vision. Many regions and communities have done "visioning

processes" that have gone nowhere and too often have
produced cynicism in their wake.

- *Thinking too small.* Some places try to take action without a compelling vision. Many regions and communities have pursued many tactics to solve specific
  problems, without stepping back, looking at the big
  picture, and developing a unifying vision to inspire
  large-scale action.

As the Founders knew, vision and pragmatic results need to
go together. To achieve this integration, however, requires the
following:

- *Moving from wishful thinking to visionary pragmatism:*
  how to generate powerful ideas that renew core values
  in light of changing circumstances, providing the glue
  that joins idealism and pragmatism

- *Transforming diverse leaders into regional stewards:* how
  to create an environment that encourages individuals
  from all walks of life to answer the call of stewardship,
  to make the long-term commitment to place and play
  a role in the continuing American Experiment

Another fundamental challenge is that of fighting fatigue in
growing and sustaining a vision and action over time. The Founders
set up a system in which responsibility could pass from generation
to generation of stewards. Seldom do regions and communities greet
the inevitability of generational change and civic fatigue with a
process of renewal. Today the added complexity and pressures of
breakneck economic change create multiple challenging tasks for
leaders, making time more precious and fatigue more likely.

The optimism of the 1990s, with a naive belief that a new
economy could rescind the business cycle or that the end of the
Cold War would create a new era of peace, has now given way to

a more realistic assessment of our future as we deal with bursting economic bubbles and continued threats and realities of war. The terrorism of September 11, 2001, has raised fundamental questions about idealism and pragmatism and has put into a harsh light a set of new realities about the balance between freedom and security. Although we cannot be guided by a false optimism about uninterrupted human progress (which may have seemed as plausible in the "long-boom" 1990s as it did during the time of the French Enlightenment philosophers), neither can we be blinded by the pessimism of those who see a clash of civilizations and a path of decline in the West.

We live in a real world of risks and challenges, just like any other period of history, but we still need visionary pragmatists who can help us forge a path between idealism and pragmatism based on our core values and faith in democracy. David Brooks (2002), political columnist, captures the need for reconciling optimism and pessimism in our time:

> It's easy from the vantage point of our present difficulties to feel superior to the paradise mentality of the 1990s—in fact, too easy. The reality is that we need both hope and experience in the cycle. We need seasons of hope to push us into the future, to pioneer innovations, to create new worlds and dreams, to unleash new energies—energies that ultimately lead to new corruptions. Then we need seasons of experience to correct the excesses of the boom times. This is the only way we can move forward—swerving from one to the other, and bouncing periodically off the guardrails of our own good sense [p. 30].

What can help serve as the "guardrails of our own good sense" are the core values that can help guide leaders during times of change.

Compounding this need for visionary pragmatism is the reality that the problems we face defy national and local solution. National directives and programs are often as inadequate as neighborhood-level or city-level initiatives in grappling with complex problems that cross jurisdictional, sectoral, and other boundaries. These problems require both knowledge close to the problem and per-spective and resources to frame and execute meaningful solutions. Today the new locus for visionary pragmatism is the region. The working boundaries of regions vary from situation to situation, the product of an organic process in which the scope of the problem and solution and the sources of regional stewardship come together. It is not likely to work if the region is prescribed by federal or state government.

The fragmentation of local governments and the anonymity of business and civic leadership in many regions have made the life of the regional steward difficult. In fact, Harvard University professors Ronald Heifetz and Marty Linsky (2002) warn about the danger of leadership in complex and often hostile political environments:

> To lead is to live dangerously because when leadership counts, when you lead people through difficult change, you challenge what people hold dear—their daily habits, tools, loyalties and ways of thinking—with noth-ing more to offer than a possibility. Moreover, leader-ship often means exceeding the authority that you are given to tackle the challenge at hand. People push back when you disturb the personal and institutional equi-librium they know. And people resist in all kinds of cre-ative and unexpected ways that can have you taken out of the game, pushed aside, undermined, or eliminated [p. 2].

In this type of complex and often hostile environment, how is it possible to achieve any vision? Examples exist of regions where tough-minded and pragmatic regional stewards have made headway in bringing visions to reality through a skillful blend of leadership, participation, and expertise. Just as the Founders discovered the right mix of idealism, practicality, and credibility, regional efforts require the same blend. Engendering confidence and motivation is always a challenge for leaders. There is only so much that one can accomplish before running into the reality that life is difficult and dangers are always present.

Regional stewards are ultimate pragmatists who understand the need to go beyond traditional forms of leadership. Established forms of leadership are still essential to communities. For example, neighborhood activists and ethnic leaders are critical to mobilizing the grass roots; social entrepreneurs pioneer new approaches to social problems; environmental activists maintain vigilance over our natural assets; government leaders focus public resources on critical needs within their jurisdictions. However, as Heifetz and Linsky (2002) suggest, a different kind of leadership is necessary to be successful in the new environment:

> Leadership would be a safe undertaking if your organizations and communities only faced problems for which they already know the solutions. Every day, people have problems for which they do, in fact, have necessary know-how and procedures. We call these technical problems. But there is a whole host of problems that are not amenable to authoritative expertise or standard operating procedures. They cannot be solved by someone who provides answers from on high. We call these adaptive challenges because they require experiments, new discoveries and adjustments from numerous places in the community. Without learning new ways—changing attitudes, values and behaviors—people cannot make the adaptive leap necessary to thrive in the new environment [p. 13].

Regional stewardship is different from traditional leadership in that it crosses boundaries, takes an integrated approach, and builds new coalitions for action (see Exhibit 6.1).

Regional stewards tend to have certain common characteristics (Alliance for Regional Stewardship, 2000, pp. 8–13):

They are civic entrepreneurs, who apply the same entrepreneurial spirit and persistence to solving regional challenges that business entrepreneurs apply to building a business. They combine two great American traditions: the spirit of innovative enterprise and the spirit of community initiative. Civic entrepreneurs are catalysts, who help regions go through the change process. Like the business entrepreneur, the civic entrepreneur operates in a time of dramatic change, sees opportunity, and mobilizes others in the community to work toward their collective well-being. Although civic entrepreneurs come from all sectors—public, private, nonprofit—they share the common characteristics of entrepreneurial business leaders. They are risk takers. They are not afraid of failure. They possess courage born of strong convictions. They are passionate and energetic. They are people of vision and persistence.

They are integrators, who see the need for more connected regional approaches to addressing economic, environmental, and equity objectives. Regional stewards have 360-degree perspective, recognizing the interdependencies between economy, environment,

Exhibit 6.1. Traditional Leadership Versus Regional Stewardship.

Traditional Leadership	Regional Stewardship
One jurisdiction, one organization	Cross-jurisdictional and cross-organizational
Specific problem or goal	Integrated vision for the region
Single network	Diverse collaborative networks
Commitment to an idea or cause	Commitment to place

and social equity. In many regions, leaders are addressing problems in each of these areas, but it is not an integrated approach. Partly because of the problem of anonymity of leadership in large metropolitan regions, leaders do not know what other leaders are doing and have a hard time linking their efforts. Regional stewards help their communities develop an integrated approach to policy and planning, based on a common set of values and a regional vision.

They are boundary crossers (a term coined by nationally syndicated columnist Neal Peirce), who reach across jurisdictional, organizational, ethnic, and other boundaries to seek solutions to community problems. They are not deterred by turf issues. In fact, it is striking how often regional stewards are building collaborative solutions outside the traditional government structures. We are entering a period of experimentation and designing new civic intermediaries to address regional challenges that transcend the ability of government, business, or community institutions to address by themselves. These intermediaries—which can be institutions or ad hoc alliances—work across multiple political jurisdictions, organizations, and networks.

They are *coalition builders*, who build support from leaders, citizens, interest groups, and policy professionals toward a shared regional vision. Regional stewards reach across their regions to create broad-based coalitions for change. These coalitions can influence and motivate policy professionals to act while neutralizing the effect of competing interest groups in the policy process. (See Figure 6.1.)

In addition, regional stewards are concerned with how people work together. They know how to get people to the table and keep them there, encourage others to join, provide the framework for problem solving without insisting on a particular solution, safeguard the process through the inevitable frustration and skepticism, help participants navigate through conflict, and use their credibility, access, and skills to include both usual and unusual voices in the conversation.

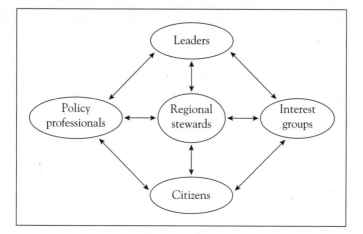

Figure 6.1. Regional Stewards Create New Coalitions for Change.
Source: Alliance for Regional Stewardship, 2000. Printed with permission.

What is also evident about regional stewards is their persistence. In the face of overwhelming obstacles, they keep going because they have a commitment to a set of core values and beliefs, a commitment to place, and a sense of *efficacy* (or a belief that they can make a difference by their actions).

Will they succeed and make a difference? In complex environments, small changes can have big results. Regional stewards are pushing toward what Malcolm Gladwell (2000) calls the "tipping point." Gladwell has noted the phenomenon in which small actions—whether social movement, fads, or epidemics—experience a tipping point, which leads to major change. First, "mavens," or the true believers, start the process. They work with "connectors," who spread the word. Finally, connectors help mobilize a wide body of "salesmen," who broadcast the message to a much wider audience. Eventually, virtually everyone in a community is involved.

What are the practical challenges for this new generation of visionary pragmatists—civic revolutionaries who are trying to move their regions to a tipping point? As the Founders made clear—and subsequent generations of stewards have demonstrated—an excess of either idealism or pragmatism is worth avoiding. By navigating skillfully between these two extremes, civic revolutionaries have experienced success in building resilience in their communities, an ability to meet challenges and continue moving forward.

Promising Experiments: Achieving Resilience of Place

To achieve *resilience of place*, civic revolutionaries must stay focused on the following goals:

- *Turning powerful ideas into practical achievements*

- *Staying focused on the big picture over the long term*

Turning Powerful Ideas into Practical Achievements

Some regions have achieved a resilience of place by blending idealism and pragmatism for several decades. In different ways, civic revolutionaries in these places have worked together on the basis of enlightened self-interest to create and sustain coalitions for change that have improved their regions. In each case, the struggle is never over, nor is progress an unbroken trend. The struggle continues through a dynamic interplay of vision and practicality.

Oklahoma City, Oklahoma

Oklahoma City's history of self-determinism goes all the way back to its founding in 1889, when the city sprung up overnight during a land run. When the cannon roared, nearly ten thousand people streamed into the town on wagons and buckboards, on horseback, on foot, and even on bicycles. Today Oklahoma City has rediscovered that same sense of self-determinism through a combination of high ideals and practical determination.

In 1992, after a decade of economic turmoil, Oklahoma City engaged in a serious effort to rescue its economy. Along with nearly a dozen U.S. cities, it was competing to be the site of United Airlines' new aircraft maintenance facilities, a prize that offered seven thousand new jobs and significant economic benefits. Despite offering the more aggressive financial-incentive package (valued at more than $200 million), Oklahoma City lost the bid to Indianapolis because United felt that Indianapolis offered a higher quality of life. Recalls Roy Williams of the Greater Oklahoma City Chamber of Commerce, "That was a hammer in the forehead. It made our leadership take a real look at this community and reassess ourselves. We have been so focused on what others wanted, we didn't know what we wanted."

That year, at the chamber of commerce retreat, which included the mayor and other city leaders, everyone agreed that there was a problem. More important, they were convinced that they could do something about it. A new initiative—Metropolitan Area Projects Plan (MAPS)—was born to improve the quality of life and physical infrastructure of the declining city. Mayor Ron Norick, with the chamber's assistance, took responsibility for driving the effort and making it a reality. He convened a committee representing the city's diverse interests, who selected nine flagship projects with input from city residents. The proposal included something for everyone—from a new downtown ballpark and arena to a canal river walk, from a new convention center to a metropolitan library-learning center. The list of projects was rolled out as one package, to be paid for by a five-year, one-cent sales tax. It was a daring proposal, one that initially prompted voter skepticism. Polls showed that MAPS would lose by twenty points just one month before the elections. Amazingly, in December 1993, voters approved the tax by a slim margin.

Countless other cities have tried—and failed—to do what Oklahoma City did. What made the difference for them? Was it an inspiring new vision for what Oklahoma City could aspire to or an effective campaign waged by supporters? It was both. Chamber and city leaders were united in the belief that Oklahoma City needed to take bold action in order to transform itself. At the same time, grassroots efforts rallied support in communities and neighborhoods. The decision ultimately came down to the fundamental and practical question of what kind of Oklahoma City people wanted. In countless speeches across the city, Mayor Norick summed up the choice: "We made it very simple. It was either a yes or no for the city's future" (Bailey, 2000, p. 66).

After the successful passage of the tax, MAPS hit some bumps during implementation. Planning for the sites took longer than expected, with project costs exceeding original estimates. The 1995 Oklahoma City bombing and its aftermath stalled new construction. Nearly five years passed before any tangible results from MAPS could be seen. Residents complained about the slow pace and became angry when MAPS announced a $10 million shortfall. Then, in 1998, the new ballpark opened and changed everyone's perspective. According to Mayor Humphreys, Norick's successor, "When people got their first look inside, they realized that MAPS was going to change this city in ways they hadn't imagined" (Bailey, 2000, p. 68). Thanks to the new ballpark—an inspiring symbol of revitalization—and an aggressive campaign led by the city and the chamber of commerce, 68 percent of residents voted to extend the MAPS tax in order to complete the other community improvement projects.

Today Oklahoma City is a vastly different place than a decade ago. Formerly abandoned downtown neighborhoods are now alive with activity, gleaming new city facilities mark the landscape, and a palpable optimism pervades. "We have a renewed understanding of our capacity to make this city what we want. Ten years ago, people did not feel that they had control over what was happening to them. We looked to outside companies to bring economic relief. Now we know that we control our destiny," describes Williams. Along with the renewed sense of confidence, Oklahoma City residents have a sensible, pragmatic attitude about their city's transformation. "I don't think of anything we did as hard; it's just hard work," says Cynthia Reid, marketing director of the chamber and longtime resident.

Through its MAPS initiative, Oklahoma City has created a new civic process that reconciles idealism and pragmatism by encouraging residents to imagine great things while demanding tangible results. The city is now embarking on a second round of MAPS, this time focused on improving the educational system. Called MAPS FOR KIDS, the combination sales tax/bond issue passed in November 2001. MAPS FOR KIDS will raise $695 million to fund a comprehensive school reform plan, making it the largest-ever capital investment package passed in Oklahoma City. Carrying forward the lessons learned from the original MAPS, the recent campaign included more up-front and open communications with residents about how the process would unfold, how long it would take, and the possible things that can go wrong. Part of the decision to focus on the educational system, acknowledges Reid, is the recognition that soft assets matter as much as hard assets. "We used to think that we could fix problems by building new buildings. We are now learning that it's not the entire solution." If Oklahoma City and its leaders can bring the same visionary pragmatism to the "soft" issues in their community (diversity, human capital, economic innovation), then they will indeed be the masters of their destiny.

Chattanooga, Tennessee

Chattanooga was declared in 1969 to be the most polluted city in America. A clear wake-up call to the city leaders, this shock led to what became known as the Chattanooga Process—the engagement of a wide number of citizens in a process of generating and implementing ideas to create a better community. Officially begun as a public-private partnership, Chattanooga Venture, the process was based on a set of simple, but effective, guidelines (see Exhibit 6.2).

Chattanooga city leaders used this process to develop and implement Vision 2000 starting in 1984, which resulted in a bold vision of regional transformation and a compelling series of specific civic improvements—including the Tennessee River Park, Chattanooga Neighborhood Enterprise, Tennessee Aquarium, and Bessie Smith Hall—totaling millions of dollars. These improvements in turn led to the transformation of the riverfront, revitalization of downtown, and dramatic improvements in environmental quality. By the early

Exhibit 6.2. Chattanooga Process Guidelines.

Any idea is worth exploring.

At the beginning, all possibilities get a respectful hearing.

Success will occur if we all sit down and put our heads together. That way we will reach a common agenda.

There is always a specific, open-ended agenda for public participation.

Collective good is always the goal, and that means the good of all citizens.

Preventing future problems and creating systematic change are always priorities in the process.

We always bring in the best people in the country to speak, advise, and participate.

When necessary, we visit other communities that have been successful to find out the nuances of how and why a solution worked there and what to avoid.

Source: Adams and Parr, 1998. Printed with permission.

1990s, most of the original goals had been achieved. In 1992, Chattanooga Ventures again invited the community to offer ideas for ReVision 2000. More than twenty-six hundred people participated, and an even more ambitious agenda was developed.

Although a visit to Chattanooga reveals the tangible results of their efforts—the revitalization of the downtown, the excitement generated by the aquarium and the river walk—perhaps the most important outcome of the Chattanooga Process is the ongoing capacity for civic innovation. Chattanooga has created a platform for regional stewardship built on civic, business, and government leadership that is constantly encouraging and rewarding civic innovation and promoting a more creative community. One part of this platform is a resource center, where citizens and planners gather to develop new ideas for civic improvement, using the most advanced tools available. Probably more than in any other American city, Chattanooga's use of new tools such as geographic information systems, modeling, visualization, and simulations has become a regular part of the development of new civic improvements. Chattanooga has become a living laboratory that blends an exciting vision of a livable community with pragmatic applications of new tools to achieve that vision.

Staying Focused on the Big Picture over the Long Term

Although all regions must grapple with the issues of the moment, some places have shown an admirable ability to stay focused on long-term transformations. Despite the tremendous barriers to success they face, they keep finding ways to make progress.

Atlanta, Georgia

Probably no American region has willed itself through more transformations or has demonstrated more effective long-term stewardship than Atlanta. A small rural railroad town founded as Terminus in 1837, Atlanta has moved through the Civil War, Reconstruction, the rise of the New South, the Civil Rights movement, and several real estate booms to become an international region—host to the 1996 Summer Olympics and home to major global companies. The story behind the story is clearly about how civic leaders promoted major change with a commitment to a set of core values.

Fortune editor and Atlanta native John Huey once said in a Metro Atlanta Chamber publication (half in jest), "I say Atlantans have had this theory for over a hundred years. They make up the most outrageous lie they can think of about Atlanta. Then they run around all over the whole world telling everyone about it until it comes true. The amazing thing is, it always comes true." Although this anecdote may illustrate an extreme version of regional stewardship (bordering on raw boosterism), Huey's statement seems to contain more than a grain of truth. Atlanta has reinvented itself several times based on an unusual mix of business, civic, government, and neighborhood leadership that has stepped up at different times to make things happen. For example, during the civil rights struggles of the 1950s and 1960s, Atlanta's leadership stepped forward to address challenges in a progressive way, in contrast to many other southern cities, becoming in the process "the city too busy to hate."

The story of Atlanta has been told many times, but the central theme seems to be the special relationship between Peachtree Street and Sweet Auburn. The white civic leadership who lived along Peachtree Street, led by Mayor Ivan Allen Sr. in the 1940s and Mayor Ivan Allen Jr. in the 1960s, promoted Forward Atlanta and Central Atlanta Progress, partnerships of business and civic leaders, who built a strong downtown economy and then reached out to black leaders who lived in the Sweet Auburn neighborhood to address racial challenges. In the end, white leaders helped make the transition to black political leadership with the election of the first black major, Maynard Jackson, in 1973. White business and civic leaders recognized that it was in their enlightened self-interest to make the changes required to ensure that Atlanta avoided the problems faced by other cities during the Civil Rights movement. Atlanta prospered because of this stewardship in the 1960s and 1970s.

The Olympics offered Atlanta the opportunity to put itself on the map internationally. But the goal for Atlanta was to use the 1996 Olympics to leave a lasting legacy for the city. As the late Dan Sweat, former head of Central Atlanta, said, "We won't emerge in September 1996 as a world class city, if all we've done is build some stadia and staged good games and entertained the visitors of the world. If we haven't significantly improved the daily lives of the people at the bottom of the economic heap, we don't deserve world class status" (Adams and Parr, 1998, p. 2). Through an extraordinary partnership between the public and private sector, Atlanta did promote an Olympics that planted ten thousand trees, built twelve miles of sidewalks, installed twelve hundred streetlights, and targeted fifteen city neighborhoods for improvement, adding a thousand units of housing in neighborhoods near downtown. It built new parks and improved existing parks. According to former Atlanta commissioner of planning and development, Leon Eplan, "We have transformed the city."

Since 1996, however, Atlanta's special formula for success has been challenged. Many people believe that the Atlanta Project, an ambitious initiative to help reduce poverty in the city, has fallen well short of expectations. The leaders of that effort now acknowledge that the project tried to do too much and was too top down. Achieving the right level of citizen participation proved difficult.

In addition, the growth of the region in a metropolitan area that now encompasses twenty counties with different ethnic, cultural, and political interests has created difficulties for Atlanta's special ways of the past. For example, Brenda Branch, director of economic development for the Gwinnett Chamber of Commerce, has said, "Most people would say Atlanta does not matter, but people in the know realize that Gwinnett exists because of the City of Atlanta. We know we must be involved in regional issues" (Adams and Parr, 1998, p. 9). The sheer size of the region and the complexity of issues facing the metropolitan area have overwhelmed the existing governance structures, including local government and regional planning agencies.

Transportation congestion and air pollution are now major challenges facing the region. Recent Environmental Protection Agency and court rulings on air-quality attainment have forced the region to take major steps to deal with transportation and land use issues on a regional basis. In 1998, then Governor Roy Barnes implemented his proposal to create the Georgia Regional Transportation Agency (GRTA), a state agency with power to oversee transportation and land use decisions in the Atlanta region to address the growing challenge facing the area. Although not fully implemented, GRTA represents one of the most aggressive attempts to deal with the problems of regional growth in the nation.

The Atlanta model of civic, business, and government partnership that worked so well for more than a hundred years has been challenged by the pressures of dealing with complex issues, including transportation, land use, and housing. Change will drive Atlanta in new directions in terms of the economy and society, but the question facing the region is whether regional stewards will continue their commitment to place. While the region continues to transform, its tradition of partnership and civic leadership will need to meet new challenges. Innovative approaches to inclusive stewardship, including efforts to connect neighborhood and regional leaders better to build new housing in the context of mixed-income communities, are under way. Atlanta remains a work in progress but has proven to be resilient over time.

Seattle, Washington

Seattle is another region that has experienced repeated transformations and has demonstrated a pattern of resilience over time. Beginning in the 1950s, civic leader Jim Ellis helped create the nation's first metropolitan regional council of governments to help save Lake Washington. In the early 1960s, Ed Carlson mobilized a group of Seattle leaders to promote and hold a world's fair, which proved to be a transforming event for both Seattle's economic and civic leadership as it opened up new international relationships, especially with Asia.

Bill Stafford, president of the Trade Development Alliance and longtime Seattle civic leader, says that a critical factor in Seattle's transformations has been "our attitude toward risk taking and failure since new ideas and companies require taking chances and therefore risking potential failure. When I worked for the mayor, other cities marveled at the experiments that we tried." Seattle has been willing to experiment in many areas, including the economy, international trade, downtown and neighborhood development, as well as culture. Stafford cites a number of ingredients for Seattle's success, including a research university, its talented people, a favorable quality of life and environment, transportation (including ports), openness and diversity, friendly business climate, foreign investment, and luck—or rather the ability to capitalize on luck and circumstance.

It was luck that Bill Boeing moved to Seattle to operate a timber business at a time when airplanes were made of wood. His hobby was flying and he started making seaplanes. The rest is history. Bill Gates was born in Seattle, and now there are sixty thousand "Microsoft millionaires" living in the Seattle area. Clearly, Boeing and Microsoft have been critical drivers of Seattle's economy. Although luck certainly played into the equation, these entrepreneurs found Seattle to continue to be hospitable to experimentation and a suitable location for growing their businesses. In fact, being located far away from the center of political power in Washington, D.C., has stimulated an independent mind-set and experimental culture in Seattle.

At the same time, as the closest mainland American city to Asia, Seattle was positioned to be a leader in international trade and investment. However, it took entrepreneurship and risk taking for the region to capitalize on both luck and location. Progressive business leaders including Jim Ellis, as well as George Duff at the Greater Seattle Chamber, began organizing major-city trips in the 1980s, which now include visits to global cities such as Barcelona, Kobe, Sydney, and Stockholm. This kind of experience led civic revolutionaries to form the Trade Development Alliance of Greater Seattle to drive the region's globalization.

Seattle has been marked by continuous transformations in leadership as well. During the 1970s, a new generation of political leaders led by Mayor Wes Uhlman overturned the traditional political elite in Seattle and opened up the process to a wider range of citizens. By the 1990s, new styles of entrepreneurial leadership emerged with the growth of Microsoft and the activities of Bill Gates, Paul Allen, and the Microsoft millionaires, early employees of the firm whose stock had skyrocketed in value over the years.

In recent years, Seattle's creative culture—spawning everything from Starbucks and alternative music to Microsoft—has played a prominent role in the city's downtown development strategy. Former Seattle Mayor Paul Schell, a real estate developer, historical preservationist, and dean of the University of Washington's School of Architecture and Urban Planning, believed that his job was to turn the city into a "platform for the creative experience. . . . You have telecommunications, biotech, software, and the Web all coming together with great music, architecture, and art. It's at the intersections of disciplines where sparks fly. That's where the ideas come from" (Kirsner, 2001, p. 143). With this perspective, Schell provided a welcoming environment for creative initiatives of several kinds.

The Experience Music Project by Microsoft cofounder Paul Allen is rapidly becoming the functional and symbolic backbone of this "creative experience." This $100 million facility, designed by world-renowned architect Frank Gehry, combines interactive and interpretive exhibits to tell the story of how American popular music is made.

Other projects are under way. The new Seattle Public Library is being designed by Rem Koolhaas. The Fuse Foundation, a nonprofit organization to help emerging artists gain a stable financial footing, gave its first grants in summer 2001. In 2002, the art museum in neighboring Bellevue moved into a new $23 million home designed by architect Steven Holl. The organizing principle behind the city's plans—the vision that most of the players seem to be working toward is expressed by Schell: "We want to be the Geneva of the Pacific, where international ideas can be exchanged" (Kirsner, 2001, p. 143).

For a creative downtown to have a strong interactive edge like Seattle, lots of threads must weave together: electronic connectivity, pedestrian-oriented squares and streets that support face-to-face encounters, airport service that makes global and regional networking easy, to name just a few. As opportunities for interaction on multiple scales and venues occur, the community's strength and resource base for creative dynamics grow. Moreover the "cleaner" nature of the new economy makes it possible to locate homes, workplaces, and recreational areas closer together.

In sum, the story of Seattle is about regional stewards like Jim Ellis in the 1950s, who wanted to save Lake Washington and formed a regional council of governments; Ed Carlson, who promoted the world's fair as a way to put Seattle on the global map; Wes Uhlman and other political leaders, who opened up the political process; George Duff and Bill Stafford, who created new international linkages through study tours and a regional trade alliance; the Microsoft millionaires, including Paul Allen, who wanted to stimulate innovation in the community; and Paul Schell, who wanted to help build a more creative downtown. Taken together, these visionary pragmatists have kept Seattle resilient over time, responding to the challenges of globalization while creating a more attractive city.

Recent events, including the World Trade Organization demonstrations, downturns in the economy with difficulties at key firms like Boeing, and even an earthquake, have shaken the confidence of this region. Paul Schell was not reelected. Questions remain about the success of key cultural initiatives launched in recent years. However, Seattle has always been a resilient region, rebounding from earlier economic downturns in the early 1970s when Boeing hit a rough spot (a local bumper sticker at the time read "last one leaving please turn out the lights") and unemployment also was high. With a tradition of risk taking and experimentation, it is likely that Seattle will once again find a way to reinvent itself.

Insights from the Field

Every region and community must find its own path to resilience, its own reconciliation of the competing values of idealism and pragmatism. At the same time, civic revolutionaries from around the country have lessons to share. Insights from the field are offered here, organized according to the major roles that civic revolutionaries play—they build a compelling case for change (discover), make critical choices in experimentation (decide), and ultimately mobilize allies for change (drive).

Discover: Building a Compelling Case for Change

Stretch the imagination with outside ideas. Civic revolutionaries help their communities expand their horizons by exposing them to the possibilities. Through intercity visits, places such as Seattle and Atlanta are relentless in their pursuit of new ideas, innovations from other U.S. and international regions, and interactions with a diverse mix of people. Both Seattle and Atlanta have a history of actively seeking out opportunities to host international gatherings, such as the world's fair and the Olympics. Cincinnati hosts the Great Cities Symposium series, attended on average by two hundred community leaders. The symposia generally include a keynote address by a national thought leader, a best-practices panel of practitioners from other regions, and ample time for discussion. Then the speaker and the practitioners join local leadership for discussion with the local media, resulting in editorials and articles that help stretch the imagination of an even larger audience. The symposia are also videotaped and broadcast on local television.

Move people along a regional pathway, exposing them to new people and ideas and encouraging their growing commitment to place and their contribution of ideas for change. Places like St. Louis involve people of all kinds in a variety of leadership programs and experiences, seeking out energy and ideas to help move the region forward. Orlando is well-known for its welcoming leadership culture, which actively engages new executives, including branch plant managers, in civic affairs. Leadership programs and experiences are important here too, along with a strong commitment by Mayor Glenda Hood to reach out to new people and ask them for their ideas for making Orlando a better place. Richmond and Fresno are good examples of places that are expanding the circle of leadership to include diverse voices.

Places need to understand their pathways to regional stewardship. Regional stewards usually develop over time. A leader may begin by identifying a specific way to give back to the community or become directly involved in a specific issue as a volunteer in something that has personal value. Based on that experience, the next step may be to join or take a leadership role in larger efforts. These leaders often become civic or social entrepreneurs, who bring their own innovative problem-solving talents to community issues. They are change agents who focus on opportunities and create new solutions. However, their efforts still tend to focus on a single issue or cause.

To become regional stewards, these leaders recognize how their efforts fit into the broader vision of the region and see the connections between the economy, environment, and society. Places such as Atlanta, St. Louis, and Pittsburgh are experimenting with regional leadership development programs for civic leaders in order to expand their networks and knowledge of regional efforts. These leadership programs can help convert civic leaders from all sectors into regional stewards by helping them see regional challenges in an integrated way. The potential is for regions to identify these diverse, high-potential civic leaders and accelerate their development along pathways to regional stewardship.

However, with traditional sources of leadership in transition in most regions, it is important to increase the pipeline of regional stewards by broadening the sources of leadership to recruit young, next-generation leaders, leaders from diverse ethnic communities and leaders from small entrepreneurial firms. This requires aggressive outreach and mentoring, not simply invitations to participate.

Decide: Making Critical Choices in Experimentation

Choose breakthrough ideas with meaningful first steps. Civic revolutionaries are not afraid of big ideas. They know, however, that they must spend time on developing meaningful first steps toward realization of a compelling vision. In fact, when getting started, begin with the purpose of considering only alternatives that are big enough to transform the community. Send the signal that you and others are only interested in breakthrough thinking and action. Otherwise, why bother? Everyone is busy, and many people are already spread thin across a range of community commitments. Only something qualitatively different, something that appeals to their imagination and deep feeling for the community, will create the motivation to join.

One way to visualize breakthroughs is to make the tipping point an explicit mission. A lot of wasted effort can go to promising, but disconnected, initiatives that do not lead to a regional tipping point or a gathering momentum for regional transformation. Up-front work is necessary to envision and articulate a plausible path to transformation. How will an initial set of actions trigger another set of actions, which in turn will lead to a ripple effect throughout the region? Map out the change process, and make adaptations if initial actions are not leading to their desired ripple effect.

Chattanooga, Atlanta, and Seattle are good examples of this tipping-point effect, because a small group of people began processes that ultimately enveloped the entire community. In each case, the guiding ideas were huge: to recover from environmental disaster by becoming one of the most attractive cities in the country, to avoid the racial disruptions of other cities and become the center of the New South, and to become an international center of trade and creativity far from traditional centers of power. Who in 1969 would have thought that Chattanooga could become one of the nation's most livable communities? Who in the 1970s would have thought that Atlanta could get the 1996 Olympics and become a leading international city? In each case, the region began with a set of big ideas that combined to provide a compelling vision of the future, one that could be broken down into explicit projects and investments but that also opened up a continuous process of change, one step building on another.

Agree to guiding principles that ensure breakthrough action but do not constrain creativity in implementation. With its Metropolis Principles, Chicago concisely lays out the guidelines for a fundamentally different land use and transportation philosophy and pattern of behavior, one where the full range of employees can efficiently get to work and where jobs, housing, and public transit are effectively connected. The actual implementation of this approach could and should take many forms. In fact, civic revolutionaries in Chicago developed a package of changes that both major gubernatorial candidates agreed in writing to help enact if elected.

In Austin, a set of sustainability criteria guides thinking and creates real incentives for a new kind of development, based more on compactness, infill, and other smart-growth principles. Similarly, in the Sierra Nevada counties of California, civic revolutionaries have put together principles that describe how to grow a region of rural communities so that they maintain their distinctiveness and preserve surrounding open space and agriculture. Along with the principles, explicit examples are provided of land use patterns, policies, and other tactics for achieving the desired outcome, leaving it up to individual communities to choose the right mix for them. In each of these cases, the common thread is providing a framework for a big idea (that is, a new development pattern), while encouraging grassroots innovation in implementation.

Drive: Mobilizing Allies for Change

Recruit with the understanding that visionary pragmatism is a team sport. A key lesson from the experience of the Founders is that idealism and pragmatism rarely reside in the same person but that visionary pragmatism is the product of a group. A critical ingredient is a rare visionary pragmatist—such as a Washington, Madison, or Franklin—who can provide the creative formulations that hold together the Jeffersonian idealists and the Hamiltonian and Adams pragmatists. But ultimately, all of these kinds of players are necessary to move a region forward. Assemble the regional stewardship "team," looking not only at an individual's jurisdictional, sectoral, and other representational qualities but at his or her visionary and pragmatic qualities as well. In places as diverse as Austin, Seattle,

Atlanta, Chicago, Chattanooga, and Denver, one can identify individuals who fit the Jefferson, Hamilton, Madison, and Washington personae, working together to reconcile idealism and pragmatism and to move their region forward.

Create laboratory settings for tinkering. Chattanooga, St. Paul, and a growing number of other communities are experimenting with a form of community design center, a physical place where community residents can come together with information and visualization tools to imagine how their communities as a whole or as individual parcels under development could be changed. This kind of setting can encourage purposeful exploration of alternatives, the tinkering with assumptions and elements to produce a desired outcome. In California's Central Valley, the Great Valley Center provides a tangible place, a platform on which new ideas and innovative approaches are nurtured. The center sponsors research, facilitates dialogue, and seeds new efforts to address regional challenges. It provides a source of information for the media and a civic voice for a region that traditionally has not been well understood or heard statewide.

Of course, spaces for tinkering need not be physical centers. They can be civic forums such as the citizens league models in Minneapolis, Oklahoma City, and other places that provide a qualitatively different environment for dialogue, the articulation of creative ideas and problem-solving approaches, and the design of innovative solutions to public problems. Boise, Idaho, created the Treasure Valley Partnership as a new civic space to focus local officials on regional issues and includes the Futures Project, which produces joint research, dialogue, and a "tool kit" for defining and implementing sustainable and livable development patterns.

Create campaigns to energize allies. Campaigns provide focus and urgency, but they can also create divisiveness and provide a false sense of completion when in fact solutions are more complicated and must play out over the long term. Nevertheless the positive attributes of campaigns can be captured in the context of a long-term commitment to change. For example, Atlanta and Seattle mobilized around campaigns to host big international gatherings that also had major impacts on longer-term infrastructure and economic vitality. Austin has used national competitions for federal R&D facilities to motivate and focus their collaborative efforts, in the process building a sense of trust among partners and a confidence that the future of the region can be purposefully shaped. In California's Central Valley, a new campaign to transform the major north-south Highway 99 corridor provides an urgency for change and a multidimensional program of action, including road improvements, regulatory changes, environmental cleanup, and economic development initiatives. It provides a new platform for creative ideas and pragmatic regional collaboration—all with the understanding that it will take years (if ever) for this "campaign" to come to an end.

Build momentum by measuring and communicating progress toward a vision. Too many regional groups do "the vision thing" and falter because there is no mechanism to track progress and communicate it in ways that help fuel the momentum for change. The civic revolutionaries who are driving Joint Venture: Silicon Valley took over a civic group that was rapidly losing its credibility with the community and the media, developed clear memorandums of understanding that laid out specific objectives in implementation, and then measured progress and reported it monthly via newsletters and through media briefings. This approach produced a documented about-face by the local media and built confidence that this effort was a serious and effective vehicle for change. That breakthrough led to others, as the group was able to launch a multi-million-dollar educational improvement initiative, negotiate sweeping changes to streamline local regulatory processes, and broker a new regional approach to economic development. Efforts such as these move from goals to measurable outcomes, measuring progress toward goals and connecting actions to those goals. And just as important, they communicate both promising results and lack of progress to stimulate further dialogue and action.

What Success Looks Like: Resilience of Place

The competing values of idealism and pragmatism not only can coexist but also can blend productively in places that make resilience their guiding civic philosophy. Building a resilience of place is the highest calling for the civic revolutionary. There are no permanent solutions, fixed formulas, or viable strategies that can wall off a community from outside forces or protect it from internal disruptions. The pragmatic reality is this: communities are faced inevitably with challenges that they cannot anticipate fully and for which they have no well-honed response. The idealistic opportunity is this: communities can ride the waves (and make their own waves) of change, confident that long-term resilience is the goal. But what does success look like?

- The community generates powerful ideas that renew core values in light of current circumstances, providing the glue that joins idealism and pragmatism.

- The community has an environment that encourages individual leaders from all walks of life to answer the call to stewardship, to make the long-term commitment to place and play their role in the continuing American Experiment.

7

The Rise of the New Civic Revolutionaries

Answering the Call to Stewardship

Leaders must not only have their own commitments,
they must move the rest of us toward commitment.
They call us to the sacrifices necessary to achieve our
goals. They do not ask more than the community can
give, but often ask more than it intended to give or
thought it possible to give.

John W. Gardner, On Leadership

To answer the call to stewardship in our own time, we must learn from the lessons of civic revolutionaries of previous generations and from civic revolutionaries in our own generation. Then we must forge our own path.

Answering the Call to Stewardship in Our Time

In the mid-1700s, a grassroots movement began as leaders in small communities across the American colonies began to recognize their common destiny as an independent nation based on the revolutionary principle of liberty. Coming together through committees of correspondence, future leaders of the American Revolution, including Benjamin Franklin, John Adams, and Thomas Jefferson, began to share their thoughts. The different voices of Virginia, Pennsylvania, Massachusetts, and other colonies joined; they spoke first through the Declaration of Independence and later through the Constitution and *The Federalist Papers*. Although these leaders from local communities were not looking for greatness, greatness was thrust upon them at a critical moment. We remember the heritage of these American revolutionaries.

Similar grassroots movements have occurred periodically throughout American history. Local leaders first discuss ideas in their communities and then join together to create sweeping change for the nation. This practice was true during the debate about slavery before the Civil War and the debates about the role of the trusts before the Progressive Era of the early 1900s. The Civil Rights movement was preceded by community organizing across the South in the 1950s. The environmental movement was inspired by Rachel Carson's *Silent Spring* in the 1960s and by local efforts to fight pollution.

A new grassroots movement is under way in the regions of America today. Once again, a movement is beginning in communities across the nation by leaders who see the need for fundamental change in how their regions define and solve problems and ultimately how they are governed. They represent a new kind of regional civic leadership more attuned to the economic and social realities of our times. Traditional, top-down leadership styles and stovepipe government models simply do not work in the fast-paced, global economy and diverse society of today. Business, civic, and government leaders know that the old way of governing is simply not working any more in solving critical economic, social, and environmental challenges, especially as these issues become more interdependent. Although the old model is failing, new models have not yet fully emerged to take their place. We are in an uncertain time of transition similar to the 1760s, 1850s, 1900s, and 1950s, just before major change.

In particular, a generation born after World War II—tempered by the social turmoil of the 1960s, the political disruptions of the 1970s, and the economic turbulence of the 1980s and 1990s—must now rise to the challenge. Many people who are part of the large baby boom generation have a commitment to place based on the communitarian values of the 1960s, combined with an entrepreneurial spirit forged by the realities of the emerging new economy. Many people of this generation are responsible for igniting the beginning of the grassroots revolution in the regions of America during the 1990s.

Just as Franklin, Adams, and Jefferson found one another to forge the America Revolution, Abraham Lincoln melded the forces of antislavery to save the Union, Teddy Roosevelt rallied the elements of an emerging Progressive movement to fight the trusts, and Martin Luther King Jr. coalesced the Civil Rights movement, the next decade may find the coming together of new civic revolutionaries to write the next chapter in the American story. We may need new committees of correspondence among our regional civic leaders, a *Regionalist Papers* to marshal the intellectual arguments for new forms of distributed governance, and new kinds of dialogue with lasting impact—like that of Abraham Lincoln and Stephen Douglas, who debated slavery, or generations of civil rights leaders, who raised the consciousness of the nation at important times during American history.

This time, new regional stewards may seek to achieve the moral imperatives of freedom, equality, and opportunity through more decentralized means rather than through centralized national government because conditions have changed. We need flexible, innovative responses based on collaboration that meet real community needs, rather than the simple top-down "mainframe," one-size-fits-all models of the earlier Progressive Era. In fact, centralized means left over from the earlier Progressive Era have themselves become captive to special interests, often leading to gridlock. Although the ends may remain the same, the means must change to meet new economic and social realities.

This book has described the journey of some of these new civic revolutionaries, who are working on promising experiments in regional stewardship. They are practicing a new style of civic leadership because it is working. As visionary pragmatists, they see the value in working in more collaborative ways to solve complex problems based on fundamental principles and shared values. Together they may change the way our country solves problems—one region at a time and then joining together as streams become rivers, building to a tidal wave of change across America.

Reconciling Competing American Values: Guiding Principles

Following the example of the nation's Founders and subsequent generations, these new civic revolutionaries are grappling with the timeless tensions of the American Experience. The struggle between competing positive values, such as individual and community, is as old as the nation itself, but every generation must address it anew. The task of every generation is to seek and find the *points of reconciliation* between these competing values—enabling the American Experiment to move forward.

The new civic revolutionaries are driving efforts to reconcile important American values in their communities in our time. Taken together, these efforts are clarifying the practical challenges and the types of transformations necessary to achieve reconciliation among these American values. The work of these new civic revolutionaries, given their experience so far, suggests the following principles for reconciliation, an answer to the question of what success may look like for our time:

Reconciling Individual and Community: Create Common Purpose

To create common purpose between individual values and community values requires that

- People voluntarily exercise their freedom to build a community of place, believing that they will gain more in social benefits than they give up in individual liberty.

- Competing interests form working relationships based on compatible values and complementary roles.

- Complex problems transform into manageable tasks, and independent efforts are channeled into collaborative action based on simple but elegant guiding principles.

Reconciling Trust and Accountability: Build Webs of Responsibility

To reconcile the values of trust and accountability, civic revolutionaries must work to ensure that the following take place:

- Both strong expectations and authentic opportunities exist to participate in civic affairs through open and influential organizations and inclusive and catalytic processes.

- Written agreements formalize the basic lines of accountability among stakeholders, creating the foundation for building trust and confidence in the system.

- People and institutions exceed the minimum requirements for accountability because they trust that the prevailing civic system is conducive to risk taking and innovation.

Reconciling Economy and Society: Strengthen the Vital Cycle

To reconcile the often competing values of economy and society, civic revolutionaries need to build strength into the following elements of the vital cycle:

- Businesses prosper as part of the fabric of communities by being both globally competitive and deeply rooted to place.

- The economy is considered an essential part of the community and operates in a productive relationship with people and the environment.

- The economy is an expanding source of opportunity and mobility for all, rather than a fixed source of opportunity for some and not for others.

Reconciling People and Place: Make the Creative Connection

Creativity is key to balancing the interests of both people and place:

- People and places are on a shared pathway to better living standards.

- People and places feed off one another in a creative interaction that fuels economic and community vitality.

Reconciling Change and Continuity: Create Vigilance for Renewal

To maintain a balance between the forces for change and the forces for continuity, civic revolutionaries must be vigilant in the following ways:

- The community expects constant, dynamic change, seeking to leaven the negative impacts and leverage the positive benefits while preserving core values.

- The community is purposeful about filling its leadership pipeline, expanding the sources of leaders and excusing no one from service.

Reconciling Idealism and Pragmatism: Build Resilience of Place

Ultimately, civic revolutionaries must work to achieve an environment that nurtures both idealism and pragmatism in stakeholders from all segments of the community:

- The community generates powerful ideas that renew core values in light of current circumstances, providing the glue that joins idealism and pragmatism.

- The community has an environment that encourages individual leaders from all walks of life to answer the call to stewardship, to make the long-term commitment to place and play their role in the continuing American Experiment.

Igniting the Passion for Community Change

This book has explored sets of competing American values, from their historical revolutionary roots to their contemporary effects, and has shown how the current generation is trying to reconcile them for our time. We do not presume to offer an inclusive list of competing values nor to offer a set of choices between "good and evil." Although clear-cut, black-and-white choices will always exist, much of what happens in communities today is more complex, operating in a gray area where no one can stake claim to the moral high ground, where reasonable people can disagree. However, even in this gray area, a case could be made for other sets of competing values—and *should* be made if those values need to be reconciled in order for a community or region to move forward.

Our purpose, instead, is to suggest that Americans can find ample common ground in the process of reconciling positive American values—values that compete with each other and can clash in a struggle for supremacy, creating a cascade of negative consequences for people and communities. By focusing on how to reconcile and maximize the positive impacts of these American values, civic revolutionaries can ignite the passion for community change.

Our purpose is also to identify practical insights from the field of experimentation, strategies and techniques that might be useful to civic revolutionaries in regions across the country. Based on these experiences and rooted in the experience of the Founders, we believe that there are three major roles that civic revolutionaries play in igniting the passion for change and navigating the process of experimentation in their communities. These roles mirror the experience and beliefs of John W. Gardner. For Gardner, life was a continuous cycle of reflection, decision, and action. For today's civic revolutionaries, like those before them, change is a continuous cycle of discovery, decision, and action.

Discover: Building a Compelling Case for Change

Civic revolutionaries build a convincing case for change in their communities—accumulating information, ideas, and allies in the process. They diagnose the challenges facing their communities, the tensions between competing values that must be addressed in new ways. They creatively describe, reframe, measure, and connect issues and root causes. They try to understand what is working, what is not working, and what might work. They seek out the experiences of other communities, to expand the view of what is possible and to find other civic revolutionaries who might be able to help them frame problems or develop solutions. At the same time, they seek out and discover allies in their communities, individuals that can help make the case and become part of the coalition for change.

Decide: Making Critical Choices in Experimentation

Civic revolutionaries use what they learn from the discovery process to make decisions. They make choices from among the many actions they could take to tackle their challenges. They may consult with those in other communities and tap into national sources of research and ideas to consider options for action, and they sort through different ideas and decide on how best to apply what they have learned. They decide about focus, scope, and priority in designing experiments in community change—immediate actions connected to an overall vision (or story) of change that will provide opportunities for continuous feedback and adaptation.

Drive: Mobilizing Allies for Change

Civic revolutionaries are relentless in their drive for change. Even though they are thoughtful and reflective in preparation and in decision making about what to do, they neither succumb to "paralysis by analysis" nor engage in an endless search for the perfect solution. They embody the spirit of experimentation—they reflect, decide, act, then reflect on initial results, make more decisions, pursue new actions, and start the process again. They drive a realistic, opportunistic, and adaptable experimentation process.

Renewing America's Social Compact to Meet the Challenges of a New Era

By playing practical roles to advance core principles of reconciliation, today's civic revolutionaries are, in effect, renewing America's social compact. Through their actions, they are redefining the relationship between Americans and their communities, regions, and nation—to better meet the challenges of a new era. In fact, we may have reached a stage similar to the period before the American Revolution, the Civil War, the Progressive Era, and the Civil Rights movement, where a new social compact will emerge from experimentation at the grass roots. What shifts would have to be made to create a new social compact based on the promising experiments of civic revolutionaries across America? They are redefining the relationship between the values of

- *Individuals and community*: shifting from compromise, conflict, and chaos to choice, complementarity, and cohesion

- *Trust and accountability*: shifting from skeptical bystanders and unclear responsibilities to engaged shareholders and mutual accountability

- *Economy and society:* shifting from short-term specula-
  tion to long-term investment, from uneven access to
  universal mobility

- *People and place:* shifting from separate paths to
  shared destinies, from common places to creative
  environments

- *Change and continuity:* shifting from stability as an
  expectation to change as a given, from leadership
  roulette to leadership renewal

- *Idealism and pragmatism:* shifting from wishful thinking
  to visionary pragmatism, from diverse leaders to
  regional stewards

To complete these shifts will require additional changes—such
as a movement from top-down pronouncements to decentralized
solutions, from interest group politics to public engagement, and
from widening inequality to shared prosperity. It will not happen
overnight, and it will not be easy. But the seeds are germinating in
communities across America.

A new social compact will have to include both rights and
responsibilities, or as Gardner was fond of saying, "Freedom and
responsibility, liberty and duty. That's the deal." Harvard professor
Michael J. Sandel (1997) claims that a new political movement
requires a new public philosophy, one that draws more on stronger
notions of citizenship and civic virtue than the philosophy that is
informing our politics currently. Central among these is an emphasis on the civic consequences of economic arrangements, what he
calls the political economy of citizenship. Such a public philosophy
would be driven by a set of simple rules, based on ethical principles,
which help guide complex behavior to address the economic and
social challenges of today.

Are we on our way to a new compact? In the 1990s, we went too far with our faith in the marketplace, losing touch with Adam Smith's original vision of the importance of "moral sentiments," or sympathy for others, as a guiding principle behind the invisible hand of markets. According to author Peter Dougherty (2002), a new civic economics is emerging, one that involves "the construction of a civic infrastructure that attracts and stimulates markets, the economics of large scale public enterprises (such as the GI Bill) without large bureaucracies, the economics of expanded assets and property ownership" (p. 16).

Perhaps the new compact will hark back to the famous nineteenth-century Cambridge University economist Alfred Marshall, who pronounced in an address to the Royal Economic Society in 1907 that the "age of chivalry is not over. . . . No one can lay his head on his pillow at peace with himself, who is not giving some time and substance to diminish the number of those who cannot earn a reasonable income and thus have an opportunity of living a noble life" (Marshall, 1907).

What makes the creation of a new social compact possible? Sometimes wars such as the Revolutionary War, the Civil War, and the Vietnam War have helped mobilize the nation and bring forth new leaders. Franklin, Adams, Jefferson, Washington, Hamilton, Madison, and others were not heroes prior to the Revolutionary War but found one another during those fateful years and created a nation based on the fundamental principles that provide the foundation for the American social compact. The Civil War brought forth the wisdom of Abraham Lincoln, who reconciled the promise of the Declaration of Independence with the practicality of the Constitution and renewed the nation's social compact.

Economic crises and excesses can also spur change, such as the downturns of the late 1800s and 1930s, which stimulated new progressive movements. Demographic shifts and social forces can also stimulate change and helped give rise to the Civil Rights movement of the 1950s and 1960s and the women's movements of the 1970s. According to Ted Halstead (2003) of the New America Foundation:

> America has so far experimented with three social contracts, each of which reflected the political forces of its time. The purpose of the first . . . was to found the nation. The goal of the second was to put it back together after the Civil War. The third—first articulated in FDR's New Deal and later expanded in Lyndon B. Johnson's Great Society—sought to build a mass middle-class society by relying on ambitious government programs and new economic regulation. It is now time for a fourth American social contract. To fit the post-industrial age, it must be able to reconcile competing demands of flexibility and fairness [and] will require new roles and responsibilities for all three parties to the contract: government, business, and citizenry [p. 124].

In the early years of the twenty-first century, a series of disruptions has opened a window for change. In rapid succession, we experienced the implosion of the Internet bubble, followed by the hard new realities of economic slowdown. These events created a wake-up call after a decade of prosperity. The events of September 11, 2001, have stimulated a new sense of communal urgency, while the collapse of Enron and other corporate lapses have created a crisis of confidence in business. Taken together, these disruptions may stimulate a new willingness to leave behind old structures and experiment with new approaches based on core values. It could hasten the renewal of America's social compact.

Renewing America's social compact was a core concern of Gardner during his long and distinguished life. It is in his memory and with the purpose of continuing his work that the national Alliance for Regional Stewardship has launched the John W. Gardner Academy for Regional Stewardship. The purpose of the academy will be much like that of Plato's academy and Aristotle's lyceum: it will explicitly link principles with practice, reflection with action. It will be based on the idea that public philosophy should be an active way of life, not simply a way of thinking or discourse. It will help civic revolutionaries, along with others, renew America's social compact—first community by community and region by region and then ultimately between Americans and their nation. Near the end of his life, Gardner issued this call to action:

> Most Americans welcome the voice that lifts them out of themselves. They want to be better people. They want to help make this a better country. . . . What you can do is to awaken them to the possibilities within themselves. Awaken them to what *they* can do for their country, the country of their children and their children's children.
>
> So those who have not succumbed to the contemporary disaffection and alienation must speak the world of life to their fellow Americans. It is not a liberal or conservative issue. It is not Democrat versus Republican. It is a question of whether we are going to settle into a permanent state of self-absorption or show the vigor and purpose that becomes us. We don't want it said that after a couple of great centuries we let the American Experiment disintegrate [O'Connell, 1999, p. xv].

Following in the footsteps of the Founders and later the civic revolutionaries of the nineteenth and twentieth centuries, we must recognize that the time has come for this generation of Americans to take its place as stewards of the American Experiment.

References

Abbott, C. *Greater Portland: Urban Life and Landscape in the Pacific Northwest (Metropolitan Portraits)*. Philadelphia: University of Pennsylvania Press, 2001.

Adams, B., and Parr, J. *Boundary Crossers: Case Studies of How Ten of America's Metropolitan Regions Work*. College Park, Md.: Academy of Leadership Press. [http://www.academy.umd.edu/publications/Boundary/CaseStudies/bcsatlanta.htm]. 1998.

Alliance for Regional Stewardship. *Regional Stewardship: A Commitment to Place*. Monograph Series, no. 1. [http://www.regionalstewardship.org]. Oct. 2000.

Alliance for Regional Stewardship. *Empowering Regions: Strategies and Tools for Community Decision Making*. Monograph Series, no. 2. [http://www.regionalstewardship.org]. Apr. 2001a.

Alliance for Regional Stewardship. *The Downtowns of the Future*. Monograph Series, no. 3. [http://www.regionalstewardship.org]. Aug. 2001b.

Austin's Economic Future: The Intersection of Innovation, Creativity, and Quality of Life. Austin: Texas Perspectives, Nov. 20, 2002.

Bailey, H. "Oklahoma City Maps: A New Frontier." *Oklahoma Today*, 2000, pp. 60–68.

Barrera, R. From a speech delivered at the Alliance for Regional Stewardship Forum, LaJolla, Calif., May 2, 2002.

Bear M., Conway, M., and Rademacher, I. *Project QUEST: San Antonio's Systemic Approach to Workforce Development*. Washington, D.C.: Economic Opportunities Program, Aspen Institute, Aug. 2001.

Berry, W. *Life Is a Miracle: An Essay Against Modern Superstition*. Washington, D.C.: Counterpoint, 2000.

Blum, J. M. *The Promise of America: An Historical Inquiry.* Boston: Houghton Mifflin, 1966.

Bonfiglio, O. "MOSES Leads the Way in Detroit." *Christian Science Monitor,* Oct. 16, 2002. [http://www.csmonitor.com/2002/1016/p16s01-lihc.html].

Brooks, D. "Lions and Foxes." *Atlantic Monthly,* Oct. 2002, p. 30.

Burke, J. *The Knowledge Web: From Electronic Agents to Stonehenge and Back— and Other Journeys Through Knowledge.* New York: Simon & Schuster, 1999.

Cohen, R. *The Good, the Bad and the Difference: How to Tell Right from Wrong in Everyday Situations.* New York: Doubleday, 2002.

Croly, H. *The Promise of American Life.* Boston: Northeastern University Press, 1989. (Originally published 1909)

Diggins, J. P. *On Hallowed Ground: Abraham Lincoln and the Foundations of American History.* New Haven, Conn.: Yale University Press, 2000.

Dionne, E. J., Jr. *Community Works: The Revival of Civil Society in America.* Washington, D.C.: Brookings Institution, 1998.

Dolan, T., Godfrey, M., and Herbert, G. "A History of Planning Is Continuing Through Envision Utah." *Salt Lake Tribune.* [http://www.sltrib.com/2002/apr/04282002/commenta/731876.html]. Apr. 28, 2002.

Dougherty, P. J. *Who's Afraid of Adam Smith? How the Market Got Its Soul.* New York: Wiley, 2002.

Dreier, P., Grigsby, J. E., III, Lopez-Garza, M., and Pastor, M., Jr. *Regions That Work: How Cities and Suburbs Can Grow Together* (M. Pastor Jr., ed.). Minneapolis: University of Minnesota Press, 2000.

Drucker, P. F. *Managing in the Next Society.* New York: Truman Talley Books, 2002.

Economic Development Administration. *Strategic Planning in the Technology-Driven World: A Guidebook for Innovation-Led Development.* Washington, D.C.: Economic Development Administration, 2001.

Euchner, C. (ed.). *Governing Greater Boston: The Politics and Policy of Place.* Cambridge, Mass.: Rappaport Institute for Greater Boston, 2002.

Florida, R. *The Rise of the Creative Class: And How It's Transforming Work, Leisure, Community, and Everyday Life.* New York: Basic Books, 2002.

Foster, K. A. *Regionalism on Purpose.* Cambridge: Lincoln Institute of Land Policy, 2001.

Fresno Area Collaborative Regional Initiative. *Community Values of the Fresno Region.* [www.fresnocri.org/main.asp?p=8]. Retrieved July 16, 2003.

Fukuyama, F. *Trust: The Social Virtues and the Creation of Prosperity*. New York: Free Press, 1995.

Fukuyama, F. *The Great Disruption: Human Nature and the Reconstitution of Social Order*. New York: Free Press, 2000.

Gardner, J. W. *The Recovery of Confidence*. New York: Norton, 1970.

Gardner, J. W. *On Leadership*. New York: Free Press, 1990.

Gardner, J. W. *Excellence: Can We Be Equal and Excellent Too?* New York: Norton, 1995.

Gardner, J. W. *A New Spirit Is Stirring: Quotations from John W. Gardner, 1912–2002*. Stanford: Haas Center for Public Service, 2002.

Gardner, J. W. *Living, Leading, and the American Dream*. New York: Wiley, 2003.

Gladwell, M. *The Tipping Point: How Little Things Can Make a Big Difference*. New York: Little, Brown, 2000.

Grayson, D., and Hodges, A. *Everybody's Business*. New York: DK Publishing, 2002.

Halstead, T. "The American Paradox." *Atlantic Monthly*, Jan. 2003, p. 124.

Harris, J. "The Regionalist's Season." Speech presented at the Alliance for Regional Stewardship Forum, San Diego, Calif., May 2002.

Heifetz, R. A., and Linsky, M. *Leadership on the Line: Staying Alive Through Dangers of Leading*. Boston: Harvard Business School Press, 2002.

Henton, D., Melville, J., and Walesh, K. *Grassroots Leaders for a New Economy*. San Francisco: Jossey Bass, 1997.

Henton, D., and Walesh, K. "The Creative Economy." *Grantmakers in the Arts Reader*, July 2002, pp. 19–31.

Institute on Race and Poverty. "Racism and Metropolitan Dynamics: The Civil Rights Challenge of the 21st Century." Paper prepared for the Ford Foundation, Aug. 2002.

Jefferson, T. Letter to Samuel Kercheval. Monticello, Va., July 12, 1816.

Johnson, C., and Peirce, N. *Boundary Crossers: Community Leadership for a Global Age*. College Park, Md.: Academy of Leadership Press, 1997.

Joseph, J. A. "On Moral Imperatives." *Foundation News*, 1995, 36(6), 10.

Kirsner, S. "Seattle Reboots Its Future." *Fast Company*, 2001, 46, 143–147. [http://www.fastcompany.com/magazine/46/seattle.html].

Langdon, P. "How Portland Does It: A City That Protects Its Thriving, Civil Core." *Atlantic Monthly*. [http://www.theatlantic.com/issues/92nov/portland.htm]. Nov. 1992.

Levin, R. Yale University President's Freshman Address. [http://www.yale.edu/opa/president/fresh_01.html]. Sept. 2001.

Marshall, A. "The Social Possibilities of Chivalry." Address to the Royal Economic Society, London, 1907.

McMillan, J. *Reinventing the Bazaar: A Natural History of Markets*. New York: Norton, 2002.

Menand, L. *The Metaphysical Club*. New York: Farrar, Straus & Giroux, 2002.

The Metropolis Principles. [www.metropolisplan.org/principles.pdf]. Retrieved July 16, 2003.

Meyerson, M. *Political Numeracy: Mathematical Perspectives on Our Chaotic Constitution*. New York: Norton, 2002.

Needleman, J. *The American Soul: Rediscovering the Wisdom of the Founders*. Los Angeles: Tarcher, 2002.

Nonaka, I., and Takeuchi, H. *The Knowledge-Creating Company: How Japanese Companies Create the Dynamics of Innovation*. Oxford: Oxford University Press, 1995.

O'Connell, B. *Civil Society: The Underpinnings of American Democracy*. Hanover, N.H.: University Press of New England, 1999.

Ostrom, E. *Governing the Commons: The Evolution of Institutions for Collective Action*. Cambridge: Cambridge University Press, 1991.

Peirce, N., and Johnson, C. "The Peirce Report: Shaping a Shared Future." [http://www.voicesandchoices.org/region/september17.asp]. Sept. 1995.

Peirce, N., Johnson, C., and Hall, J. S. *Citistates: How Urban America Can Prosper in a Competitive World*. Santa Ana, Calif.: Seven Locks Press, 1994.

Polanyi, K. *The Great Transformation*. Boston: Beacon Press, 1980. (Originally published 1944)

Polanyi, M. *Personal Knowledge: Toward a Post-Critical Philosophy*. Chicago: University of Chicago Press, 1974.

Quinn, F. *The Federalist Papers Reader*. Santa Ana, Calif.: Seven Locks Press, 1993.

Reich, R. B. *I'll Be Short: Essentials for a Decent Working Society*. Boston: Beacon Press, 2002.

Ridley, M. *The Origins of Virtue: Human Instincts and the Evolution of Cooperation*. New York: Viking Penguin, 1997.

Rischard, J. F. *High Noon: Twenty Global Problems, Twenty Years to Solve Them*. New York: Basic Books, 2002.

Sandel, M. J. "The Political Economy of Citizenship." In S. Greenberg and T. Skocpol (eds.), *The New Majority: Toward a Popular Progressive Politics*. New Haven, Conn.: Yale University Press, 1997.

Schumpeter, J. A. *Capitalism, Socialism, and Democracy*. New York: Harper, 1942.

Smith, A. *The Theory of Moral Sentiments*. Indianapolis: Liberty Fund, 1984.
    (Originally published 1759)

Smith, V. "Veteran City Civic Group Champions Regional Issues." *Baltimore
    City Paper*. [http://www.citypaper.com/2002-04-17/mobs.html]. Apr. 17,
    2002.

South Florida Regional Resource Center. *Summary of SFRRC Board Retreat*.
    [www.sfrrc.net/documents/RRC_strategy_revised.doc]. Retrieved Jan.
    2003.

Stiglitz, J. E. *Globalization and Its Discontents*. New York: Norton, 2002.

Wallis, A. "Rebirth of City States and Birth of Global Economy." *National
    Civic Review*, 1996, p. 15.

Williams, S. "Stan Williams Presentation." Speech given at the Next Twenty
    Years Series conference, San Francisco. [http://www.tnty.com/press/
    transcripts/sftech-williams.html]. 2000.

Wood, G. S. *The American Revolution: A History*. New York: Modern Library,
    2002.

Yankelovich, D. *The Magic of Dialogue: Transforming Conflict into Cooperation*.
    New York: Simon & Schuster, 1999.

Index

This page constitutes a continuation of the copyright page.

The quotation by John Gardner at the beginning of the Introduction is from John W. Gardner, *Living, Leading, and the American Dream* (San Francisco: Jossey-Bass, 2003, p. 173). It is reprinted with the permission of John Wiley & Sons, Inc.

In Chapter 1, the comments and recollections about San Diego Dialogue by Malin Burnham and Mary Walshok are used with their permission.

The comments about Voices & Choices by Betty Chafin Rash in Chapter 1 are used with her permission.

The comments about the Housing Action Coalition by Carl Guardino in Chapter 1 are used with his permission.

The comments and recollections in Chapter 1 by Karen Greenwood about the Smart Valley regional initiative and the NetDay event are used with her permission.

In Chapter 2, the excerpt on Baltimore's Citizens Planning and Housing Association (CPHA) is from V. Smith, "Veteran City Civic Group Champions Regional Issues," *Baltimore City Paper*, Apr. 17, 2002, and is reprinted with permission.

The comments in Chapter 2 on Chicago Metropolis 2020 by executive director Frank Beal are used with his permission.

In Chapter 4, the comments by Andrew Michael on the San Francisco Bay Area's Community Capital Investment Initiative (CCII) are used with his permission.

The comments on WIRE-Net by John Colm in Chapter 4 are used with his permission.

The comments in Chapter 4 on the Mixed Income Community Initiative (MICI) in Atlanta by N. von Nkosi and on Atlanta Neighborhood Development Corporation by Hattie Dorsey are used with permission.

The comments in Chapter 4 on Burlington, Vermont, by its mayor are used with his permission.

In Chapter 5, the comments on economic clustering in Akron, Ohio, by Bob Bowman, senior vice president of the Greater Akron Chamber, are used with his permission.

The account in Chapter 5 of regional cooperation in the Washington, D.C., area by George Vradenburg, chair of the Potomac Conference, is used with his permission.

The comments in Chapter 5 on the Louisville–Jefferson County merger by Joan Riehm, deputy mayor of the new metro government, are used with her permission.

In Chapter 6, the comments by Roy Williams of the Greater Oklahoma City Chamber of Commerce on Oklahoma City's rescue of its economy are used with his permission, and the comments by Cynthia Reid, marketing director of the chamber, are used with her permission.

In Chapter 7, the epigraph by John Gardner is from John W. Gardner, *On Leadership* (New York: Free Press, 1990). It is reprinted with the permission of The Free Press, a division of Simon & Schuster Adult Publishing Group. Copyright © by John W. Gardner.